THE BLYTON PHENOMENON

The Blyton Phenomenon

*The controversy surrounding
the world's most successful
children's writer*

SHEILA G. RAY

BA M.Phil FLA

*Senior Lecturer
Department of Librarianship
Birmingham Polytechnic*

ANDRE DEUTSCH

FIRST PUBLISHED 1982 BY
ANDRE DEUTSCH LIMITED
105 GREAT RUSSELL STREET LONDON WC1

COPYRIGHT © 1982 BY SHEILA RAY
ALL RIGHTS RESERVED

PRINTED IN GREAT BRITAIN AT
THE THETFORD PRESS LTD, NORFOLK

ISBN 0 233 97441 5

Contents

Enid Blyton

Born 11 August 1897
Educated St Christopher's School for Girls, Beckenham,
    Ipswich High School and the Froebel Institute
Married Hugh Pollock 1924 (divorced 1942)
Two daughters, Gillian, born 1931, and Imogen, born 1935
Married Kenneth Darrell Waters 1943
Died 28 November 1968

Acknowledgements

This book developed from an M.Phil.(CNAA) thesis written at the City of Birmingham Polytechnic under the supervision of Dr Keith May and Dr Geoffrey Nelson, for whose help and encouragement I am grateful.

Thanks are due also to the following people who provided me with information which is quoted in these pages: Mrs Doris Aubrey, Miss Phyllis Baker, Miss Elizabeth Bewick, Miss Joan Butler, Dr Eileen Colwell, George Edmundson, Miss Olive Jones, Miss Olga Newman, Miss Phyllis Parrott, Mrs Mary Spickermell and Miss Joyce Taylor.

I am also grateful to the students and ex-students of the Department of Librarianship, Birmingham Polytechnic, and to those librarians, booksellers, publishers, teachers and others in the children's book world who directly or indirectly contributed information or influenced my ideas; and, of course, to those many librarians who have developed the libraries which I have used.

To those who read this book, my debt to newspapers and periodicals will be obvious, but I should like to mention specially the *Guardian* and *New Society* and, amongst the specialist children's literature journals, *The Junior Bookshelf* which, under Mr Woodfield's editorship, provided such a good picture of the children's book world in the late 1930s.

I must acknowledge my debt to two books in particular, Barbara Stoney's *Enid Blyton*, which is an invaluable source of biographical information and which also saved me hours of bibliographical searching, and Tony Thompson's *Censorship in Public Libraries*, which gave me access to the archives of Manchester Public Libraries.

I should also like to thank the trustees of Darrell Waters Limited who kindly gave me access to the collection of Enid Blyton books which they maintain.

Three young relatives, Catherine and Simon Mitchell, and Elizabeth Wells are referred to and quoted in these pages; and, finally, I must pay tribute to the patience, at times sorely tried, of my husband, Colin.

Part I

Enid Blyton and the Librarians

Chapter One

Introduction

❦

THE WORD that is most frequently used in discussion of Enid Blyton and her work is undoubtedly 'phenomenon'. This usefully describes her tremendous output, amounting to something over six hundred books, her popularity with children and the reaction of many adults to mention of her name. Its first use seems to have been in the early 1950s. In 1951 Eileen Colwell, Children's Librarian at Hendon, in a paper which she gave at the first weekend school of the Youth Libraries Section, referred to Enid Blyton as 'a phenomenon',[1] while in the following year Frank Eyre, in *20th Century Children's Books*, wrote, 'The innumerable and invariably successful contributions of Enid Blyton to this field must also be noted – they are a phenomenon.'[2]

By 1952 Enid Blyton was in her mid-fifties and had already passed the peak point of her production (in 1951 she published thirty-seven titles, the greatest number recorded for one year).[3] She and her work were phenomena which crept up on librarians, teachers and all the other adults concerned with children's reading, including the critics, and this fact must be kept in mind when the subject generally is being discussed.

In the early 1950s it was assumed that Enid Blyton's work was ephemeral, that its popularity was due to a passing fad, and that she would quietly pass from the scene before long. In the 1980s she is still a household name and there are almost certainly more references to her and her characters in the mass media than to any other writer for children. The name of Enid Blyton produces an instant response, while Noddy and the Famous Five are characters familiar to many who have never read her books. References to Enid Blyton and the characters she created can be found tucked away in the midst of news items and comments which have nothing to do with her work. For example, during the trial of the book *Inside Linda*

Lovelace, in 1976, John Mortimer, QC, was reported in the *Guardian* as saying:

> The test the jury had to apply was not 'is this a book which is suitable for kids to read?' If that were the test all of us in this country, which must have one of the most literary and sensible publics in the world, would be reduced to a perpetual diet of Enid Blyton and the life and times of Noddy.[4]

The following year, a writer in the *Sunday Times*, tongue slightly in cheek, could suggest that Enid Blyton was responsible for the fact that most young people

> . . . still hold orthodox good-citizen views of a kind which were thought to have found a last refuge on the right of the Conservative party . . . Those children who read at all read Enid Blyton . . . It is from her that these vigorous attitudes arise. Topped off by emulation of the Famous Five, they will have been first nurtured on Noddy . . .[5]

and could assume that the significance of these remarks would be understood by the majority of his readers.

Amongst eight- to twelve-year-olds, Enid Blyton's popularity is supreme. In surveys of the reading tastes of children in this age group, she is invariably shown to be the most popular author and is usually well ahead of any other claimants. The reasons for this are not hard to establish and if her books are examined alongside the proven facts about children's reading tastes, the impression which remains is that if Enid Blyton had carried out systematic market research, she could not have produced books more guaranteed to please.

Although ultimately children, as consumers, can select or reject books, they are, in the first place, dependent on a whole series of adults from the original producer, be it author or illustrator, through the publisher, the bookseller, the critic or commentator, to the buyer who is usually an adult, a parent or other relative, a teacher or librarian. Only rarely, in the case of hardback books at least, is the child the buyer. Ever since children started reading, adults have been anxious to ban some of their favourite books. In 1568 the schoolmaster Roger Ascham attacked Malory's *Morte d'Arthur*; two centuries later *Robinson Crusoe* was criticized because the reading of it might lead to 'an early taste for a rambling life' and because it emphasized the importance of accumulating material goods, while at the beginning of the nineteenth century *Cinderella* was castigated by Mrs Trimmer and her friends because it contained 'some of the worst passions that can enter into the human breast ... such as envy, jealousy, a dislike to mothers-in-law and half-sisters, vanity, a love of dress etc., etc.'

No author, however, has been attacked to the extent that Enid Blyton has during the last thirty years. Many adults, although not necessarily hostile to her work themselves, are well aware of the undercurrent of criticism, although there is some evidence that adults for whom children's books are very much a peripheral concern tend to class all writing for children together. This is demonstrated in a recently published study of treatments of the Robin Hood legend, for example, where Enid Blyton's *Tales of Robin Hood* (1930) is ranked alongside Carola Oman's *Robin Hood* (1937),[6] although Mary Thwaite describes the latter as 'outstanding' in her history of children's literature.[7]

Adult concern about the quality of Enid Blyton's writing is demonstrated mainly by teachers, parents, librarians and children's literature specialists (who are frequently teachers, parents or librarians as well), those adults who are most influential in the matter of what children read. Of these groups, it is the librarians whose attitudes towards Enid Blyton have undoubtedly received the most publicity. Since the middle of the 1960s there has been a general belief that her books are 'banned' by public libraries, frequent references being made to this fact by people outside the library profession.

Writing in the *Daily Mail* in 1968 at the time of Enid Blyton's death, Diana Norman said, '. . . many, maybe most, of the public libraries in this country as well as Australia and New Zealand do not stock her books. Some have openly banned them. Others tacitly do not buy them.'[8] In an article in *New Society* early in 1970, after 'Billy Bunter' books had been removed from the open shelves at Ipswich Public Library, Nicholas Tucker pointed out that the 'extreme opinions' held by children's librarians had affected the book supply of whole neighbourhoods and that in some areas Enid Blyton's works had disappeared because of her 'snobbishness'.[9] Later in the same year, reviewing *Only Connect*, a collection of readings about children's literature, in *New Society*, he regretted the lack of knowledge about how librarians select books for libraries and continued, 'Apart from the odd eccentricities, like banning any of the three Bs — Biggles, Blyton or Bunter — one hears very little of how librarians' taste works, and in what direction so far as children's books are concerned.'[10]

In 1970 George Greenfield listed the reasons why librarians 'banned' Enid Blyton's books,[11] in 1974 Ruth Inglis, in *A Time to Learn*, said, 'British librarians have certainly decided that children can learn to live without Enid Blyton',[12] while in 1975 a comment in *New Society*, under a heading of 'A bias of books', stated:

> The bookworms are creeping out of the woodwork — in the shape of a new group of librarians who want actively to influence library users by their selection and promotion of materials. Their predecessors, who refused to stock Enid Blyton, would applaud the principle, if not the practice.[13]

This refers to the activities of Librarians for Social Change and the remark about Enid Blyton is the journalist reporter's own contribution. Also in 1975, Gillian Avery wrote, 'It was only in the 1950s when [Enid Blyton] was increasing her output ... that a storm of indignation broke out. Educationists thundered, librarians vetoed, the fastidious mother drew back her skirts.'[14] Another example comes from the *Nottingham Evening Post* in November 1977, when, describing the Library Association's centenary exhibition, it was said 'that some librarians turned against Enid Blyton's Noddy books because they had "mediocre plots", "weak characterisations" and the use of language was "unimaginative" '.[15] Much was made of the fact that Enid Blyton's work was represented in this exhibition of children's books published during the last hundred years. A report of the exhibition which appeared in the *Guardian* under the headline 'Noddy and co. come in from the cold' began with the words, 'Enid Blyton, the children's author whose work was banned by many librarians from the 1950s onwards, was rehabilitated yesterday at the opening of a major centennial exhibition of children's literature by the Library Association.'[16]

In August 1979, writing in *New Society*, Cedric Cullingford said, 'One librarian in Cumbria, with the agreement of all the local schools, banned Enid Blyton completely',[17] a statement which was promptly refuted by the Cumbrian County Librarian. Later in the year, also in *New Society*, Christina Larner, in an article about Dennis Wheatley, wrote, 'His mastery lies in the presentation of exotic "information" in an undemanding vocabulary and style of the type which had Enid Blyton banned from the children's section of public libraries.'[18]

These references to the 'banning' of Enid Blyton are taken from only a limited range of newspapers and magazines—unless they are picked up at the time, they are difficult to trace—but it seems reasonable to assume that they represent merely the tip of an iceberg of such comments. It is interesting to note that, with the exception of Cedric Cullingford's comment, which was immediately contradicted by the authority concerned, none of them refers to an actual case of banning, censorship or selection, but merely makes a sweeping generalization.

As can be seen from Diana Norman's comment, Enid Blyton's books are available — and, apparently, sometimes banned — overseas. In 1974, six years after her death, she was the fourth most translated author in the world, following on after Lenin, Marx and Jules Verne, with 149 translations being made in fifteen different countries,[19] and in translation her books have penetrated to many foreign countries as well as being available in English-speaking America and the Commonwealth countries. Since she is often criticized for her Englishness and insularity, her popularity abroad seems surprising. I once discussed this with two Indian girls. One of them had been brought up in English-speaking Malawi while the other had been educated in a French-speaking convent in Iraq and had read the books in French. They both claimed that they had not been puzzled by the books and the second girl said that it had never occurred to her that Enid Blyton was not French.

In some cases, the books have been not only translated but also adapted. Antony Kamm, writing about the lack of supplementary reading material and good children's literature in Malaysia, said, 'the hypnotic power of Blyton still prevails to the extent that her books are not just being translated into Bahasa Malaysia, but actually Malaysianised into the bargain.'[20] The responses of Malaysian students to a questionnaire circulated to students at Birmingham Polytechnic confirmed the impression that Enid Blyton's books are freely available in their country. A correspondent in *Books* once suggested that the school stories in particular were popular in Malaysia because of the great desire for British-type education.[21]

In fact the evidence suggests that in overseas countries the Enid Blyton situation is very similar to the British one. Wherever her books are available, whether in English or in translation, she is popular with children, known to adults and thought to be of inferior literary quality by many of the experts.

However, the reluctance of public librarians to include Enid Blyton's work in their stocks is by no means as widespread as is sometimes suggested. There certainly was a period of about twenty years, from the early 1950s to the early 1970s, when a number of public libraries either did not buy her books at all or bought them only in limited quantities, but this policy was by no means general.

Although Nicholas Tucker has complained that little is known about the selection policies of British librarians,[22] the results of such policies are there for all to see. Public librarians spend public money on books in a very public way and if they choose not to buy books written by a particular author or do not buy enough copies to meet the demand, then this is easily observable too. In most cases where librarians' selection policies are criticized, it is because they have bought a book which happens to have offended some member of the reading public. Again Enid Blyton is a phenomenon because in her case, almost uniquely, librarians have been criticized for *not* buying her books. Although other people have questioned or criticized the value of her work, no-one has ever supported any librarians who have rejected her books. No non-librarian is on record as saying: 'It is a good thing that public libraries do not buy her books.'

Librarians have obviously been very much involved in the development of adult attitudes towards Enid Blyton because their actions are so public, and some pattern of trends can be discerned in their activities. Up until the outbreak of the Second World War in 1939 there were few specialist children's librarians and the quality of library provision for children was variable. As children's books were mostly bought for libraries by non-specialist librarians, comparatively little attention was paid to their content in many cases. During the Second World War, the period when Enid Blyton's books first became widely available, librarians were happy to buy them, if only because there was little else. In the early 1950s, however, the supply of children's books improved considerably, both in quantity and quality, and librarians were then overwhelmed by the sheer quantity of Blyton titles and tried to rationalize the situation either by limiting their choice to specific series or by eliminating her books altogether on the grounds of their inferior quality. Although very few library authorities can be identified as ever having excluded her books altogether, it seems likely that few have ever provided enough copies to meet the demand.

Since the early 1970s, however, there have been signs that adults involved in the world of children's books are more prepared to discuss Enid Blyton's work. Michael Woods, in a *New Society* article, has suggested that 1974 was the year when Enid Blyton came in from the cold.[23] This was the year when the BBC, which had never used any of her work, included a programme about her in its series 'Success Story' and later in the year based a week of 'Jackanory' programmes on her book, *The Island of Adventure*. It was also the year when Barbara Stoney's biography of Enid Blyton appeared, was widely reviewed and stimulated a great deal of interest and discussion.

As far as librarians and teachers are concerned, attitudes have changed in the last few years because of the current worries about literacy standards. There is a general feeling that the kind of books which Enid Blyton wrote are needed to help children achieve fluency in reading, and that no other author has been able to meet this need so effectively.

What has happened in the period of over forty years since

1937, when Enid Blyton's first full-length story, *Adventures of the Wishing Chair*, was published? How far is the prevailing critical opinion the result of serious consideration or how far is it an assumption which has just grown? How much help have those concerned with children's reading received from those in a position to make an informed judgement?

Now the time seems ripe to document the changing attitudes of adults towards Enid Blyton, to bring together the evidence of her popularity with children and to attempt some critical assessment of her work. It seems appropriate that this should be done by one of the first generation of Enid Blyton readers, children who grew up in the late 1930s and early 1940s. The facts are phenomenal: here is the story behind them.

Chapter Two

The Early Years

❀

AT AN EARLY STAGE in the gathering together of the evidence, it became obvious that Enid Blyton was very much a product of the period in which she lived and wrote, and it is unlikely that she would have risen to such a commanding position at any other time. She was born in 1897 and trained as a teacher of young children largely because she believed that this training would provide a useful background to her writing, for which she had already shown some ability and in which she had a deep interest from an early age. Her first published poem was accepted for *Nash's Magazine* in 1917 while she was still training. She took up her first teaching post at a boys' preparatory school in 1919 and the first book for which she was wholly responsible, *Child Whispers*, a small, twenty-four-page book of verse, was published in 1922.

During the 1920s and early 1930s she wrote prolifically: verse, stories and articles appeared in *Teachers' World* and other magazines. In 1923 five of her poems were used in a special edition of *Teachers' World* which also included contributions by John Drinkwater, John Masefield, Walter de la Mare and Rudyard Kipling. Enid Blyton's verse was published for an age which admired Rose Fyleman's 'Fairies', with its famous opening line, 'There are fairies at the bottom of our garden', and Walter de la Mare's 'Bluebells' and 'The Buckle', and contained much the same kind of sentiment, conjuring up a rather cosy middle-class suburban world full of fairies and elves. Enid Blyton's 'Nobody knows' is not perhaps to modern taste:

> Nobody hears
> With pricked-up ears
> The plash of a weeping fairy's tears

but it belongs to an age when Rose Fyleman wrote:

> The fairies have never a penny to spend,
> They haven't a thing put by[1]

and Rose Fyleman enjoyed such a high reputation amongst librarians at the time that she was invited to give a talk to the Library Association Conference in 1934. Her verse, much of which was published in *Punch* in the 1920s and early 1930s, contained the same whimsical sentiments as Enid Blyton's. In 1930 an even more distinguished poet, Walter de la Mare, published *Poems for Children*, made up of *Songs of Childhood* and *Peacock Pie*. Amongst the first, originally published in 1902, were such verses as:

> I had a bunch of cowslips
> I hid them in a grot
> In case the elves should come at night
> And me remember not.[2]

Another of Enid Blyton's verses, 'Put to bed', recalls Robert Louis Stevenson, while 'Goblins' is reminiscent of James Whitcomb Riley's 'Little Orphant Annie'. This kind of verse was widely admired up until at least the outbreak of the Second World War and some of Enid Blyton's verses compare favourably with those of the poets mentioned, all of whom, unlike Enid Blyton, are represented in *The Oxford Book of Children's Verse*, edited by Iona and Peter Opie.

Barbara Stoney's book reveals the enormous energy and self-discipline which Enid Blyton must have had to produce all this work in addition to carrying out the commitments of her full-time teaching posts. In 1924 she married her first husband, Hugh Pollock, and from this time forward she devoted herself to her writing which was already providing her with a steady income.

From the point of view of adults, the fact that much of her work had an educational bias undoubtedly gave her a sound reputation. Her articles in the *Teachers' World*, the plays, verses, natural history and other simple information books and the retellings of traditional stories, all helped to establish a favourable image.

As far as children were concerned, the major publication which established Enid Blyton's reputation must have been the weekly magazine, *Sunny Stories for Little Folks*, which she began to edit for Newnes in 1926. During the first ten years of this magazine's existence, the contents seem to have been very similar to her work that was being published elsewhere, consisting mainly of retellings of traditional material and simple information features, but in 1937, with the change in title to *Enid Blyton's Sunny Stories*, the emphasis shifted to creative fiction and the weekly issues began to contain the original short stories and regular serial story, which were later published in book form. The publication in 1937 of *Adventures of the Wishing Chair*, which had formed the serial in the first issues of the new-style *Sunny Stories*, marks the date when Enid Blyton really emerged to stand alongside other writers for children. By this time she had already been a published author for twenty years with an established reputation of educational respectability. Barbara Stoney describes how Enid Blyton interviewed A. A. Milne for *Teachers' World* in 1926, the year of publication of *Winnie-the-Pooh*, and quotations from the article show that Enid Blyton was fully in command of the situation.

The following examples of her work will perhaps serve to show the position which she had achieved by the early 1940s. One of the classic picture book series of the 1930s was the series of books about Babar, the elephant, by the Frenchman, Jean de Brunhoff. In 1941 Methuen published *The Babar Story Book* 'told by Enid Blyton' and well produced, with black and white illustrations and endpapers reminiscent of those of *Winnie-the-Pooh*. (Milne's books were also published by Methuen, and Milne had written an introduction to the first volume of *Babar* to appear in Britain.) In 1942, part of Enid Blyton's retelling of Babar was published in Methuen's 'Modern Classics' series, edited by E. V. Rieu and Peter Wait, a series which also included books by A. A. Milne, Kenneth Grahame and a simple narrative version of Maurice Maeterlinck's *The Children's Bluebird*. This contains an editorial by E. V. Rieu who comments that Babar 'returns triumphant (though in black-and-white) and with a full-length biography by Miss Enid Blyton'.

The second example consists of two books about the Brown Family called *London to the Seaside* and *Building a New*

House. During the early months of the war, when nursery education was being developed, attention was drawn to the need for more and better instructional picture books for very young children and the *News Chronicle* sponsored a competition, 'Nursery Education Contest for Artists and Art Students', for which the panel of judges included Sir Kenneth (now Lord) Clark and John Piper. A series of pictures by E. and R. Buhler was awarded a prize and, as the pictures were considered particularly suitable for reproduction as a book, Enid Blyton was asked to write the text to accompany the illustrations. The illustrations are excellent and must have been outstanding at the time of their original publication, while the text is in Enid Blyton's usual style. The fact that her name was associated at this period with enterprises in which A. A. Milne, E. V. Rieu, Lord Clark and John Piper were also involved, is some indication of her standing by the end of the 1930s.

Having found a successful formula and an appropriate style by 1940, Enid Blyton's work changed little from then until her death in 1968. Her early work, in *Enid Blyton's Sunny Stories* and in her first full-length stories for children, must be seen in the context of the 1930s. At this time, as Geoffrey Trease has pointed out, the young book-reading public was still predominantly 'a sheltered middle-class public'.[3] Junior public libraries were in their infancy, school libraries were to be found mainly in the traditional grammar schools and catered largely for older children, while book-buyers came mostly from the middle class. In the 1930s the middle classes developed a new way of life. As Jane Waller shows in *Some Things for the Children*:

> The 'House' of the Twenties had, by the Thirties, come to be called 'the Home' . . . a bungalow, semi-detached or detached residence with a garden at the back and a garage at the side . . . lived in by the now small middle-class family, 'Hubby', 'Wifey' and the 'Kids', acting as a closely knit unit.[4]

The family image was essentially a cosy one. Children had moved to the forefront of family life and parents believed that children should be told happy and cheerful stories. It was thought that many of the traditional nursery tales had a bad effect on children and Walt Disney's cartoon version of *Snow White and the Seven Dwarfs*, released in 1937, was thought to be frightening for sensitive children. This protective world which middle-class parents sought to create for their children may well have been a conscious or sub-conscious reaction to the growing threat of another world war. It certainly created an environment in which children's books tended to be bland, free of anything too alarming and frightening, an environment in which Enid Blyton's work would have a wide appeal. In an article published in the *Daily Mail* the day after Enid Blyton's death in 1968, Diana Norman wrote of 'the great quality that pervades her books – security. For more than 40 years, in a frightening and perplexing world, her books remained the same.'[5] Her writing, in terms of the world she portrayed and of the style in which she wrote, was very much to the taste of the 1930s.

Although the Second World War proved to be something of a watershed for children's literature, there were already signs in the 1930s that children's books were changing. The year 1930 had been a landmark in the development of children's books for this was the year in which Arthur Ransome's *Swallows and Amazons*, the first modern story of holiday adventure, was published. This kind of story proved to be very popular and many of its type were published in the years that followed. The best had a strong regional flavour and contained a certain amount of practical information; the worst relied heavily on smugglers, lost treasure and the capturing of criminals, although the fact that Ransome, one of the best writers, included the recovery of stolen goods to provide a climax in *Swallows and Amazons* should not be overlooked. In 1938 Eleanor Graham wrote *The Children who Lived in a Barn* partly as a corrective to some of the wilder flights of fancy about what could happen to children whose parents conveniently went away and left them to fend for themselves; this was in the same year that Enid Blyton's first book of this kind, *The Secret Island*, was published.

Mystery stories, in which children assumed the detective role and where the tracking down of criminals was at the centre of the story, received a new impetus with the first translation into English of Erich Kaestner's *Emil and the Detectives* in 1931, described by Marcus Crouch in *Treasure Seekers and Borrowers* as a major landmark and highly praised by May Lamberton Becker in *Choosing Books for Children*, an American book published in England in 1937, where mystery and detective stories received detailed attention just because they were so popular with young people.

School stories were also very popular, especially with girls. In mentioning these, May Lamberton Becker quotes an entry from the catalogue of the Children's Book Club of London to the effect that they 'are generally very badly written'. A headmistress writing in *The School Library Review* in 1936 said 'I never allow school stories' and Angela Brazil, the writer of girls' school stories, was in the 1930s frequently used as an example of a popular but worthless writer. Gillian Freeman describes how, in 1936, the headmistress of St Paul's School expressed the wish to collect the books of Angela Brazil and burn them, and comments on the fact that Angela Brazil's vocabulary was extensive with 'no paucity of words, no repetition as was prevalent in, say, Enid Blyton, who in 1936 was rapidly ascending to prime popularity'.[6]

Enid Blyton's holiday adventure, mystery and school stories are probably her most popular books. She also wrote family stories which, like most others of the period, tended to be about middle-class families. Eve Garnett's Carnegie Medal-winning book, *The Family from One-End Street*, published in 1937, stood very much alone in the 1930s and has come to be regarded as the first notable children's story about a working-class family, although even this is today criticized for its condescension.

Career stories and pony stories also emerged in the 1930s but these Enid Blyton never attempted, except in so far as she wrote a number of stories with a circus background, a setting which seemed to have a special attraction for her. The first career story was Noel Streatfeild's *Ballet Shoes*, published in 1936, while the fashion for pony stories was firmly set by Joanna Cannan's *A Pony for Jean*, which appeared the same year. Both ballet and ponies have continued to be popular themes with girls as can be seen by looking at almost any girls' comic today. In the *Enid Blyton Magazine* in 1953, Enid

Blyton explained to children who had written in to ask for notes on ballet to be included in the magazine, that this would interest only girls and her magazine was intended for both sexes. Even if one accepts that her knowledge of the technicalities of ballet and ponies was limited and that this was why she avoided them, it is surprising that she did not make any use of her musical knowledge (her father had intended that she should train as a musician and she gave up a place at the Guildhall School of Music in favour of training as a teacher only at the last moment).

Nor did Enid Blyton ever write any historical fiction, which also turned in a new direction in the 1930s when Geoffrey Trease, with his first children's book, *Bows Against the Barons*, published in 1934, placed emphasis on social history rather than on cloak and dagger adventure and paved the way for a new generation of writers. Although some excellent historical fiction has been written for children since 1934, it is not very popular with children of the age group for which Enid Blyton primarily wrote. Whether she recognized this and acted accordingly or whether the research which would have been required just did not fit in with her way of writing is a matter for speculation.

Before 1930, some of the best twentieth-century work for children had been in the field of fantasy by writers of the stature of Walter de la Mare, John Masefield, A. A. Milne, Kenneth Grahame and J. M. Barrie. In the 1930s, however, the publication of P. L. Travers' *Mary Poppins* in 1934 and J. R. R. Tolkien's *The Hobbit* in 1937 went almost unnoticed. The fact that Enid Blyton's fantasy stories were intended for young children of about seven to nine reflects the fact that in the 1930s fantasy was still regarded as something very much for younger children.

For the youngest, there were picture books, but the modern picture book, with its use of lithography, was scarcely established in this country before the outbreak of the Second World War. Babar, already mentioned, was imported from France; Edward Ardizzone and Kathleen Hale were almost alone among British picture book author-illustrators in the modern style; even at the end of the 1950s, British librarians and teachers were still dependent on American imports of good quality picture books and in 1949 the gate was wide open for the arrival of Enid Blyton's Noddy.

Overall, one can see that in the writing that was being done for nine- to thirteen-year-olds in the 1930s, there was a definite trend towards writing books that would appeal to both boys and girls. Arthur Ransome, Malcolm Saville, Geoffrey Trease, Eve Garnett and even Noel Streatfeild, whose themes tended to appeal to girls, included children of both sexes amongst their central characters. Before 1930, books about everyday life had tended to be about boys for boys or about girls for girls. It is significant that when one looks for the popular authors who preceded Enid Blyton the names most frequently mentioned are those of Percy F. Westerman, who wrote for boys, and Angela Brazil, who was surely read only by girls. Enid Blyton, as she made clear to readers of her magazine, hoped to be read by children of both sexes and in order to achieve this she even set her first series of school stories in a co-educational school.

A number of authors who, like Enid Blyton, began their careers as writers for children in the 1930s, such as Noel Streatfeild, Malcolm Saville, Geoffrey Trease and M. E. Allan have also written prolifically, but have shown more awareness of the changing scene. Only three other writers for children have been the subject of the same kind of hostile criticism as Enid Blyton; these are W. E. Johns, the author of the Biggles books, Richmal Crompton, the creator of William, and Frank Richards, the creator of Billy Bunter. These three authors were all popular in the 1930s and have continued to be so, but their work was, of course, much more limited in scope.

There must have been good reasons for the changes which were taking place in children's books in the 1930s and although these were partly social and economic, including the sheer increase in the size of the middle classes, they may also have been due to the changes in the adult literary scene. In the nineteenth century, fiction was fairly homogeneous. Books were written for young people up to the age of about ten or eleven; after that children read adult fiction which happened to appeal to them and authors such as Scott and Dickens, who told a good story, were widely read by the young. Girls, their mothers and grandmothers read Charlotte M. Yonge and

Frances Hodgson Burnett, while boys, their fathers and grandfathers read Robert Louis Stevenson and Rider Haggard. The books of Henty and Scott have something in common as have those of Charlotte Yonge and Mrs Gaskell. No great leap forward is required of the reader who graduates from one to the other. However, by the 1930s and 1940s the names most frequently mentioned in critical discussions of modern fiction were those of D. H. Lawrence, Virginia Woolf and James Joyce, whose main concern was not with telling stories and whose novels, for various reasons, were unlikely to be read by young people. At the same time that the mainstream literary tradition passed into the care of such writers as these, popular adult fiction started to become more outspoken in themes and style. This second development is more clearly illustrated by comparing the work of John Buchan and Ian Fleming, although Fleming merely represents the culmination of a gradual change in this respect. Whereas parents and teachers were happy for young people to move on to read Buchan when they outgrew children's books, they were not quite so happy for them to move on to the sex and sadism of Fleming. The changes in both the literary novel and the popular novel meant that there was a greater need for fiction written specifically for children in a style with which they could cope and with suitable content. Enid Blyton established herself as a writer, therefore, at a period when most adults who cared about children's reading were more concerned with suitability of content than with literary quality.

Apart from parents, the two groups of adults most closely involved with children's reading are teachers and librarians. Developments in education and in public libraries led to an increasing interest in, and subsequently a concern for, the standards of children's literature but in the 1930s these developments were still very much in the early stages.

Teaching in both primary and secondary schools was still very formal and little encouragement was given to most children to read beyond the texts used in the classroom. In 1936 the School Library Association and the School Libraries Section of the Library Association were both established, evidence of the developments in school library provision, but an examination of *The School Librarian* and *The School*

Library Review in their early, pre-war years, shows that these developments were mainly in the traditional grammar schools, some independent schools and comparatively few secondary modern schools. In these schools books written for children by contemporary writers were virtually ignored and although nineteenth-century children's classics such as *Treasure Island* and *Alice in Wonderland* were promoted to some extent, the main aim was to get children on to reading Dickens, Scott, Dumas and H. G. Wells as soon as possible. A. J. Jenkinson's survey of children's reading interests, *What Do Boys and Girls Read?*, published in 1940, suggested that teachers of English might select 'set books' more realistically for younger secondary school children, relating them more closely to the books which the children themselves would select for leisure reading. Jenkinson's survey was based on research carried out in the late 1930s and Enid Blyton's name does not appear at all in his commentary. Whether any of the young people who participated in the survey listed her as one of their favourite authors we shall presumably never know. Nor was she mentioned in the report of a survey of children's reading carried out by Sheffield City Libraries in 1938. At this stage of course, her output was still fairly small and if titles by her were mentioned by any of the children who replied to questionnaires, they were obviously not in sufficient quantities for it to cause comment.

In primary schools in the 1930s some teachers promoted children's books through reading them aloud. In 1937 a teacher read aloud to a class of six- or seven-year-olds, of which I was a member, some chapters from *Adventures of the Wishing Chair* which, at that period, was being serialized in *Sunny Stories*. This was, as far as I can recall, my introduction to Enid Blyton (since it was the first full-length story which she published in book form, this seems highly probable) and I was very impressed, although it was perhaps a year or so later before I at last read the whole of the story. It is significant that it is one of the only books which I can remember being presented to me at school in this way, although the fact that I later read it for myself may have something to do with this. The images stayed in my mind throughout childhood and it was only when I re-read it some twenty years later that I found it disappointing, compared with other children's books of the same kind. Although one might take the view that such reading aloud sessions would have been better used in reading Tolkien's *The Hobbit* (this would have been available in 1937, the year of its publication), one must also recognize that the images conjured up by Enid Blyton's prose may well be more within the comprehension range of the average seven- to ten-year-old. Is there something to be said for reading aloud a book from which the least able in the class may gain something, rather than catering for the able few who might get more satisfaction from *The Hobbit*?

Although some public libraries had provided books for children from the beginning of the century and some major figures in public librarianship, such as John Ballinger in Cardiff and W. Berwick Sayers in Croydon, had taken an active interest in promoting library work with young people, the few specialist children's librarians that there were in the 1930s tended to work in the large city conurbations, mostly in London. One of the few, Eileen Colwell, who had become children's librarian at Hendon in 1926, has since written, 'Any modern librarian would have thought the children's libraries of the early 1930s very drab.'[7] The Library Association became involved in producing lists of books recommended for young people in 1926 when it was asked to prepare lists for the guidance of club leaders engaged in spending Carnegie United Kingdom Trust grants made to boys' and girls' clubs. These early lists now have a rather old fashioned air but although there was a heavy reliance on nineteenth-century children's classics, popular authors such as Angela Brazil, Percy Westerman and Richmal Crompton were also included in *Books to Read* (1930) and *Books for Youth* (1936).

In 1936, the Library Association established the Carnegie Medal, to be awarded annually to an outstanding children's book. In doing this and in publishing lists of recommended books, the Association clearly saw itself as having a responsibility for setting and maintaining critical standards. Looking back at the record of the Carnegie Medal on the occasion of its twenty-first birthday, Marcus Crouch concluded that it had helped to raise standards:

> The general standard of writing for children is much higher now than it was in 1936, and the quality of selection for public and school libraries is proportionately higher. At best, six British publishers have a recognisable policy in the children's book department: of how many could this have been said in 1936?[8]

The first award was made to Arthur Ransome, whose *Swallows and Amazons* had been such an innovation in 1930, for a later book about the same characters, *Pigeon Post*.

In 1937, an Association of Children's Librarians was formed and from such evidence as exists, it seems that the small number of British children's librarians working in this pre-war period supported the view of their colleagues in America, where children's librarianship was rather more advanced, that the public library's function was to provide only the best children's books and that good books would drive out bad. Constance Stern, children's librarian at Croydon in the 1930s (later to become Constance Martin and children's librarian at St Pancras at the time of a major Enid Blyton controversy in 1963), stated, 'Reading should be a stimulant not a drug', and in particular condemned girls' school stories as a cause of young people 'wasting creative energy on unpractical daydreams'. She particularly admired the standards of book selection in Russia, 'the only country which has made any contribution to the art of living in the last few decades'.[9]

At this time Enid Blyton was scarcely visible above the horizon and there is certainly no evidence of what, if anything, children's librarians thought of her work. In the two years 1936–7, which saw the establishment of the Carnegie Medal and the Association of Children's Librarians, she had added only five books to the handful of works already published which might have been considered for public library stock.

In the period immediately before the Second World War, one of the leading county library authorities in the field of children's work was Derbyshire County Library, whose County Librarian at that time was Edgar Osborne, later to become famous as a collector of early children's books. In the late 1930s and early 1940s Derbyshire County Library produced regular annual booklists. A collection of Enid Blyton's plays, *The Wishing Bean and Other Plays*, was included in the list of 1939 and *The Children of Willow Farm* and *More Adventures on Willow Farm* appeared in the list for 1942. These lists were highly praised in *The Junior Bookshelf* and it is to the pages of the early issues of this specialist reviewing journal that we must turn for any serious discussion of children's books in the 1930s. When Enid Blyton began to publish her first full-length story books, there was little activity in the field of criticism of children's books. The reminiscences of Eleanor Graham, who worked in bookselling and in publishing at this time, provide evidence of this lack. She has pointed out that in the 1930s, 'No one, of course, would stop to consider critically the work of Angela Brazil [at that period – Enid Blyton later], but there were many people who assumed that *all* children's books were on that level.'[10] Geoffrey Trease, in the article which he contributed to Edward Blishen's *The Thorny Paradise*, also commented on this lack of critical discussion of children's books in the 1930s and suggested that it was perhaps not surprising in view of the quality of much of the writing.[11]

The first sign of a change came in 1936 when H. J. B. Woodfield, an ex-librarian, who worked for the library supply firm of Combridge in Birmingham and who later set up his own firm of library suppliers, Woodfield and Stanley, established the first British specialist reviewing journal for children's books, *The Junior Bookshelf*. It was modelled on *The Horn Book Magazine* which had been successfully launched in America in the previous decade. Mr Woodfield very much admired the developments which were taking place in America in the field of children's books and libraries and he believed that the British could learn from the Americans in this respect. He felt that public libraries for children should set high standards of selection and that the good would drive out the bad. These beliefs were put forward consistently through-out the period which coincides with much of Enid Blyton's career, from November 1936 onwards. Mr Woodfield was continually pressing for higher standards from the publishers and urging librarians to select critically, and he praised and encouraged anything which he thought would support these improvements.

Even before there was any reason to suppose that the most prolific children's writer ever was in our midst, *The Junior*

Bookshelf expressed a less than enthusiastic opinion of Enid Blyton's work. In the second issue, in February 1937, there was a note about *The Famous Jimmy*: 'The value of this book is in its pictures. Rabier's animals have a great deal of character. The story, however, is not worthy of them. It is of a little duckling whose adventures are far too human to ring true.'[12] Benjamin Rabier was one of the most popular and competent author-artists in France and this book was a translation or rewriting by Enid Blyton of the original text, similar to the work she later did on Jean de Brunhoff's Babar. *The Babar Story Book* was reviewed unfavourably in *The Junior Bookshelf* in December 1941:

> . . . the book depresses me . . . crowded text and lack of colour. I have not had an opportunity of comparing it with copies of the original folios, but we are informed that *The Story of Babar* is 'written' by Enid Blyton. What in heaven's name can she have done to it? Did de Brunhoff's fine prose need rewriting? That would indeed be gilding the lily. Let us hope nothing so horrible has really happened.[13]

It is interesting to compare this comment with E. V. Rieu's words of praise quoted earlier.

Both the reviews quoted are for books originating in France and rewritten by Enid Blyton. It was not until 1946 that a review of one of her own books appeared in the pages of *The Junior Bookshelf*, which was presumably pursuing the normal policy of critical reviews and concentrating on those books considered to be of significance.

There was, therefore, little written guidance for librarians. There were few books about children's literature. F. J. Harvey Darton's *Children's Books in England*, published in 1932, was concerned only with the history of children's books, and finished at 1901. Paul Hazard's *Books, Children and Men*, published in France in 1932, was not translated into English until 1944 and was then published in America rather than England. The only available book about contemporary writers, the American May Lamberton Becker's *Choosing Books for Children*, adapted to the English market and published by the Oxford University Press in 1937, seems to have been scarcely known. Certainly, when Geoffrey Trease published *Tales Out of School* in 1949, it was claimed as 'a new departure' and the 'first' book to look at contemporary children's literature.

May Lamberton Becker was one of the first writers on children's reading to show concern about the influence of the cinema, adopting a rather puritanical attitude towards it and suggesting that children should be protected from the premature experience it vicariously offered. Throughout the rest of the 1930s, the 1940s and the early 1950s, commentators from both the educational and the library worlds were very much concerned about the adverse effects upon children of both the cinema and comics. The concern about the cinema seems to have disappeared only with the increasing availability of television, while the concern about comics also lessened in the 1950s after the passing of the Children and Young Persons (Harmful Publications) Act. During the period of Enid Blyton's greatest output, therefore, from 1937 to 1955, her books could well have appeared to be a useful antidote to the supposed harmful effects of the cinema and comics. In the period before 1939 there were no signs of hostility towards Enid Blyton and by 1939 most people were deeply concerned with a far greater threat to Britain's children as the Second World War began.

Chapter Three

The War Years
1939–45

❁

THE SECOND WORLD WAR had a twofold effect on children's books generally. First, there was the damage caused by bombing raids on London, when publishers' stocks and printing plates were destroyed; secondly, there was the paper shortage. The war was something of a watershed in children's literature: many nineteenth- and early twentieth-century minor children's books went out of print at this time and with the stocks and printing plates destroyed, a conscious decision had to be taken as to whether it was worth the cost and effort of setting up in type and republishing a book which was probably out of date in its setting, theme and attitudes. Many books must have been rejected as not being in tune with the post-war society. Enid Blyton's books, on the other hand, were fresh from the press and reflected very much the ideas and beliefs of the parents of most of her readers.

The paper shortage also seems to have worked positively to Enid Blyton's advantage. By the time of the outbreak of war in 1939, her position as a children's writer was secure. Her various publishers must have respected her capacity for work, her business-like approach to writing and her commercial popularity. This was important because it meant that publishers managed to find the paper for her books even when it was in short supply and as, by this time, she was producing material for a number of different publishers, she had multiple paper allocations and was, therefore, at an advantage compared with other authors who worked only for one publisher.

Most publishers are in business to make money, and an Enid Blyton title was (and still is) an almost guaranteed commercial success. In the comprehensive bibliography of her work in

Barbara Stoney's biography,[1] fifty-three publishers are listed, although the majority of these are responsible for comparatively few titles. Her major publishers are Newnes, who published her first full-length story book, *Adventures of the Wishing Chair* and the weekly magazine, *Sunny Stories*, Methuen, Hodder and Stoughton (with its subsidiary firm of Brockhampton), Sampson Low and Collins, while the Lutterworth Press and Evans each published over twenty of her books.

While Newnes was her first major publisher, and indeed it was through working with them that Enid Blyton met her first husband, the firm of Hodder and Stoughton gradually came to regard itself as her main publisher, responsible for what were undoubtedly her two most popular series, the 'Famous Five' and the 'Secret Seven', and issuing her offical biography in 1974. John Attenborough, in his history of the firm, tells how Enid Blyton first came onto the Hodder list, via the Brockhampton Press. The latter was set up (as the Brockhampton Book Company) in 1938 to get rid of overstocks of theological works. The manager of this subsidiary, Ernest Roker, wanted to publish children's books and in 1940 was given permission to do so provided that he did not claim any of the Hodder wartime paper allocation; he therefore arranged to buy paper off-cuts from *Picture Post* to produce little booklets measuring three by six inches and, realizing that Enid Blyton was one of the most productive children's writers in the country, commissioned her to write a series of suitable stories; these emerged as the 'Mary Mouse' books. Two hundred thousand copies of each title were printed at a time and by the end of the 1960s, a total of four and a half million had been sold. In the same year that the first 'Mary Mouse' books appeared, 1942, the first 'Famous Five' story, *Five on a Treasure Island*, was also published by Hodder. Later on, in 1954, the 'Famous Five' Club was founded and forty thousand children enrolled in the first eight months.[2]

Both Paul Hodder-Williams and John Attenborough, of Hodder and Stoughton, were genuinely proud of Enid Blyton's connection with the firm, although they could not help but be aware of the criticisms which were made of her. Paul Hodder-Williams was annoyed about the supposed banning of her books by public libraries, even though he knew that this would increase her bookshop sales. In his address at her memorial service at St James', Piccadilly, he said: 'She really loved children and understood instinctively what would interest them.'[3] John Attenborough suggests that her royalty earnings 'provoked a critical reaction built more on jealousy than reason. Children from five to eleven, as most parents were aware, came to love reading *because* of Enid Blyton.'[4]

Although some leading publishers never took any Enid Blyton titles onto their lists, some of the firms that did have been responsible for publishing outstanding post-war children's writers. The profits that were made on Enid Blyton's books must have made it possible for them to experiment and to publish writers who could never be bestsellers to the same degree as Enid Blyton.

Despite the wartime paper shortages, one important event in the development of children's books did take place. Allen Lane, after establishing his first Penguin paperbacks in 1935, moved into the field of publishing for children. Having successfully launched Puffin Picture Books, which were simple information books, in 1940, he published the first Puffin Story Book in 1941. The first Puffin editor was Eleanor Graham, already experienced in writing, publishing and selling children's books, who shared the viewpoint of those who wanted to set high standards for children's reading. She describes her selection of Puffin titles as 'something of a counterblast to those who were thinking in terms of Angela Brazil and Enid Blyton . . . I was, of course, frequently urged to get some Blyton on our list but I never did. It was not intended for that kind of public.'[5] However, during this period and for a long time afterwards, paperbacks for children were published only by Penguin and the number of titles available in this format was therefore fairly small. Hardbacks, of course, were still relatively cheap.

Wartime restrictions on paper led not only to a shortage of books but also to a change in their appearance: the feather weight, bulked paper, commonly used for children's books in the 1930s, disappeared. However, the greatest effects of all were to be seen in the book shortage. An article in *The Library World* in 1943 drew attention to the fact that Lord David

Cecil had commented on the difficulties faced by parents who wanted to buy children's books as Christmas presents.[6] *The Junior Bookshelf* over the same period monitored the situation very closely and bemoaned the lack of newly published books. Lorna Lewis, a reviewer and writer of children's books, wrote an article for the *Wilson Library Bulletin*, an American library periodical, to describe what British children were reading in wartime. This could be summarized as 'whatever they could get' and this voracious and uncritical appetite was attributed to the paper shortage which had hit children's books 'especially hard'. Some firms, she said, had closed down their juvenile departments, others had lost large stocks in the blitz of 1940–1 and it was impossible to buy copies of *David Copperfield*, *Villette* or *The Vicar of Wakefield*.[7] Writing just after the war, in 1946, the Chief Librarian of Bethnal Green, reporting on a children's essay competition, said that his shelves were almost denuded of popular books such as *Peter Pan*, *The Water Babies* and *Little Women*, new copies of which had been almost unobtainable since the beginning of the war.

Although this situation seems difficult to believe forty years later, I personally can recall the problems and difficulties of spending book tokens in the early 1940s. One can see that it was not merely a question of the popular and meretricious driving out the good and worthwhile: there was actually a vacuum to be filled at the time when Enid Blyton was entering her most prolific period (she published 13 titles in 1940, 9 in 1941, 18 in 1942, 17 in 1943 and 22 in 1944).[8] Almost by chance, it seems, her books were being published at a time when well-established children's books were not being reprinted in sufficient quantities to meet demand. The lack of classics was particularly regretted. For example, the Bethnal Green librarian wrote that the place of the classics 'has to be taken in large part by books which, though healthy in tone and passably written, can by no indulgence of appraisal be called literature'.[9] In *The Junior Bookshelf* Mr Woodfield, also commenting on the lack of copies of classics, said: 'Let us forgo our Blyton, our Johns. Let us even manage without Ransome, Uttley, Farjeon, Lynch if necessary, but give us our classics.'[10]

Although some of the librarians involved in providing

services for children were of the view that it was the duty of the public library to set standards, there were as yet no signs of a desire to exclude Enid Blyton's work from stock. In 1943, Muriel Lock, a librarian at Croydon, expressed the view that: 'Most children have a latent good taste . . . The process will have to be one of gradual abolition of the inferior quality . . . certain standards should be kept in view.'[11] She did not, however, specify any particular author as not meeting those standards. The Bethnal Green librarian in the report already mentioned, explaining that the essay competition had been organized in order to get an assessment of the 'real value to the children in terms of good healthy reading of the service provided in public libraries', actually said, at least without disapproval, that there was a need to acquire more copies of popular books 'such as those by Enid Blyton'.[12]

The one carping note, apart from that struck by Eleanor Graham in retrospect, appeared in the pages of *The Junior Bookshelf*, which was published throughout the war years, though paper shortages and other causes meant that its appearance was sometimes irregular. Advertisements for Enid Blyton's books appeared from time to time and, of course, the fact that Mr Woodfield needed support of this kind from the publishers may have prevented him from giving his reviewers a free hand or from allowing them to be quite as outspoken as they might have liked to be. However, some comments were made, apparently tongue-in-cheek, such as the following which appeared in 'Notes from the attic' in March 1945:

> ENID BLYTON – Miss Blyton has written some hundred and fifty books and aims at a steady twenty a year. She is reported as saying, 'It is like pulling cotton off a reel.'[13]

As far as the children were concerned, Enid Blyton had already established herself as a favourite author. The first evidence of this comes in Lorna Lewis's article in 1945, where she reported that: 'Enid Blyton, writer for audiences anywhere between four and fifteen, has a big following . . .'[14] The youngest prize winner in the Bethnal Green essay competition, Gladys Smith, aged seven, was obviously a great admirer (the first on record) and in her essay she reflected the enthusiasm of her contemporaries:

I had a book out called *Round the Clock Stories* by enid blyton it was lovely I took it back and has I walked in there were three girls ask me whether I had an enid blyton book when I told then I had an enid blyton book they nearly went mad I think and they said O let me have it please so I didn't have a chance to say yes it was gone . . .[15]

The Bethnal Green report is one of the earliest accounts of children's reading interests in which the name of Enid Blyton appears.

Individually, of course, children at this time drew on different sources and the classics would be available to many, handed down by parents. Personal recollections of people who were children during this period show that they read widely and without much discrimination. Patricia Beer, the poet, born in the early 1920s,[16] and Anne Ellis, a children's librarian, born about a decade later,[17] both demonstrate a similiar range of reading. Both mention an enthusiasm for school stories at one stage, for *Little Women* and *Anne of Green Gables* and both also mention D. K. Broster's *The Flight of the Heron*. Patrica Beer belongs to the pre-Blyton generation while Anne Ellis says that she was only introduced to Enid Blyton's books through her younger sisters. Beryl Bainbridge, born in 1934, recalls that 'when I was nine I was reading *Just William*, *What Katy Did*, *The Mill on the Floss* and Enid Blyton. Also my mother's library books which had a strongly romantic flavour.'[18] David Benedictus, born in 1938, remembers that as a child he read *Just William*, fairy stories, *King Solomon's Mines*, Enid Blyton's adventure stories, *Thirty-Nine Steps*, Biggles, the Saint and *Bulldog Drummond*. He thought Arthur Ransome was 'wet' and would rather borrow his sister's Angela Brazil and *The Naughtiest Girl is a Monitor* (Blyton again).[19] As a child, I read most of the books which Enid Blyton had published by the time I was eleven, but very few of the later ones, even though I had a sister five years younger who was also a great Enid Blyton fan. I also read the classics and a wide range of contemporary children's authors who were being praised in the pages of *The Junior Bookshelf*. Children born as the 1930s wore on were less and less likely to escape reading Enid Blyton at some stage in their childhood.

For children growing up during the war, radio with its

regular 'Children's Hour' was influential. Anne Ellis mentions being introduced to *The Flight of the Heron* through this programme, which used many children's books, both classic and contemporary, as material for drama and story readings. Unlike the cinema, radio never seems to have been regarded as anything but an influence for the good, perhaps because it did maintain rigorous standards in the selection of the material which it used. Its influence in popularizing certain children's books was mentioned by Eileen Colwell in a paper given to the Library Association Conference in 1947 to mark the establishment of the Youth Libraries Section.

Enid Blyton's work was never used in this way. Barbara Stoney writes that she tried to 'interest the BBC in broadcasting some of her work but nothing came of this, despite the fact that both she and Hugh [her first husband] repeatedly sent in material they considered suitable for the children's programmes'.[20]

Enid Blyton did not need the assistance of the BBC to make her popular. Instead she established her public through her weekly magazine which provided good publicity for her books. In her weekly letter, readers were told when a story which had appeared as a serial was going to be published in book form or when stories about certain characters who regularly appeared in the pages of the magazines were to be gathered together in a book. The fact that the readers had already enjoyed the stories once did not appear to discourage them from acquiring the books so that they could read them again. Richard Bourne has recently written:

> I am sure that this awareness of a child's need to enjoy books, to be entertained as well as stimulated, lies behind the success of many school bookshops. It is the reason why children queued up at the counters of bookshops in the 1940s to buy Enid Blyton at a time when some high-minded public librarians were refusing to stock her.[21]

Although there is no evidence that any librarians were at this time refusing to stock her and although 'queues' may be an exaggeration, it is clear that by the end of the war Enid Blyton was well established. She shared the advantages of some earlier popular authors who are held in affectionate regard by their readers. Like Dickens, she had the discipline of serial publication; like Conan Doyle she had the advantage of cheap magazine publication. By 1945 she was a successful and popular storyteller, and her books were readily available in bookshops, newsagents and libraries.

Chapter Four

The Period of Recovery
1946–58

WARTIME SHORTAGES continued for some time after the end of the war in 1945 and it was not until the early 1950s that children's books became so plentiful that librarians could be selective in what they chose for the shelves of their children's libraries. This period was also a period of development in public libraries, particularly in the field of children's librarianship. In the late 1940s the first librarians in charge of work with young people were appointed in counties such as Nottinghamshire, Lancashire and Hertfordshire. Development was slow, however; the West Riding (of Yorkshire) County Library made its first specialist appointment in 1953, but the second city, Birmingham, did not make one until 1960. A survey carried out by the Youth Libraries Section of the Library Association in 1958–9 showed that there were only 253 designated posts on APT grades for children's specialists in 168 library authorities; 43 authorities had designated posts on other, lower, grades while 189 authorities had no designated posts.[1]

These early children's librarians were largely self-taught. They were qualified as librarians, often through correspondence courses or part-time classes, but they had had no formal training in working with young people. When the schools of librarianship were set up after the Second World War to meet the needs of returning servicemen, little attention was paid to teaching about the special library needs of young people and it was not until 1964, when the full-time course in librarianship changed from being a one-year course to being a two-year course, that it became possible to take courses in librarianship and literature for children as part of the basic librarianship qualification.

Immediately prior to this, the North-Western Polytechnic in London had offered a series of short courses lasting first six and then eight weeks, between 1958 and 1962, and it was also possible to take two papers in the Final Examination of the Library Association leading to the Fellowship.

In 1947, however, a Youth Libraries Section was formed within the Library Association, replacing the earlier Association of Children's Librarians, and this gave children's librarians an opportunity to meet each other to discuss matters of common concern and interest, and in 1955 a newsletter, edited by Stanley C. Dedman, began to appear. In the period between 1947 and 1955, a critical period in the publication of Enid Blyton books, the existence of the Section seems to have led to more comment on children's reading amongst librarians generally, but there were no signs of anti-Blyton hysteria.

In 1947 Ernest Savage, the City Librarian of Edinburgh, who was regarded as one of the leading chief librarians of this period, published *A Librarian Looks at Readers*, the first three chapters of which are concerned with children's reading. There is, in fact, very little about reading for girls and Savage, in talking about books for boys, seems to look back nostalgically to what he himself must have read as a boy. The picture that he paints is very similar to that depicted in Jenkinson's survey, that all children were still happy to read Henty, Scott and Stevenson. Savage's chief dislikes were 'bloods', girls' school stories and the influence of the cinema and he again took the view that the best books, provided in sufficient quantities, would drive out a liking for the worst. He totally ignored the much-praised writers for children who had begun to write since 1930, such as Arthur Ransome, Noel Streatfeild, Geoffrey Trease and J. R. R. Tolkien, some of whom at least should surely have come to his notice as winners of the Carnegie Medal. Interestingly enough, the only post-1930 children's writer who is mentioned is Enid Blyton. Referring to Jenkinson's finding that girls read more plays than boys, he comments that 'Enid Blyton's *Plays for Younger Children*, *Plays for Older Children* and like volumes, are Christmas cake to them.'[2] This favourable mention of Enid Blyton suggests that Savage did not include her books amongst the rubbish he obviously despised.

Of course, there is a lapse of time between a book being written and its publication, but there is little evidence in the periodical articles of 1947 that librarians regarded Enid Blyton as a producer of sub-literature. Yet by this time she was well established as a writer and her peak publishing year, 1951, was only four years away. An article in *Librarian and the Bookworld* in May 1947, by 'F.P.P.' comments on the desperate need of libraries for more copies of good popular books and classics, and the desirability of librarians being more discriminating, but she does not name the undesirable books and the only ones that are hinted at are those with a definite religious bias, which presumably refers to the books published for the Sunday school market.[3]

In June 1947, to mark the founding of the Youth Libraries Section, a special session was held during the Library Association Conference at Brighton, at which Eileen Colwell gave a paper surveying developments in children's books during the previous twenty years. She mentioned many of the authors who had established themselves during this period; some of these are no longer in print, but she did also refer to the three authors who were to become so controversial in the next decade, acknowledging their popularity. Speaking of W. E. Johns, she said, 'I do not suppose that his books will have any lasting fame for they are topical and his heroes are of the kind who will be superseded by still more up-to-date supermen.' She paid tribute to Richmal Crompton, saying, 'Our children – and grown-ups – are none the worse for the many laughs William has given them in these depressing times', and then went on to say, 'But which will survive the verdict of the years – the latest Enid Blyton or *The Wind in the Willows*? I venture to predict that Enid Blyton's stories, although they meet a popular need, are ephemeral, for their characters are puppets.'[4] However, the main message of her paper was to reflect the prevalent feeling of the idealistic children's librarians of the 1930s and 1940s, that: 'All we can do is to give them the best books available and leave the selection to them, for their taste, in the long run, is always good.'[5]

The following month, July, found G. A. Carter giving a paper to a meeting of librarians at Wallasey. He revealed that a survey carried out amongst 109 children of twelve to fourteen in the north-west of England showed that Enid Blyton was their fourth most popular author. More popular were W. E. Johns, mentioned 34 times, Angela Brazil, with 29 mentions also reflecting the very great popularity of school stories, and Percy Westerman, who received 28 mentions. Enid Blyton had 25. No comments were made on this order of popularity or on these particular names.[6]

In the October of the following year, 1948, a conference paper given by Hilda McGill, Organizer of Library Work with Young People in Manchester, although in many ways forward looking, still reflects a world of public libraries where there was little or no provision for children before they could read fluently, where silence, clean hands and good behaviour were required and where it was believed that these could be obtained by high expectations. There is a comment on the generally low standards of book selection in children's libraries and a plea for higher standards but there is no specific mention, favourable or otherwise, of Enid Blyton.[7] The following year, in 1949, Charles Nowell, the City Librarian of Manchester, conducted a very amicable correspondence with Enid Blyton, who had written to him after her attention had been drawn to his favourable mention of her work in his annual report.[8] It seems clear from this that Enid Blyton's books were stocked in Manchester libraries at this period.

The first public manifestations of what soon came to be regarded as the 'Blyton problem' came really in 1949. Early in that year Geoffrey Trease published the first critical survey of contemporary children's fiction by a British writer. After a short career as a teacher, Trease had begun writing for children in the early 1930s and had made a major contribution to the development of the children's historical novel. After the publication of *Tales Out of School* in 1949 (a second edition appeared in 1964), he was regarded as one of the leading authorities on children's books and has written and talked widely on the subject. In *Tales Out of School*, he describes Enid Blyton as 'perhaps the most prolific English author for younger children'.[9] He had written to her to obtain her views about writing for children, which he quotes, and he mentions her in the context of school stories, citing *The Naughtiest Girl in the School* as 'an example of Miss Blyton's school fiction at its best'.[10] He also describes a children's librarian as speaking of Enid Blyton's 'intense mediocrity', but his final suggestion that authors should set to work and write equally popular books with more stimulating themes and vocabulary seems to be a counsel of despair. As an author himself, he probably realized that this was more easily said than done. In a paper given at the Library Association Conference in May 1949, Stanley Dedman referred to this verdict of 'intense mediocrity' recorded by Trease. He had carried out a survey amongst children in Leyton in the East End of London and although twenty children had named *Treasure Island* as their favourite book and eight children *Black Beauty*, making these the two most popular titles, forty-seven children had listed an Enid Blyton title. After this, in surveys intended to establish children's favourite authors, Enid Blyton seldom appears in other than first place as far as children of eight to twelve are concerned. In the discussion which followed Stanley Dedman's paper, Hilda McGill, who had omitted any reference to Enid Blyton in her own paper the previous year, is described as 'deprecating the fact that once again a discussion on children's reading tastes had degenerated into a discussion upon Enid Blyton'.[11] Dedman himself seemed to take a more moderate view, making a good case for the value of reading widely a catholic selection of books, as the best way of acquiring a taste for the best literature. He was more concerned about the need to prevent children from reading comics and also believed that radio, in introducing good books to children, was a good influence, while the cinema's influence was bad because children were able to see lurid and violent films. Dedman saw quite clearly that 'whether we like it or not, we must face this fact of Enid Blyton's great popularity',[12] and refers to the overwhelming demand for her books. His remarks show that arguments against stocking Enid Blyton's books on the grounds that they are light, escapist literature were already being aired, but he suggested that 'although the Blyton books may be light and easy to read, they are morally sound, right always triumphs, and the child characters are real and normal, and act in much the same manner as the children who read the books'.[13]

As a result of his paper, Dedman received a letter from Enid Blyton, which was subsequently published in the *Library Association Record* and which showed no sign of the resentful feelings which she was later to express about librarians. In this letter and her letters to Charles Nowell, she was full of praise for librarians and their 'fine work'.[14] Certainly at this time relations between Enid Blyton and librarians seem to have been harmonious.

However, by the early 1950s the country was beginning to recover from the effects of the war years and at last the book-supply situation began to improve. Librarians could afford to be selective although critical opinions still tended to develop in isolation since there were so few specialist librarians at this time. W. A. Taylor, then Chief Librarian of St Pancras in London, has shown that he decided in the early 1950s that as there was only a limited amount of money to spend, it should be spent on 'the best in children's literature' and books by Enid Blyton, W. E. Johns and Richmal Crompton were not replaced as they wore out.[15]

There were few important landmarks in children's literature in the 1950s and the main developments lay outside mainstream children's fiction, with picture books and information books. In 1956, the Library Association established the Kate Greenaway Medal to be awarded annually to an outstanding illustrator of children's books and, after this, though not of course necessarily as a result of it, the quantity and quality of British children's picture books improved significantly. The successful 'Noddy' books, the first of which was published in 1949, therefore established themselves at a period when there was still a comparative shortage of good quality books for the youngest children.

Towards the end of the 1950s the growth of heuristic methods in primary schools led to an upsurge in the publication of information books for younger children. The accompanying growth in primary school libraries may also have accounted for a new movement among the leading publishers of children's books, the production of simple formula stories for five- to eight-year-olds. However, as the pioneer publisher in this field was the Brockhampton Press, which was associated with the 'Secret Seven' and 'Famous

Five' books, another reason may have been the feeling that Enid Blyton had passed her production peak. The example of Brockhampton was followed by most of the other important publishers for children and a number of series for this age group came into existence (and are still flourishing). Although they have helped to fill an undoubted gap, for the most part the stories lack the excitement and the immense readability of Enid Blyton's stories for children of the same age.

These publishers' series began to appear at a time when the age appeal of mainstream children's literature was beginning to move upwards. During the 1960s, for example, fantasy was written for older children, possibly as a result of Tolkien's new popularity and the success of C. S. Lewis's 'Narnia' books, while the barriers which had hitherto been firmly erected around subjects considered suitable for children's fiction were slowly pushed back. A new sophistication in style and content was heralded by the work of William Mayne, whose first book was published in 1952. His books are demanding and provide the challenge for which Eileen Colwell looked in her papers of 1947 and 1951.

In 1951 the Youth Libraries Section held its first weekend school and a paper given by Eileen Colwell on this occasion reflects the state of children's literature at this time. She made two references to Enid Blyton, one of which contains an element of adverse criticism:

Almost everything about the school story – an English speciality – is artificial. The humour is facetious, the plot hackneyed, the characters typed, and the atmosphere snobbish in some way. This can be seen in the books by Rita Coatts, Enid Blyton, Sylvia Little and similar authors.[16]

She also reiterated the point she had made in 1947, that Enid Blyton's books would not endure, commenting:

In any survey of modern children's literature, the work of Enid Blyton cannot be ignored. Miss Blyton is a phenomenon in the history of children's books for she is the most prolific and widely publicised of children's writers, enjoys an immense popularity and writes on an infinite variety of subjects. She has undoubtedly found the formula for success in writing for children. Time alone will show how enduring her fame will be.[17]

While these comments are far from enthusiastic, they do not suggest that libraries banned Enid Blyton's books completely. Her fame has, incidentally, endured considerably longer than that of other authors who are praised in the same paper and one has the feeling that by the time librarians were aroused to the dangers, if any, of Enid Blyton, she had already firmly established herself as a popular children's writer, likely to extinguish or at least overshadow all other children's writers of the same period. The general outlook for children's literature was none too good in 1951. Eileen Colwell could see little indication of progress since her conference paper of 1947; there were no new authors to be mentioned, and she commented:

> The general standard of children's literature today is commonplace . . . too many children's books are written to a formula and are uninspired and lacking in the challenge that children need . . . we must do all in our power to reject the second-rate and to encourage quality.[18]

In the early 1950s, children's librarians, in public at least, seem to have continued to be most concerned about the effects of the cinema, of comics and of horror stories.

In the second issue of the Youth Libraries Section newsletter, *Spotlight*, a children's librarian opened a debate with a chilling letter about children wanting to borrow *The Scourge of the Swastika*, a book about the German concentration camps, and obtaining horror comics.[19] The only mentions of Enid Blyton in the early issues of *Spotlight* are fairly non-committal. For example, a child's remark that 'Enid Blyton writes some good books with exciting stories, but, if you read them once I find you don't want to read them again' is quoted under the heading 'Without Comment',[20] and a report from Kirkcaldy Public Library says that Enid Blyton and W. E. Johns are still the most popular authors, again without adding comment.[21]

When I began to search for documentation of the Blyton phenomenon as it affected libraries, I accepted the general view that many libraries did not buy Enid Blyton's books. The only evidence I had for this was the unsubstantiated comments of critics and journalists of the kind already quoted, and the knowledge that, following the example of several more experienced children's librarians in neighbouring library authorities, I had bought very few of her books for use in the two library systems in which I worked between 1958 and 1968. The only real evidence that libraries were not buying Enid Blyton's books dated from the early 1960s, although it was clear from this that these policies must have been introduced in some libraries in the early 1950s.

I therefore talked to a number of friends who had been children's librarians or who had held senior positions in libraries in the early 1950s, and the following pages are an amalgam of their opinions and recollections. I tried to pin them down to 1951 as this was the year of the first weekend school of the Youth Libraries Section and also the year in which Enid Blyton published the greatest number of titles (thirty-seven). This was also a year when public libraries were in the first stages of post-war development and, although there were sufficient children's librarians to make the holding of a weekend school a viable proposition, there were still very few specialist posts.

The ten librarians, some now retired, who kindly helped me with their recollections and impressions were, in 1951, working in a variety of library authorities including London boroughs, provincial cities and boroughs and counties, ranging over the whole of England. They either represent the first generation of children's librarians or were in senior posts in authorities which at the time did not have specialist posts. They have one thing in common: from their recollections, it seems that they lacked, both in their initial training and through post-qualification opportunities, external guidance about the standards to be applied in book selection, but felt some need to rationalize their buying of Enid Blyton's books which otherwise threatened to swamp the stock of the children's library.

Reference has already been made to the fact that there were few opportunities for specialist training in children's librarianship and literature until 1964. One of the ten recalled attending the course in librarianship provided for returning ex-service people at University College, London, in 1946–7:

some lectures were given by Eileen Colwell who talked 'good sound common sense' and who obviously must have influenced many young librarians at this time and for some years afterwards. Some of the others were given responsibility for buying children's books without knowing anything about them. As one said: 'In those days one didn't select one's job, one did as one was told.' Another confessed that her hair now curls at the thought of some of the things she did but her chief librarian was a great believer in staff learning by trial and error. She had access to *The Horn Book Magazine* and *The Junior Bookshelf* and went to Combridge's to buy books 'under the watchful eye of Mr. Woodfield'.

Asked for recollections of when the controversy about Enid Blyton began, most were vague and placed the beginning sometime after the end of the Second World War in 1945, either the late 1940s or the early 1950s, commenting also about the shortage of other children's books in this post-war period. One recalled that in her London borough they bought most of Enid Blyton's titles, but that there was very little else. One wrote that she still remembered the moment of revelation when she discovered for herself that Enid Blyton used a certain number of basic plots and she decided at that point that the library did not need to have every variation of the theme. Another described how her 'moment of truth' came after an unpopular book published under the name of 'Mary Pollock' in 1947 was reissued under Enid Blyton's own name in 1950 and suddenly became popular. She then decided it was the name and a good publicity campaign which induced children to read Enid Blyton's books and from then on she bought very few of them.

Only one of the ten librarians stated that Enid Blyton's books were eventually not bought at all in her library, saying that Enid Blyton, W. E. Johns and other authors of the same kind were 'phased out' from 1948 onwards. The others bought 'only a few' or 'the best'. One suggested that it was a dangerous practice to praise or criticize any author on a generalized basis, since this might lead to good books being overlooked and bad books being bought. Another pointed out that it was undiplomatic to exclude one author from stock; it could appear to be a criticism of parent's tastes if they encouraged children to ask for Enid Blyton's books and the children were then told that they were not stocked because they were 'bad'.

One librarian recalled an incident which can be traced to 1951. She took a group of children to an Enid Blyton tea party at which the children played games and had tea. Enid Blyton then came onto a platform, talked about her latest book and offered to tell the children a story about one of her characters chosen by them. The children all went home with balloons, feeling that they had had a wonderful time. This librarian suggests that as, about this time, there was a relaxation in economy standards for paper, new, good writers were emerging and that possibly the party was held because Enid Blyton's publishers felt that she just might be on the downward side of the crest of the wave.

During one discussion of the public libraries' attitude to Enid Blyton, the Library Association was quoted as saying, 'The job of the public library is to educate and entertain. In the children's departments we put a heavier stress on education. It is thought that Miss Blyton does not present enough of a challenge to children.'[22] The educational role of the children's library was beginning to be recognized more strongly and widely by 1951 and this put many librarians into something of a quandary. Enid Blyton was in great demand for she had created a public for her books, but librarians were conscious of the fact that increasingly there was so much more that was worthy of children's attention. In the West Riding, there was a policy, under the direction of B. Oliph Smith, County Librarian from 1940 to 1957, of raising the general level of reading and much of what he considered sub-literature was not bought. He was very conscious of the educational role of the public library and in 1955 stated:

It is time that the public library was recognized by ratepayers and their representatives as the major instrument of adult education. It is perhaps above all time that library authorities and librarians took their courage in both hands, and by recognizing and proclaiming that the real role of the public library is to educate and inform, began to earn that respect and that financial support which the service needs and deserves, but which it will never command while it is so largely and obviously engaged in the provision of light entertainments.[23]

I am particularly interested in what was happening in the West Riding as I used two branches of the County Library as a child and as an adolescent from 1939 to 1948, worked in one during vacation periods as a student between 1948 and 1952, and in 1952 joined the staff, working first at headquarters in Wakefield and then as a mobile librarian until 1958. During the whole of this period, 1939 to 1958, the only Enid Blyton title which I can remember seeing was *Bom*, a book similar in style and format to the 'Noddy' books, which was bought in quantity when it first came out in 1956.

However, memory can play false, and one of the librarians who was in charge of a West Riding branch in the 1940s recalls that there were long waiting lists for Enid Blyton's books which seems to indicate that there were some in stock. Librarians who held senior administrative posts in the late 1940s and early 1950s could not recall that there had been any actual ban on Enid Blyton titles although they felt that at one time only the 'better type' were bought. They did agree, however, that her books were so popular that they were never on the shelves and enthusiasts 'had to be pretty fast on the returned trolley to get hold of one'.

Apart from a very few libraries which had adopted a phasing-out policy by the early 1950s, the situation seems to have been that libraries were not anti-Blyton but that Enid Blyton's great output made it necessary to be selective. The sheer quantity of her books made her name the one that 'every parent remembered', 'it was always a question of quantity that was under consideration,' she wrote for such a wide age range 'that a child could read nothing but Blyton during its reading life', and the books flooded the market. The problem of how to cope with the demand and the inevitable requests was not an easy one to solve. One library apparently put up a notice saying that 'all books could be reserved except those by Enid Blyton'. Some librarians recalled authors who could be offered as substitutes or alternatives in the early 1950s – Malcolm Saville, Kathleen Fidler and Ian Serrailler seem to have been popular choices in this respect. One librarian remembers that at her London library she once produced a booklist on the lines of 'If you like the "Famous Five" you will also like . . .' The aim was to make children realize that 'Blyton' was not synonymous with 'book'. This problem still occurs over twenty years later and Walsall Public Library, for example, issued a list called 'Alternatives to Blyton' in January 1977. In 1973 Janet Hill, emphasizing the need to have a book selection policy which relates to the needs of the community, wrote:

> Many libraries refuse to buy Blyton books. I don't think this is a very helpful attitude, but if a library provides them in such quantity that there are always Blyton titles on the shelves, some children will continue to borrow them in preference to everything else . . . in Lambeth we buy only three of the most popular series. A small selection of titles is bought for each library, and complete sets of the same series are bought for a reserve stock . . . children . . . can reserve specific titles, which will be supplied direct from reserve stock, and returned to it when the request has been satisfied.[24]

A picture emerges of the series which are most likely to be bought by libraries: the 'Famous Five', 'Secret Seven', 'Faraway Tree' and 'Noddy' series, the two series of school stories, 'St Clare's' and 'Malory Towers', and, the most universally approved series of all, the 'Adventure' series, published by Macmillan.

By the early 1950s teachers were also becoming aware of the popularity of Enid Blyton. Surveys carried out in schools began to indicate this popularity during the 1940s. In an article published in *Life and Letters* in November 1945, Gwen Marsh reported on an inquiry which she had recently carried out amongst secondary school children, where Enid Blyton had proved to be the third most popular author amongst girls in an elementary school (i.e. non-selective secondary school).[25] A report published in 1950 showed that in a Glasgow school, in a class library used by ten-year-old girls, the only book which was issued during each of the sixteen weeks of the survey was Enid Blyton's *Castle of Adventure*. Essays produced by the same class on 'My favourite book' demonstrated quite clearly that Enid Blyton was well-established as the favourite author.[26] Another survey of the same period, carried out by Brighton Training College amongst 1803 children of nine to eleven, asked children for the titles of books which they had read more than once because they had particularly enjoyed them. Enid Blyton titles were mentioned by 332 children; the next most popular groups were annuals and collections (158), *Robin Hood* (105) and *Black Beauty* (82).[27]

Two more surveys were published in 1957. J. D. Carsley's survey, amongst junior school children on Merseyside, involved a sample of 1054 boys and 986 girls, aged ten, chosen to represent schools of different patterns of organization (mixed, single sex, single stream and four-stream) and social backgrounds. Children were asked to give their favourite book and Enid Blyton was the author mentioned most frequently by both boys and girls. The boys listed 116 Enid Blyton titles, of which 50 were 'Famous Five' books, the next most popular being 'Biggles' books (49) and *Treasure Island* (31), while the girls produced 249 mentions of Enid Blyton, of which 50 were of 'Famous Five' titles, with *Black Beauty* (57) and *Little Women* (45) following on.[28] The 8,000 children who were surveyed in the Harrap and W. H. Smith survey in the same year were grouped into four categories: boys at public and grammar schools, boys at secondary modern schools, girls at public and grammar schools, and girls at secondary modern schools. Only in the case of the first group was Enid Blyton not mentioned enough times to appear in the final analysis. With the secondary modern boys, she was the second most popular author, and with both groups of girls she was the most popular author, although the fact that Agatha Christie appears as the second most popular author amongst the girls suggests that many of the girls in the sample would be beyond the stage of reading Enid Blyton.[29]

The authors of the Black survey (1958) were concerned with the reading of grammar schools girls and drew their sample from both single sex and co-educational schools in different types of area. They comment that the extreme popularity of adventure stories amongst the first years is largely due to Enid Blyton's popularity. A third-year girl is quoted as writing,

'When I was younger, I used to be very enthusiastic about the adventure stories of Enid Blyton. Now I think they are terrible. They are based on a very simple plot that could be explained in a few pages, but are drawn out into full-length books by the description of meals that the children had.'

This comment emphasizes the fact that, as the survey shows, children do outgrow Enid Blyton, who wanes in popularity with the second and third forms and disappears altogether from the reading of the fourth years.[30]

Amongst teachers, the idea that Enid Blyton's books are useful as material on which children can practise their reading skills seems to have established itself at an early stage. Geoffrey Trease commented in 1949 that, 'A teacher remarked that their simplicity of style, combined with their entertainment value, made them useful in the early stages of reading, because they broke down the child's resistance to print.'[31] Even those librarians who felt strongly that the function of the public library was to promote the best children's books, realized that teachers might justifiably regard Enid Blyton's books as a useful means of helping children to practise reading skills. Teachers were in a much better position to see that the reluctant readers who might profit from Enid Blyton's books got them and, conversely, to ensure that keen and able readers moved on to more demanding books.

Teachers probably hold as wide a range of opinions on Enid Blyton and children's books generally as any other section of the population although a recent survey suggests that they are not generally hostile.[32] Their views have not received quite so much publicity as those of librarians, partly because children's leisure reading is a relatively small part of their concerns and partly because their book selection policies can be carried out much less publicly. However, by 1958, controversy about the value of Enid Blyton was well established amongst members of the teaching profession as we can see from the following comment made by John Cutforth in 1956: 'As we might expect, the reformers and improvers are in full cry; few assemblies of teachers are not sharply divided on the subject of Miss Blyton's work!'[33]

Comparatively little has been written about the attitudes of parents to Enid Blyton. The first children to read her books in quantity, who would have been born between 1930 and 1936, would themselves start to become parents soon after 1950. Many of them must have taken the view that as they had enjoyed her books, their children would do the same. Since little adverse criticism of her work had appeared by the early 1950s, there was no reason why they should not encourage the reading of her books and, by this time, even those parents who had not themselves come across her books in childhood must have realized that they were an effective source of entertainment for many children. In *20th Century Children's Books*, published in 1952, Frank Eyre refers to Enid Blyton as 'the best-selling children's writer of today',[34] which suggests that by the early 1950s her books were readily accessible in bookshops and no doubt the situation which certainly existed at the end of the decade, when the average bookshop gave as much display space to Enid Blyton titles as to all the other children's books put together, was already to be seen. Such a situation meant that these books easily caught the eye of grandparents, godparents and other adults in search of children's books as presents.

The picture which emerges from such evidence as does exist, however, shows that since the early 1950s some parents have become aware of the fact that Enid Blyton's books are poorly regarded by some teachers and librarians and tend to be on the defensive, while other parents, who try to encourage children to read what are thought to be good books, have adopted the accepted critical attitudes. Certainly by the late 1950s children's librarians talking to groups of parents at meetings of parent-teacher associations, mothers' clubs and the like, found that one of the most frequently asked questions was about the effects of reading Enid Blyton.

Whatever advice they receive, parents of small children in particular are likely to be influenced by the fact that as well as having Noddy books read to them, their children may well have Noddy soap, Noddy toothbrushes and Noddy cereal, since the Noddy character has been commercially exploited in nursery food and equipment. This kind of exploitation is not uncommon nowadays but in the 1950s Noddy was one of the few book characters who gave his name to other nursery products. One librarian, in a letter to me, quoted the experience of a young mother saying to her, after she had talked to a young wives' group about the variety of books available to children, about the not-yet-reading baby in the pram, as she fixed on his Noddy safety-harness, 'He loves Noddy, it means we are going for a walk.'

In the early 1950s, like librarians and teachers, thinking parents who cared about their children's cultural experiences, were probably far more concerned about the effects of horror comics and the cinema. This was the period when a campaign against the worst form of comics was mounted and brought to a successful conclusion with the passing of the Children and Young Persons (Harmful Publications) Act in 1955. To parents *Sunny Stories* no doubt seemed a very desirable antidote. In 1951 the British Research Bureau carried out a survey of the reading of children's periodicals and comics on behalf of the Hulton Press who wished to establish the market penetration of one of their comics, the *Eagle*, which had been launched as a quality comic. This survey showed that 13% of the total child population between the ages of eight and fifteen read Enid Blyton's *Sunny Stories*. It was far more popular with girls than with boys, 22% of the girls in the age group reading it as compared with 5% of the boys. A further breakdown of the figures showed that 30% of the eight- to ten-year-old girls read it.[35]

What kind of guidance did librarians, teachers and other adults receive from the specialist booklists, reviewing periodicals and monographs available during this period? By the 1950s the Library Association, through three of its branches, was producing lists of recommended books under the title of *Books for Young People*. These were concerned to identify books 'of positive value' which have 'sound writing, lively imagination and accuracy in observation'.[36] The list of books for under-elevens, published in 1952, included four fiction titles by Enid Blyton, *The Children of Cherry Tree Farm*, *Five Fall into Adventure*, *The Green Story Book* and *The Island of Adventure* with other books in the same series mentioned in the annotations.[37] *The Children's Life of Christ* and *Let's Garden* were included in the appropriate non-fiction sections. No Enid Blyton titles, however, were included in the list for slightly older children which appeared the following year. *The Children of Cherry Tree Farm* and *The Island of Adventure* survived in a revised list in 1955,[38] and *A Story Book of Jesus* alone was to be found in the revised edition of 1960,[39] where the annotation reads, 'A simple version that retains some of the original wording of the Gospel story.'

One of the standard guides to British children's books in the 1950s was Kathleen Lines' *Four to Fourteen*, compiled for the National Book League and published by the Cambridge University Press. An introduction by Walter de la Mare described it as a 'manual' and Kathleen Lines herself described it as a list from which a child's own library could be chosen, or as a buying list for school librarians. It had come out originally as a pamphlet in 1940 and at that stage it included no Enid Blyton; the 1950 edition included *The Children's Life of Christ* and *The Valley of Adventure*, the annotation for the latter being: 'Miss Blyton has written some two hundred books for children: omnibus books, nature books, family, school and adventure stories, which are issued by various publishers. Her popularity is immense.'[40] In the preface to what is described as the 'second' edition (1956), Kathleen Lines wrote, 'It is not for me in a list of this sort to add to the publicity of already well-publicized contemporary writers,' and the only Blyton title included is *Let's Garden*, described as 'simple directions for little children who want to grow things'.[41]

Until 1958 the periodical read most regularly and assiduously by librarians selecting children's books was likely to be *The Junior Bookshelf*, whose editor, H. J. B. Woodfield, stands out, along with Eileen Colwell, as one of the most influential figures in thinking about children's books during this period. Not only was he able to express his view in *The Junior Bookshelf*, but, as a bookseller, he must have influenced what books librarians bought to some extent, especially after he set up his own library supply firm, specializing in selling children's books to libraries, in 1946. In 1949 he drew comparisons between British librarians and their rather more critical American counterparts, commenting, 'The fact that little Tommy wants to read the latest counterpart to Biggles or little Elsie wallows in every new Enid Blyton would not be used as a reason for buying these books if, in the librarian's judgement, they were not of a sufficiently high standard.'[42] Elsewhere Enid Blyton is clearly implied although not named in phrases like 'the numerous titles that flow from the pen of one very popular, but not first rate writer'.[43]

However, during this period of recovery, there were only two reviews of Enid Blyton's books, both for titles in the 'Adventure' series published by Macmillan and generally regarded as the best of Enid Blyton's work. In March 1946, *The Castle of Adventure* was said to lack 'body and background', the scene was 'vague', the characters had little 'reality or individuality', although the reviewer added 'this book is as good as anything I have read by this author.'[44] The July 1948 review of *The Sea of Adventure* by Eileen Colwell contained the much-quoted comment, 'But what hope has a band of desperate men against four children?' and complained of the lack of atmosphere and indistinguishable characters.[45]

The School Librarian and *The School Library Review* continued to reflect a scene where young people were encouraged to read the classics or middlebrow bestsellers, although there were some signs of support for the view which Jenkinson had put forward in his survey of children's reading, that books suitable for children at every stage of their development should be available in the school library. In *The School Library Review*, which ceased publication in 1952, I found only one reference to Enid Blyton. This was in an article by Elizabeth Bewick, a children's librarian, who, writing about children's fiction in 1952, said, 'But by far the most popular children's author today is Enid Blyton, whose phenomenal output includes books of every conceivable type for children of all ages, each of them an instantaneous success with her devoted public but not one of them of any real or lasting literary value.'[46] In *The School Librarian* the first mention of Enid Blyton came rather earlier, in 1947, when a teacher, writing about the library for eight- to thirteen-year-olds at St Dunstan's College, commented, 'The boys who enter at the age of eight or nine, who are fee payers, are quite different. Enid Blyton is generally their first choice with Arthur Ransome a good second.'[47] There is no hint here that there might be a world of difference between these two writers and perhaps in the 1940s most teachers did not take the trouble to investigate the actual contents of children's books since the main aim was to get the readers on to Kipling, Scott, Dickens and Dumas as soon as possible. Trash, according to a letter from a Northampton teacher in the same issue, meant comics, near-pornography and women's magazines.[48]

A teacher-librarian and a children's librarian, both working in the East End of London, commented on the popularity of Enid Blyton in *School Librarian* articles in 1949. The librarian pointed out that although her books are light, ephemeral and not outstandingly well-written, they are also completely innocuous.[49] The same issue includes an amusing review of *The Mountain of Adventure* (significantly it is an 'Adventure' title which is being reviewed yet again), commenting on the food, the incredible plot and the 'accommodating mama' who allows the children to set off to explore the Welsh mountains with a guide who 'can't read a map, doesn't know the way, doesn't speak English and is discovered somewhat late to be a simpleton'.[50] A list of books recommended for retarded readers in December 1950, includes three Enid Blyton titles.[51] The standards set by *The School Librarian* and *The School Library Review*, the main specialist sources of information about children's books for teachers at this time, were therefore marginally less discriminating than those set by *The Junior Bookshelf*.

The first number of the special *Children's Books* issue of the *Times Literary Supplement* appeared in July 1949. The editorial described it as 'one means of breaking the almost total silence which greets the appearance of a new book for children' and certainly it would have a wider circulation than either *The Junior Bookshelf* or the two school library journals. Geoffrey Trease, reviewing the first few issues in *The School Librarian*, suggested that it was hypercritical,[52] but as books by Elinor Brent-Dyer, Richmal Crompton and Ruby Ferguson were reviewed in the first issue, the standards set were not particularly high. In the second issue, an article mocked holiday adventure and school stories, 'Valery Towers' being an obvious dig at Enid Blyton's Malory Towers.[53] In the issues up to the end of 1954, a period of six years during which Enid Blyton published 184 titles, including titles in many of her more important series, only six of her books are reviewed or mentioned in short notices. *The Yellow Story Book* is praised for its 'gift of invention' and 'range and style',[54] other of her books are said to be 'pleasing' or 'pleasant'. There is no outright criticism except in the case of *The Secret of Moon Castle* which is reviewed along with other holiday adventure stories by such writers as Malcolm Saville, Monica Edwards and the Pullein-Thompson sisters (all going strong nearly thirty years later); all the books receive the same sort of comments – 'drab', 'perfunctory writing', 'mechanical plot', 'occupationless children' and 'vulgar little story'.[55]

Reference has already been made to the comparatively few histories and critical works which were available in the 1930s and the situation in the 1940s was little better. In 1958, when I first became involved in buying children's books for libraries, there were two books which were highly regarded by experienced children's librarians in Britain, as a guide to selection standards: *About Books for Children* by Dorothy Neal White, a New Zealand children's librarian, published in 1946, and *The Unreluctant Years* by Lillian H. Smith, a Canadian children's librarian, published in 1953. Both Mrs White and Miss Smith had been influenced by American children's librarians and both set high standards, subscribing to the belief that good books drive out bad. Lillian Smith wrote, 'Children will defend themselves against encroaching mediocrity if the books of genuine quality are put within their reach.'[56] Neither of them mentioned Enid Blyton although Dorothy Neal White criticized Frank Richards' Billy Bunter stories because they describe 'an unreal world which is dangerous because it sometimes pretends to mirror actuality and is often accepted by children as doing so. The adventure story in which callow and inexperienced youth outwits maturity and experience may be condemned for similar reasons.'[57] Twelve years later in a correspondence in *New Zealand Libraries* a Mrs D. White, undoubtedly the same person, said that there was no justification for 'spending money on rubbish' and that, by her standards, Enid Blyton was 'rubbish'.[58]

The two standard American works on children's literature at this time were *A Critical History of Children's Literature*, edited by Cornelia Meigs, and May Hill Arbuthnot's *Children and Books*. The first, published in 1953 (a revised edition appeared in 1969), undertook to offer a critical analysis of 'what has endured and why',[59] and was concerned only with what the authors believed to be the best. There is scarcely any indication that the popular and widely-read series books existed, although the following sentence can be seen as disapproval of both Caroline Keene and Enid Blyton: 'During the forties and fifties a trend could be noticed toward a type of mystery story in which groups of children track down criminals, with far from childlike purpose and technique, finally outwitting not only the criminals but the police.'[60]

The first edition of *Children and Books* was published in 1947 to provide a guide for adults to contemporary children's literature and was primarily concerned with quality books. The 1947 edition dealt briefly with the influence (generally regarded as bad) of comics, radio and the cinema. The 1957 edition introduced television as a serious rival to the reading of quality books.

The books by British writers published before 1958 were much less critical. For the most part they were factual surveys or histories. Geoffrey Trease's coverage of Enid Blyton in *Tales Out of School* (1949) has already been mentioned. Roger Lancelyn Green's *Tellers of Tales*, published for young people in 1946, was concerned largely with nineteenth- and early twentieth-century writers. Frank Eyre's *20th Century Children's Books* mentioned Enid Blyton briefly, calling her a phenomenon, a bestselling author and referring to the Eileen Colwell review already quoted.[61] The various histories and critical works available to British children's librarians by 1958, therefore, offered little guidance.

One of the earliest comments on the 'low-brow manufactures of Enid Blyton'[62] appeared in a periodical called *Life and Letters* where it was unlikely to be seen by many teachers or children's librarians. During the 1950s two important periodical articles about Enid Blyton appeared and they too were published in periodicals where they were unlikely to be seen by most of the librarians and teachers who might have profited from them. In 1955, Janice Dohm, an American children's librarian, contributed an article to the *Journal of Education*, using Enid Blyton as an example of a formula writer. It was the first time that criticism of the triviality of Enid Blyton's world, her undemanding style and superficial characterization had been made *and* backed up by specific examples. Janice Dohm pointed out that it is Enid Blyton's adventure stories which are the most attractive to children and concentrated her attention on these.[63] Frederick Woods, following up this article by a letter, expressed the view that 'there is a positive danger for children in these books' and stated his belief that the desire to increase word power is stultified by them, that children are lulled into a false sense of literacy and that they need to be given a critical sense if they are not to develop mediocre standards and grow up to read nothing more demanding than *Reveille* and strip cartoons.[64]

Three years later, in 1958, Colin Welch published an article in *Encounter* which began, 'If you have small children and they don't like Noddy, you are very lucky. I have, they do; I am not.'[65] Welch was concerned with the quality of stories which parents read aloud to their small children, suggesting that when parents read classics, the essence of which is that they can be enjoyed at different levels, they experience a 'complex harmony of pleasures' and the books form a link between the generations. Welch admitted that Enid Blyton undoubtedly entertained the people she meant to entertain although, he suggested, 'It is hard to see how a diet of Miss Blyton could help with the 11-plus or even with the Cambridge English Tripos.'[66] He concentrated his attention on Noddy, comparing the stories about him to those about Winnie-the-Pooh and pointing out that although they appeal primarily to the same age group, the latter are written with wit, taste and an almost 'magical felicity of form', while the books about Noddy are the 'book for children' carried to extremes. Like C. S. Lewis, he suggests that good children's books appeal to both adults and children. Noddy does not appeal to adults, therefore he is bad.[67]

In the form in which they first appeared, neither of these articles was likely to come to the attention of most children's librarians. Janice Dohm's article became more widely known and quoted when it was reprinted in *Young Writers, Young Readers* in 1960. Colin Welch's article was publicized in a rather less direct way. It was reprinted in *New Zealand Libraries*, evidently caused some debate in New Zealand and this was reported in the *Library Association Record* in 1960 under the headline 'Noddy a Blight on Libraries "Down Under" '. Readers were told that Enid Blyton's books are now 'totally banned from the pubic children's libraries throughout New Zealand'. The report has a rather holier than thou tone, giving the impression that Enid Blyton was freely available in British libraries at that time.[68] However, a check of *New Zealand Libraries* for the 1950s suggests that there was an ambivalent attitude towards Enid Blyton there too. In an article about a subscription library which had been set up in Upper Riccarton in 1953 in response to mothers' concern about their children reading horror comics, it seems that they wanted the provision of 'clean, wholesome reading' ('wholesome' is used three times) and although there is a hint of apology in the statement that there is 'a proportion of the scorned Enid Blyton, W. E. Johns type of book on the shelves' and Enid Blyton's books are referred to as 'pot-boilers', there is also justification for their inclusion.[69]

In 1958, debate about the merits of Enid Blyton was widespread but nowhere was there a total 'ban' on her books, and there were plenty of adults, including librarians, who felt that her work had merit as far as children were concerned.

Chapter Five

The Second Golden Age
1958–74

By 1958 Enid Blyton was firmly established as the best-known contemporary children's writer and as one of the most popular and easily accessible. In May 1959, along with William Mayne, James Reeves and Geoffrey Trease, she contributed to a feature, 'Writing for children', which appeared in the *New Statesman*. By this time she had in fact passed the peak of her writing career. All her best-known characters and series had been created. *Sunny Stories* had been handed over to another editor and replaced by *Enid Blyton's Magazine*, which came into being in 1953 and closed down in 1959: the demands of producing three short stories and an instalment for the serial each week became too much when she wanted to spend more time with her husband, then retired. In 1958 she published fifteen new books and, with the exception of 1960 when there were seventeen new titles, there was thereafter a steady decline in the amount of work which she produced each year until her death in 1968.

The late 1950s and more especially the 1960s saw important developments in children's literature, both in terms of quality and in the amount of interest taken in children's books by adults. John Rowe Townsend ended the first edition of *Written for Children* (1965) by suggesting that:

> . . . by the end of this century the great names of the 1950s and 1960s will stand out for all to see. There will be quite a number of them, and they will rank with the best from former times. The half century before 1914 was the first golden age of children's literature. The second golden age is now.[1]

This idea of a 'second golden age' became a topic for discussion, although it did not meet with universal acceptance.

Some feared that the wish to please the critics or to reflect current social issues or to produce books which would serve a therapeutic purpose would detract from authors' creativity. As a result of this debate, John Rowe Townsend later pointed out that although 'No golden age can be gold all through . . . One could compile a "team" of children's writers of the 1960s which I believe would far outshine any team that could have been assembled in any previous decade.'[2]

Authors who produced their first books in the 1960s included Helen Cresswell (1961), Penelope Farmer (1960), Leon Garfield (1964), Alan Garner (1960), Mollie Hunter (1963), John Rowe Townsend (1961) and Jill Paton Walsh (1966). These writers have made a major impact on children's fiction; more, such as Penelope Lively, emerged in the early 1970s to join them. Alongside these outstanding writers, there have been others who have been concerned, and increasingly so in the 1970s, with current problems, to the extent of allowing this concern to mould their work. In 1969, Geoffrey Trease commented that children's reading had become more sophisticated than it was in the 1930s. The children, he said, see 'people talking without embarrassment about their illegitimate babies, drug habits, abortions, mental break-downs and sexual difficulties. I do not mean that all these themes should, or are likely to, become the material for children's stories.'[3] In fact, by the end of the 1970s, all these themes, if not commonplace, had been treated in books for children. Ideas about the kind of language that was appropriate in children's books changed too; swear words and blasphemies which would have been unthinkable even ten years before in books for children were now to be found in otherwise innocuous texts, and not everyone was happy about these changes.

Not only did Enid Blyton reach her production peak before the dawn of the golden age, but the changes which came may have helped to perpetuate her popularity. Nothing that she wrote can be criticized on the grounds of bad language or unsuitable topics; the kind of story which she wrote is still apparently needed by many, perhaps most, children at a certain stage in their development and is approved of by their guardians, and no author has appeared to take her place.

As well as being a decade of new, outstanding writers, the 1960s were a period of new interest in children's literature. A landmark in criticism was the publication of Margery Fisher's *Intent Upon Reading* in 1961. During the 1960s, Margery Fisher gained recognition as the leading British expert in the field of children's literature, serving on the international Hans Andersen awards committee, being the first recipient of the Eleanor Farjeon Award for services to children's literature in 1966 and subsequently being invited to give the first May Hill Arbuthnot lecture in the United States in 1970. Although she had previously reviewed children's books for a woman's magazine, her book, *Intent Upon Reading*, brought her to the fore and was quickly recognized as an important milestone by those involved with children's books. It has only one mention of Enid Blyton, when she says *en passant*, 'Simplicity does not mean short, blunt sentences, and it does not mean short blunt words . . . if Beatrix Potter wanted to use a long word, or an unfamiliar word, she did. Enid Blyton and others think that children are taxed too much if they are confronted by so much as a polysyllable . . .'[4] Margery Fisher was following the accepted practice of giving space only to those authors whose work is felt worthy of mention. The question arises as to whether this practice is valid in the case of children's books and later a correspondent from Malaysia commented: 'In selecting children's books one is always torn between what they should read and what they will read. For example, I thought the biggest fault with Margery Fisher's *Intent Upon Reading* was the tiny coverage given to all the most popular authors, i.e. Blyton, Crompton and W. E. Johns.'[5]

Following upon the success of *Intent Upon Reading*, Margery Fisher launched a regular reviewing periodical, *Growing Point*. This carries no advertisements so that editorial policy cannot in any way be said to be influenced by the need to encourage publishers to advertise their wares in its pages, and almost all the reviews are written by Margery Fisher herself, thus ensuring a consistent viewpoint. Four reviews of Enid Blyton titles, including two reprints, have appeared in *Growing Point* over the years. In the fourth issue, *Five Have a Mystery to Solve* is criticized for its weak plot and lack of verisimilitude.[6] Ten years later *The Land of Far*

Beyond is criticized for its static characters and triviality[7] and *The Mystery of the Strange Bundle* for its flatness and absurd plot; it is in her review of the latter that Margery Fisher comments: 'I am sorry to see that a new generation is to be encouraged to feed on what I honestly believe to be slow poison.'[8] Only a retelling of the story of the Good Samaritan is reviewed favourably, in the following words: 'The style is quiet, colloquial but not sloppy, and there is a welcome absence of sentimentality, so that the story, with its added explanatory details of place and time, is both interesting and pleasant to read.'[9] *Growing Point* represents a rational view of Enid Blyton, neither frivolous nor spiteful, and it is regrettable that it was not in existence in the early 1950s when it might have helped teachers and librarians to develop reasoned arguments for their attitudes towards Enid Blyton.

Another specialist reviewing periodical, *Children's Book News*, began in 1965 as a house magazine for the Children's Book Centre; it later became an independent journal as *Children's Book Review*, before going out of existence in 1975. Its usual attitude towards Enid Blyton is one of disparagement, and reviewers frequently use her writing as a standard of comparison. In the issues from 1968 to 1975, only one Blyton title, *Before I Go to Sleep*, a reprint, is reviewed. Here the tone is sympathetic, the reviewer commenting that the book is a work of love by 'somebody who cares' and that 'Enid Blyton has had a lot to put up with.'[10]

Because new titles by Enid Blyton were coming out in smaller quantities after 1958 it is reasonable to find very little coverage of her work in the reviewing periodicals. With the steady improvement in the quality of children's books after 1960, compilers of booklists became more selective and after 1960 no Enid Blyton titles were included in any of the nationally-available lists published by such bodies as the Library Association, the School Library Association and the National Book League.

Margery Fisher was not the only critic of children's literature to emerge in the early 1960s. Next to her, John Rowe Townsend is probably the most widely-known British commentator on children's books. He conducted extra-mural classes on the subject for the University of Sheffield when he was on the staff of the *Guardian* in the early 1960s. In 1969 he gave up his post as editor of the weekly international edition of the *Guardian* in order to have more time for writing and lecturing, but he retained a connection with the paper as its children's books editor until June 1978. He continues to write regular columns for the *Guardian* on the subject, has written a number of novels for young people and, as well as contributing articles to periodicals, has written two books about children's literature: *Written for Children*, first published in 1965 with a second edition in 1974, and *A Sense of Story* (1971, updated and revised 1980). This latter is a collection of essays about leading contemporary writers for children and Enid Blyton is legitimately excluded. However, *Written for Children* is a history of children's literature and she is also excluded from the main text of this, although William and Billy Bunter are both mentioned briefly. Townsend says that he is concerned with the best children's books, commenting: 'I assume that what we require of a child's reading at any level above that of keeping him quiet, is that it should stretch his imagination, extend his experience, give him some new awareness of people and the world around him.'[11] In an 'Afterword' he acknowledges, however, that children also need the not-so-good, saying, 'Tom Swift and the Bobbsey Twins, Biggles and the Famous Five go down easily, the ideas and vocabulary are simple for the intended age group, the plots and situations are such as the authors know from long experience will touch off a ready response.'[12] The fact that William and Billy Bunter are dealt with in the main text is perhaps a reflection of John Rowe Townsend's age in that he enjoyed those books himself as a child, but was too old to have read Blyton as a child. It is very difficult to be objective about children's books that one remembers from childhood.

Two critics who came from the educational world condemned Enid Blyton fairly thoroughly. In *English for Maturity* (1961), David Holbrook was very much concerned with the quality of literature teaching in schools. He made several references to Enid Blyton, describing her style as being 'deficient in the rhythms and imagery of experienced difficulty', her prose as 'journalism at its most bloodless and fleshless', and he criticized Noddy in particular, commenting that adults 'feel safest with little Noddy, whose experience rules out everything mysterious, discomforting and troublesome: in Toyland every difficulty may be overcome by some such device as a jolly magic rubber, and everything is tractable.'[13]

Aidan Chambers is a critic with a background of teaching experience: in the 1960s he was associated particularly with the problems of the reluctant reader. At the time when he began to write about children's literature, Enid Blyton was regarded by many as the way into reading for reluctant young teenage readers. However, to Aidan Chambers, even at this time, Enid Blyton was seen to be synonymous with both popular and bad, and although in his first book, *The Reluctant Reader* (1969), he admired her 'market-place tale-teller's ability to hold our attention',[14] in his second, *Introducing Books to Children* (1973), he criticized her writing for 'its triviality, linguistically impoverished style, anaemia in plot and characterisation, and clichéd, stereotyped ideas.'[15]

An indication of the increased interest in children's books amongst adults was the appearance of new editions of two books mentioned in the previous chapter, Roger Lancelyn Green's *Tellers of Tales* and Geoffrey Trease's *Tales Out of School. Tellers of Tales*, published originally for young people in 1946, was published in a rewritten and expanded form for adults in 1953, with further revised editions in 1956, 1965 and 1969. Concerned mainly with nineteenth-century writers, comparatively little space is allocated to contemporary writers. In the latest, 1969, edition, Chapter 23 is concerned with Ransome and holiday adventure stories and one might have expected to find some mention of Enid Blyton here, particularly as Malcolm Saville is included as an author of 'improbable but entertaining tales of children foiling spies and burglars with the greatest of ease'.[16] In a chronological list of 'famous representative children's books', published between 1800 and 1965, one Enid Blyton title is included, *The Naughtiest Girl in the School*, although there is no mention of this in the chapter on school stories. It is significant that this title is one of the books recommended by Trease in *Tales Out of School*, although as Green mentions both Malcolm Saville and Anthony Buckeridge, his omission of Enid Blyton from the main text of his books seems rather arbitrary.

The Library Association marked the increasing interest in children's books by publishing two books covering their history from earliest times to the present. The first of these, Mary Thwaite's *From Primer to Pleasure* (1963, later published, 1972, as *From Primer to Pleasure in Reading*), finished at the early years of the twentieth century; the second, Marcus Crouch's *Treasure Seekers and Borrowers* (1962), was a factual account of children's books in the twentieth century. In the three passages in which he mentions Enid Blyton, Marcus Crouch emphasizes her fame, her considerable output and her variety, but says that her books 'could not perhaps be called very good'.[17] Although Marcus Crouch was never a children's librarian, he had a longstanding interest in children's books and libraries and was, at different times, both Secretary and Chairman of the Youth Libraries Group of the Library Association. He has written many articles for *The Junior Bookshelf* and monographs about a number of children's writers, and has reviewed children's books for both *The Junior Bookshelf* and the *Times Literary Supplement* over a long period of time. Throughout his writing he reflects very much the view of children's librarians in the immediate post-war period and this is particularly clear when one looks at his later book, *The Nesbit Tradition* (1972) which, according to the sub-title, is an account of 'the children's novel 1945–1970' and in which, rather surprisingly, there is not a single mention of Enid Blyton.

In the early 1960s British library schools began to appoint specialist lecturers in the field of children's libraries and literature. One of the first appointments was that of Alec Ellis to the staff of what was later to become Liverpool Polytechnic. In 1963, no doubt appreciating the shortage of introductory texts on the subject, he published *A History of Children's Reading and Literature*. In this and in subsequent writings he recognizes Enid Blyton's popularity and suggests that, 'It is an injustice to single out the books of one writer for ostracism when so much similar material is still available on those same library shelves.'[18] This seems to be the first time that anyone pointed out the fact that although Enid Blyton was the subject of widespread criticism, there were other authors of no greater merit whose books were stocked by libraries unquestioningly.

Anne Ellis, who had previously been a children's librarian, makes one brief mention of Enid Blyton in her book about the family story in the 1960s, saying: 'In Britain, the 1940s was a barren period in the development of the family story, apart from the various popular adventure series by Enid Blyton . . .'[19]

Amongst non-specialist commentators on children's books, Enid Blyton was given her due as a popular and well-known writer. She was the only children's author to be included in the *Sunday Times'* series, 'The Thousand Makers of the Twentieth Century', published in the mid-1960s, which aimed to record 'every person who had coloured the imagination of the twentieth century'.[20] In his *Who's Who of Children's Literature*, published in 1968, Brian Doyle, a freelance journalist, whose main interest in children's literature lay in the popular writers of boys' adventure stories, included a factual account of Enid Blyton's career and pointed out that:

> Certain educationalists, teachers and librarians tend to frown on Enid Blyton's stories, saying they are trivial, indifferently written and unimaginative, among other things. Some public libraries in Britain have actually banned Blyton books from their shelves. This is no place to enter into the controversy.[21]

This comment was published in the year of Enid Blyton's death, and it was perhaps Brian Doyle's journalistic approach which led him to write an article in *Books and Bookmen* in the following year, on Enid Blyton, W. E. Johns and Richmal Crompton, all of whom died within a space of five months at the end of 1968 and the beginning of 1969. Doyle seems to have been the only commentator to draw attention to this coincidence, speculating on who might take their place and concluding that 'it will be a long time before children's literature produces such a triumphant trio of popular writers'.[22] Doyle took the popular view that Enid Blyton's works 'form a very good "jumping-off" place and get children into the all important reading habit'.[23]

In 1970 writing about children's literature increased quite spectacularly in terms of quantity. In the spring two new journals on the subject were launched: *Signal: Approaches to Children's Literature*, edited by Nancy Chambers, and

Children's Literature in Education, a journal which grew out of the Exeter Children's Literature Conferences and in the early numbers of which papers given at the first conference were published. Neither of these journals was concerned with the reviewing of children's books, but both have included references to Enid Blyton while the latter has included whole articles about her.

In the autumn of 1970 three books were published, providing an interesting representation of the various groups concerned with children's books and reading. One of them was my own *Children's Fiction*, which was intended as a handbook for librarians and in which I was consciously trying to pick out the popular features of Enid Blyton's books and then identify what I considered to be better quality books which had the same features and which therefore should appeal for the same reasons. I feel that the remarks which I made at that time about specific Blyton titles were reasonable, particularly when compared with what else had been written on the subject by 1970. I accepted the general view that Enid Blyton's work is of poor quality, referring to *The Naughtiest Girl in the School* as being 'less insipid and trite than much of her work,' the warm mish-mash of cosiness and wish-fulfilment in *Mr Galliano's Circus* and *The Secret Mountain* as 'the level to which this type of story can sink'.[24]

I wrote as a librarian; the authors of the other two books published at the same period came from a background of teaching. However, by 1970, Gladys Williams was a journalist and writer of children's books, and in *Children and Their Books*, she was writing for parents. She is very much concerned with quality, although there is no attempt to explain to parents why some books are better than others. There is one reference to Enid Blyton and another to Noddy; it is taken for granted that Enid Blyton, Walt Disney and comics are undesirable entertainment for the young and that, although they should not be banned, the reading of them should be discouraged by the caring adult.[25] Wallace Hildick, no longer a practising teacher but a popular writer for children himself by the time he published *Children and Fiction*, discusses the topic very much within the context of adult literature. Considering *Five Run Away Together* in some detail, Hildick criticizes Enid Blyton's style for its lack of density, her poor characterization and her moral unevenness, but does find some good qualities in her work. He praises her for her storytelling skills, for her understanding of child psychology, for the fact that her books can be read and enjoyed both by able children, who use her books as an effective screen on which to project their own fantasies, and by children of limited intelligence, thus providing all children with a common bond, and for the fact that her books promote basic reading fluency. Hildick suggests that one reason why Enid Blyton is disliked by parents and teachers is that she very accurately reflects the nastier traits of middle-class children. (Her ability to do this suggests some degree of skill although, as Hildick points out, she fails to show that such behaviour is undesirable.) He concludes that we cannot make do solely with the criteria we apply to a good adult fiction when judging children's fiction.[26]

In the early 1970s there was more consideration of Enid Blyton's work. Nicholas Tucker contributed an article to the *Times Literary Supplement* in 1970, Colin Field one to *The School Librarian* in 1972. They were both concerned to try to explain what Nicholas Tucker described as her 'phenomenal success'.[27] In 1973 Brian Alderson, Children's Books Editor of *The Times*, commented on the new edition of Enid Blyton's *The Land of Far Beyond* and demonstrated, by comparing it to Bunyan's *Pilgrim's Progress*, on which it was based, that its faults did not lie solely in the fact that it was an adaptation.[28]

Although Colin Field, at least, expressed the view that Enid Blyton might provide a useful jumping-off point for some children, another kind of criticism was gathering momentum in the field of children's literature. This arose from a concern about attitudes expressed by and reflected in the work of writers for children. This was not entirely new, for in 1940 George Orwell had called attention to the undesirable attitudes perpetuated in boys' comics,[29] but in the 1970s Britain became conscious of the fact that it was fast becoming a multi-ethnic society.

As has been shown, Enid Blyton wrote against the background of the 1930s. Not surprisingly her work has come under attack from those concerned about the stereotypes of race, sex and class to be found in children's books. Librarians in particular had, even before 1970, tried to rationalize their criticism of Enid Blyton by expressing disapproval of the attitudes seen to be reflected in her books. Her middle-class view of life had been criticized for many years: now she was criticized for racism and sexism.

One of the earliest attacks on Enid Blyton on the ground of racism was made by Lena Jeger in *The Guardian* in 1966, when she looked in some detail at *The Little Black Doll*, 'a Sunshine picture story book', which had recently been given to a child of her acquaintance. Sambo, the little black doll, belongs to Matty who does not love him because of his black face. Because all the other toys feel the same, Sambo runs away, meets a pixie, looks after her and when he runs through the magic rain to fetch the doctor, all the black is washed off him. The pixie is delighted and so are the toys. In commenting ' "No wonder he's happy – little pink Sambo," writes Miss Blyton', Lena Jeger suggested that stories like this could be insidiously dangerous.[30] Since this article appeared Helen Bannerman's *Little Black Sambo* and Hugh Lofting's *The Story of Dr Dolittle*, both accepted nursery classics, have come under fire for much the same reasons.

Surprisingly, *The Little Black Doll* was reprinted in 1976 in a reissue of *Story Party at Green Hedges*; the editorial of *Books for Your Children* commented 'We can't decide whether they are being daring or just plain insensitive'.[31] This, however, is by no means the only example of such insensitivity: Katherine Tozer's 'Mumfie' books were well reviewed when they were published in the 1930s but when *The Wanderings of Mumfie* was reprinted in 1976, this too was quite rightly criticized for the racial attitudes demonstrated via a golliwog who is portrayed as a subservient, 'cotton-pickin' nigger'. Mumfie, like Noddy, lives in a nursery world of toyland, peopled by Father Christmas, scarecrows, children, animals and goblins and the books about him are typical of the books which were acceptable and welcomed in the nurseries of the 1930s.

Enid Blyton has also been attacked for her sexism, the way in which girls usually take a supportive part while the boys have the really exciting adventures, and mothers are usually seen in a very stereotyped domestic role, dispensing food and comfort at appropriate intervals. The most extensive case against Enid Blyton, on grounds of both racism and sexism, has been made by Bob Dixon in two articles which first appeared in *Children's Literature in Education* and *Hard Cheese* and were subsequently reprinted in his two-volume book, *Catching Them Young*, in 1977.

It must be said, however, that to Enid Blyton plot was all important. In some cases, it suited the plot if the native African boy or the working-class boy were independent and knowledgeable, and one of the reasons for her popularity may well have been that the girls stay back at the camp site, filling the traditional female role, while the boys go off on the really dangerous part of the adventure. At the same time, Enid Blyton, like Helen Bannerman, Hugh Lofting and Katherine Tozer, was writing for a very different kind of society from the one in which today's children live: the attitudes which they reflected were those which were taken for granted by the majority of adults at that time and they are scarcely to blame if the books which they wrote are reprinted unthinkingly by publishers in the 1970s, however undesirable it may be.

A rather different concern with the content of Enid Blyton's work was demonstrated by Gillian Freeman in *The Undergrowth of Literature*, an examination of publications devoted to sexual fantasy, published in 1967. Looking at the references to caning, slapping and whipping in children's books, she spent a couple of pages discussing *The Folk of the Faraway Tree* and other Enid Blyton stories in which there is physical punishment. However, it is only fair to say that in this book examples of such fantasies are also quoted from the works of Arthur Ransome, Beatrix Potter and other notable writers.[32]

Throughout this period, however, despite the critics, Enid Blyton's popularity amongst children continued. Whether the surveys were carried out in schools or in public libraries, Enid Blyton invariably appeared as the favourite author. Even where she did not rate as a favourite author, she was obviously being widely read, as was demonstrated by a survey carried out in a junior boys' school and reported in the magazine, *English*, in 1960. Here she is described as 'ubiquitous'.[33]

It is with girls, of course, that Enid Blyton is most popular and any survey which excludes girls is likely to reduce her position in the ratings. However, as reading fiction is, on the whole, a far more common activity amongst girls than amongst boys, her popularity soars when children of both sexes are included in the survey. In 1962, for a survey carried out at Otley Library in West Yorkshire, a questionnaire was completed by 300 children who visited the library during a period of six weeks. Although the four to fifteen age range was represented, the largest number of respondents came from the nine to twelve age group. Amongst the under-elevens, Enid Blyton was the most frequently mentioned author, mentioned by 9 boys and 76 girls. To give some idea of her overwhelming success amongst the girls, the next most frequently mentioned authors were each mentioned 9 times – Robert Louis Stevenson (by the boys) and Joyce Lankester Brisley (by the girls). Enid Blyton is not mentioned at all by boys over eleven, but is still popular with the girls, receiving 48 mentions as compared with the 33 of Louisa M. Alcott, the next most popular author. For both groups of girls, therefore, she was easily the most popular author, although she scored only modestly with the boys under eleven and not at all with the older boys.[34]

Dennis Butts' survey in 1963 was concerned with the fiction reading of 'A' stream children of eleven to fifteen in secondary modern schools. Asked for the name of their favourite author, 22% gave H. G. Wells while 21% named Enid Blyton. Butts commented on the 'relative decline' of Enid Blyton's popularity amongst older children and pointed out that 'over three-quarters of her support came from first and second formers, and over 70% from girls'.[35]

For the survey reported by A. Percival in 1963, two second-year English forms in a small rural secondary modern school kept reading diaries for three months. Percival was concerned with the quality of children's private reading and as a measure of quality he used Kathleen Lines' *Four to Fourteen* as a guide: he was thus able to establish that the 'A' stream girls read at a higher level than the 'B' stream girls, but as far as the boys were concerned *Four to Fourteen* proved to be of little help as the kind of book in which they were interested is scarcely represented in it. In the tables, Percival treats Enid

Blyton's books as a separate category. The 16 girls in 2A had read 31 Enid Blyton books and only 3 girls had read none at all: the girl with the highest reading age had read 6, but even the girl with the lowest reading age had read 3. The 9 boys in 2A had read only 5 Blyton titles but these were accounted for by only 2 boys and 4 of them had been read by the boy with the lowest but one reading age. The 12 girls of 2B had read 32 Blyton books but 6 of them had read none at all while one girl had read 9 and another had managed 10. Four of the 13 boys of 2B had read 13 Blyton books between them. This survey underlines the fact that although Enid Blyton is widely read by girls of all abilities, she tends to be read only by low ability boys.[36]

A survey sponsored by the Committee of the *National Froebel Foundation Bulletin* in 1964 surveyed 913 children in the seven to fifteen age group, divided more or less equally between the two sexes and drawn from different parts of the country. 'Biggles' books were most popular with boys, being mentioned 13 times as compared with the 8 mentions of Enid Blyton, but Enid Blyton is reported to be the most popular author amongst the girls, although the number of times that she was mentioned is not given. Two of the 4 quotations given from the children's replies refer to Enid Blyton. A boy of fourteen wrote: ' "Enid Bliton's Five on a tresher Iland. Robinson Crusos by Danyl Dufay tresher iland by Robert louis Stevenson." ' A rather more literate girl of the same age wrote, ' "I have read *Five Go Off to Camp Again* by Enid Blyton. The five are five children who are very adventurous sometimes too much so. The print is just the right size, the illustrations are not too bad, but rather too many of them." '[37] It is interesting to speculate what lies behind these answers; the boy, although not very good at spelling, seems preoccupied with the island theme and had perhaps met both *Robinson Crusoe* and *Treasure Island* in abridged or even comic strip versions or through having them read aloud to him at school. The girl, although still reading Enid Blyton at fourteen and having a rather imperfect recall of the title and of the fact that one of the 'Five' is a dog rather than a child, is articulate and faintly critical; she seems to be aware of the fact that the book is somewhat below her level but has read enough Enid Blyton to catch the spirit of the author.

The Middlemiss survey of 1966, carried out in secondary technical schools and colleges of further education, shows that while Enid Blyton is the most-mentioned author amongst the first-year children at secondary school, she falls to second place amongst the second years and is not mentioned at all by the third years. Middlemiss comments that the support given to her in the early years of secondary education is still very strong. Some of the children, when asked their reasons for choosing the 'Famous Five' books, admitted they had read most of them before, and Middlemiss suggests that in this case the books were probably providing an easy escape into comforting fantasy from the big new world of the secondary school.[38]

The Society of Young Publishers carried out their survey, published in 1967, in a girls' comprehensive school which, as a school, was enthusiastic about books and reading. The survey team, a sociologist and a publisher, identified three types of girls. Just over 10% were 'Annas', girls involved with intellectual or educational pursuits, in the top intelligence group, reading a lot and likely both to borrow books from the public library and to come from homes supplied with books. Nearly a quarter of the girls were 'Marthas', orientated towards a typical adult female life-style, with a romantic conception of marriage, home and children, their reading material most likely to be provided by mother or an older sister. The majority, a little over 60%, were 'Junes', involved in pop culture, reading very little, least likely to be members of the public library, most likely to leave school early and most likely to come from a working-class background. However, as far as books were concerned they did share common favourites and amongst the eleven- to fourteen-year-olds Enid Blyton was by far the most popular author. The tastes of the 'Annas' matured, however, whereas those of the 'Marthas' and the 'Junes' did not change significantly after the age of eleven.[39] This survey serves to demonstrate the fact that Enid Blyton appeals to a very wide range of tastes and that children who continue to read do grow out of her work in due course.

The survey carried out by I. J. Leng and published in 1968 is the most detailed ever carried out in the context of the public library. For a whole year, every book issued to every child of seven to twelve, using the children's library of an unspecified town in North Wales, and living within one mile of the library and attending one of the five primary or two secondary schools in the area, was recorded. Leng does not give the facts and figures about the most popular authors because he was more concerned with underlying tastes and interests, which he felt are relatively constant, but he does provide useful evidence of how children's reading tastes develop and shows how well Enid Blyton caters for these tastes.[40]

The Warwickshire survey, 1969, was concerned with the leisure reading of eleven- to sixteen-year-olds in nine Warwickshire schools. Asked for the names of authors whom they had particularly enjoyed, pupils in the first three years were very much in favour of Enid Blyton, and the 'Malory Towers' and 'Secret Seven' books were particularly popular with girls in the first year.[41]

Yarlott and Harpin's survey in the East Midlands, 1970, aimed to discover the 'top ten' authors amongst a thousand grammar school pupils. The pupils surveyed were taking 'O' and 'A' levels and one would not anticipate much mention of children's writers. The great majority are obviously moving towards an adult pattern of responses and only three children's writers are mentioned at all, Enid Blyton, C. S. Lewis and W. E. Johns: of these, Enid Blyton ranks highest, being bracketed forty-fourth with Dylan Thomas![42]

'The White Rose Award', organized by the West Riding County Library in 1971, to find the most popular children's book published in the previous five years, was designed in such a way to minimize Enid Blyton's chances of being nominated. Despite this, 85 of her books were mentioned, compared with a total of 44 fantasy books and 88 non-fiction books.[43] Here, Enid Blyton's considerable output obviously influenced the result. The same year, the *Observer* newspaper carried out a survey amongst its readers but no Blyton titles appeared amongst the 'top ten'.[44] This may reflect the *Observer* readership or, more likely, the fact that children who have to make the effort to write to a national newspaper to make their nominations are likely to be more disciminating.

A survey carried out by Nottinghamshire County Library and the Nottinghamshire County Youth Service, 1971, was concerned with the reading tastes of thirteen- to nineteen-year-olds and again one would not expect to find much mention of Enid Blyton. The respondents were divided into four groups, boys at school, girls at school, boys at work or college and girls at work or college. Not surprisingly only amongst the girls at school was Enid Blyton the most popular author.[45]

In 1971, a student in the Department of Librarianship at Birmingham Polytechnic surveyed the reading tastes of 50 nine- to eleven-year-olds in an independent primary school in West Yorkshire (27 girls and 23 boys) and notes the great popularity of 'Famous Five' and 'Secret Seven' books. Thirty-six of the children mentioned Enid Blyton or one of her books. One boy managed to list 11 'Famous Five' titles while another listed 9.[46]

In a survey carried out amongst 31 Girl Guides in Gosport, 1972, only 3 post-First World War authors were mentioned amongst the top 11 authors and of these the most popular was Enid Blyton, the others being C. S. Lewis and Ian Serraillier. Enid Blyton was mentioned by 29 of the girls, only E. Nesbit and Lewis Carroll doing better with 30 mentions each.[47]

The sample surveyed by *Where*, 1972, which consisted of 1,000 children under the age of twelve, was admittedly based on its supposed middle-class readership of parents interested in education and therefore likely to encourage their children to read. Amongst the five-year-olds, Beatrix Potter was the most popular author but at every other age Enid Blyton was the most popular although she was also the most frequently cited 'disliked' author, comments ranging from 'Her books aren't punctuated properly' to 'Enid Blyton (ugh!)'. Nicholas Tucker, reporting the findings of this survey, suggests that there is probably some element of bravado in this, 'almost as if the ability to dislike Miss Blyton is a necessary proof that one is now older and more mature'.[48]

J. J. Taylor's survey, 1973, examined the leisure reading habits of children in the first four years of two secondary modern and two grammar schools during a four-week period. An author was recorded by the survey if he was mentioned at least three times by at least one of the year groups. Although Ian Fleming was mentioned most frequently by both secondary modern and grammar school boys in all four years, Enid

Blyton was the most frequently mentioned author by girls in all four years, with the exception of the fourth-year grammar school girls. Enid Blyton was also noticeably popular with all boys in the first two years and with secondary modern boys in the third year. Taylor comments: 'One is compelled to discuss the phenomenon of Enid Blyton in any paper on children's voluntary reading habits in the post-war era.'[49]

Despite the optimistic views of some of the investigators who saw evidence of a falling-off in Enid Blyton's popularity, the evidence that is available suggests that she was just as widely read and as popular in 1974 as she had been in 1958. The writers of the 'Second Golden Age' had failed to make an impact on many children.

This situation undoubtedly owed something to another major development of the 1960s: this was the revolution in children's paperback publishing. For twenty years, Puffin Books, launched by Allen Lane of Penguin Books in 1940, had been virtually the only paperbacks published for children. The policy of publishing as Puffins only the 'best' children's fiction, instituted by Eleanor Graham, the first editor, and continued by Kaye Webb, meant that there were no Enid Blyton titles in paperback until 1962 when the first 'Armadas' were published. Frank Eyre, in *British Children's Books in the Twentieth Century*, comments on the 'Armada' paperbacks: 'This was soon seen to be a bringing together of the tried and tested rather than the best, such authors as Enid Blyton, W. E. Johns and Richmal Crompton predominating.'[50] Edward Blishen has also described 'Armadas' as being free of 'all lofty aims', remarking, 'here are the Blytons, the amiably silly school stories, the cobbled-up thrillers — an essential series, offering to all either an escape from the peaks or the germ of a habit that could lead a child upwards as easily as strand him on the humdrum level.'[51]

Since 1962, the flow of children's paperbacks has increased rapidly and titles by Enid Blyton have been issued in paperback by a number of publishers. Because of the great sales that can safely be predicted, they have tended to be cheaper than other paperbacks and so have an extra appeal for the child spending his pocket money. This means that at the very time in the early 1960s when more people were beginning to look critically at children's books and when a new generation of children's writers was emerging, Enid Blyton received a new boost to her popularity by becoming so cheaply and readily available in paperback. Through paperback editions, children's books have become much more accessible to children since they have been brought within the range of pocket money, have reached more sales points, the supermarkets and the corner newsagents as well as the retail bookshops in town centres, and have also appealed to children's collecting instincts.

If publishers quite clearly saw, and still see, the profits in publishing Enid Blyton, they did not necessarily defend her literary quality. Antony Kamm, Children's Book Editor at Brockhampton during the 1960s, launching 'Knight Books', a paperback series, as another part of the Hodder empire, issued the Blyton titles as 'Green Knights', denoting them as being of low literary quality but popular with children, as opposed to the 'Red' and 'Black Knights' which were books of literary merit. In the expanding paperback business Collins, publishers of 'Armadas', subsequently felt the need to establish a quality paperback series and, in 1971, started 'Armada Lions'. The sub-title of an article describing an interview with Rosemary Sandburg who, after working on 'Puffins' with Kaye Webb, became editor of 'Armada Lions' in 1973, was 'Doesn't go in much for the Enid Blyton approach'. Although she admitted that she had read Enid Blyton as a child herself, she was somewhat disparaging of her work.[52]

In an article in *Top of the News*, Jean Karl, the children's book editor at Atheneum, an American publishing firm, describes how they included some 'Famous Five' titles in a new paperback series in order to get the series accepted in book stores where a speedy turnover is essential. Despite statements about the importance of quality in children's books and the fact that it is clear from her article that she considers Enid Blyton's work to be of low quality, five Blyton titles were included amongst the first ten that they published. She believes that it helped but still tries to convince her reader (and perhaps herself) that 'good can outdo bad'.[53]

Like publishers, booksellers are to an even greater extent affected by commercial pressures. In most of the bookshops and newsagents to which children have direct access, Enid Blyton usually seems to be available in inverse proportion to the total number of children's books on display – the larger the number of books on show, the smaller the proportion of Blyton titles. During the 'Second Golden Age' most of the bookshops which sold children's books seemed to have about a third to a half of their stock in Blyton titles and they would often have a section heading for 'Blyton' in the same way that they had a section for 'Classics'. But now that there are so many more children's books available in paperbacks, the Enid Blyton titles are rather less obvious.

Public librarians were the adults who were in the best position to take advantage of the increasing number of good children's writers who emerged after 1960. On the whole, public libraries cater for children who are committed readers and in the late 1950s and 1960s, the feeling still prevailed that if good books were made available in sufficient quantities, the children would not want the bad.

It seems that by 1960 Enid Blyton's book's were not being bought by a number of public libraries, having been phased out, but this fact only became publicly known in 1963 when the policy of St Pancras library made headlines in the national press. W. A. Taylor, then Borough Librarian of St Pancras, has since pointed out that this policy dated from the early 1950s[54] and it seems likely that quite a number of libraries simultaneously in the mid-1950s adopted a policy of phasing out Enid Blyton and other prolific writers as children's books by other authors became more plentiful. The St Pancras case seems to have been sparked off by a report in the *Daily Herald* in April 1963, entitled 'Noddy and Biggles banned by libraries'.[55] This affair was revived the following year when, in September, Mr Taylor was appointed City Librarian of Birmingham.

Meanwhile, another well-documented incident took place in Nottingham in February 1964, when the local paper, under the headline 'Noddy and Big Ears fall from favour' stated, 'Junior members of the Nottingham City Libraries who have toddled along to their local branches to read about Noddy and Big Ears, or perhaps relive the adventures of the Famous Five, have had a shock.'[56] The only Blyton title to be found in

Nottingham libraries, it was reported, was a collection of Bible stories. F. C. Tighe, the City Librarian, criticized Enid Blyton's books for their limited vocabulary and the caricature of characters, and these unfortunate remarks were repeated in newspapers up and down the country. Enid Blyton herself was quoted as accusing the Nottingham library staff of 'bearing a grudge against her'[57] while provincial papers sought the views of their local librarians. The City Librarian of Manchester was reported as saying that he liked both Noddy and other Enid Blyton books, which 'are written with such facility and understanding of children',[58] while the Sheffield City Librarian said, 'As far as I am concerned, Enid Blyton is not going to be taken out of our libraries. Her books are an extremely useful way of introducing children to the written word.' This particular report went on to say, 'The most guarded Yorkshire comment was from a spokesman for Hull City Libraries. He felt that Blyton books often kept the more intelligent child from reading something more advanced.'[59]

The *Daily Mail* questioned the right of the Nottingham librarian to set himself up as a censor and included an Illingworth cartoon and a Noddy-style story by Roy Nash which began, 'One day Noddy came home quite tired out . . . He had gone all the way to Nottingham in his little car. And when he got there a nasty man called Librarian had kicked the poor little car very hard.'[60] Although *The Teacher* came out in support of Mr Tighe's view,[61] the *Daily Express* announced with satisfaction that 'Nottingham's chief librarian has been told to explain to the city libraries committee why he is not replacing Enid Blyton's story books.'[62]

The St Pancras case had repercussions when Mr Taylor was appointed City Librarian of Birmingham in September 1964. On 24 October, with the headline 'Biggles may be on way out', the *Evening Mail* reported, 'Mr Taylor . . . said today that children's libraries [at St Pancras] did not contain books by Enid Blyton, or Biggles or William books.'[63] Mr Taylor was reported as saying that he believed that children's libraries must serve a constructive purpose and that he would be discussing the selection policy in Birmingham when he took up his new post. An eight-year-old wrote a letter to the paper, commenting, 'I felt cross when I heard that the new City

Librarian of Birmingham wants to stop having Enid Blyton and "William" books in the library.[64] A parent wrote in to say that she believed that enthusiasm for Enid Blyton was just a phase in children's development.[65]

On 3 November, the *Birmingham Post* reported Councillor Jonas, the Chairman of the Library Committee, as saying:

> 'I understand Mr Taylor was saying that there was today a far better choice of good children's books than in the days when Noddy and Biggles were the standard fare, and it was necessary to keep a proper sense of proportion about books like William. We are already doing that in Birmingham' . . . and added jokingly 'Besides which I like Noddy'.[66]

The same information was repeated in the *Evening Mail* under the headline 'Relief all round at Noddy "reprieve" ' and relief was expressed, according to the report, by Mr Cashmore, the City Librarian from 1928 to 1947, and by two headmasters, while Enid Blyton, asked to comment, said:

> One librarian thought my books were far too popular and the hordes of children swarming into the library for them on Saturday morning became a nuisance. 'If only you could see the children swamping the shelves,' he told me. 'It makes us far too busy.'[67]

After Mr Taylor took up his post, work with children in Birmingham libraries developed quite considerably and on 12 April 1969, a letter appeared in the *Evening Mail* under the heading, 'Enid Blyton and the public libraries' from 'an ordinary mother', saying: 'May I make an appeal through your column for books by Enid Blyton to be restored to the public libraries . . . we cannot beg or borrow one from anywhere.' Mr Hargreaves, the Deputy City Librarian, commented, ' "Enid Blyton books have never been banned in Birmingham though many authorities in this country and abroad will not spend money on them." ' He went on to say that they tried to keep a balanced stock – other authors' books were ' "better and more real . . . Blyton books [do not] really present a very balanced view of life . . . [do not] stretch the imagination . . . are being published in paperback form." '[68]

In 1971, another letter in the *Evening Mail* complained, 'On a recent visit to the public library I was informed that they did not stock any Enid Blyton children's books . . . the reason given was that they were not popular . . . I find this unacceptable.'[69] On this occasion Mr Taylor was quoted as saying that 'Enid Blyton's books are stocked in all children's sections of branch libraries' and, suggesting that they were probably all out on loan, drew attention to the reservations service. Neither of these last two letters seems to have given rise to an outburst of complaint and this policy of taking a more reasonable attitude is one perhaps generally and wisely adopted to stem the tide of criticism.

This kind of incident probably occurred regularly in various parts of the country throughout this period, but as most of the evidence for such incidents appears in local newspapers it is difficult to track down. In the magazine *Censorship*, in 1967, reference was made to 'reports which told of Enid Blyton's children's books (Noddy) being rejected by several libraries as being sub-literature' and in support of this quoted not only the cases at St Pancras and Nottingham, but another at Sittingbourne.[70] In the article by Diana Norman, Hertfordshire County Library is specified as not having a single Enid Blyton book.[71]

In 1969 the Brighton children's librarian wrote, 'I cannot see that a collection of 15,000 books is restrictive because it lacks the Blyton opus, as is the case with my library.' This last comment drew angry letters from parents protesting that they had to buy Enid Blyton's books for their children because they could not be borrowed from the local library.[72] Another debate arose in Worcester in 1970 when, under the headline 'Worcester hang on to Noddy', it was reported that Worcester City Library would continue to buy 'Noddy' books although the County Library had decided to stop buying them. While the City Librarian was quoted as saying, ' "We treat the Noddy books as the sprat to catch the mackerel . . . if children are told that no Noddy books are stocked, we think they will leave the library for good"', the County Librarian took the view that ' "It is our business to put the best books in the way of people who come in and use out libraries." '[73]

In Limavady in Northern Ireland in 1972, a councillor asked why the local branch library did not stock Enid Blyton books and accused the library of censorship. He is quoted as saying, ' "It is unfair to refuse to provide them just because some tinpot twit thinks Big Ears and Noddy are queers." '[74]

It is clear that from time to time the press sees a good news story in the discovery that there are no Enid Blyton books on the shelves of the local library. In most cases these stories are localized but on at least two occasions they have been taken up and exploited in the national popular press. One of the reasons why the Enid Blyton controversy makes good newspaper copy is that many people know her name and most adults under the age of forty-five have probably read her books at some time.

From 1964 onwards, after the matter had first been aired in the national press, the debate about Enid Blyton continued amongst librarians and others concerned with children's reading. Margaret Payne, a children's librarian, commented somewhat bitterly on the situation:

> One mention of banning Enid Blyton or Biggles brings a spate of letters in defence of these books, mostly on the grounds of the citizen's right to read anything and the fact that 'they never did me any harm', but are these really the reasons and standards we should set for our children's reading?[75]

The debate tends to have focussed around library policy because librarians publicly spend public money: the results of whatever policy they implement are there for all to see, and those librarians who decided not to buy Enid Blyton's books found that they had to justify their reason. In *Books* in 1970, George Greenfield, Enid Blyton's agent, listed the five reasons given by librarians for banning her books, including her snobbish values, the fact that the simple events and simple language do not stretch the reader's imagination and vocabulary, the fact that the moral concepts are too neatly encapsulated, that life is not like this and because the books are too popular. He suggested that librarians feel that if they do not stock Enid Blyton's books, then children will read more worthy books by less popular writers.[76] In the same issue of *Books* Constance Martin, *née* Stern, who had been the children's librarian at St Pancras at the time of the incident previously described, said that Enid Blyton was a 'trivial writer' and that every subject she explores 'has been more subtly done by someone else, with a finer use of words, a more original imagination and certainly with more admirable heroes'. She criticizes the 'nastiness' of the Secret Seven, the Famous Five and Noddy, the confusion of nature and the supernatural in the nature stories and the sugary sentiment in the treatment of genuine religious themes. She also makes the point that reading too much Enid Blyton may destroy the taste for reading anything at all.[77]

The idea that reading too much Enid Blyton might destroy children's desire to read anything more difficult was widespread amongst librarians, but it was probably a sneaking feeling rather than a real conviction and the comments of many librarians quoted in the press showed that they believed that there was probably no great harm in her work as long as the whole thing was kept in proportion, and that she served a useful purpose with many children at a particular stage in their development.

The same range of views is held by the other group of adults who are professionally concerned with children's reading, teachers. A survey carried out by Michael Woods amongst teachers in 1974 suggests that teachers in general have a favourable view of Enid Blyton. Woods believed that teachers would be most likely to reflect 'informed' adult opinion about Enid Blyton and questionnaires were sent out to a hundred schools in various parts of Britain, including infant, junior and middle schools. Each school was asked to complete two questionnaires, one to be completed by the head teacher, the other by an assistant teacher chosen at random. The returns represented a good range of schools and regions.

The majority of teachers were well disposed to Enid Blyton – 72% were 'generally favourable', 8% were 'very favourable' while only 10% were 'unfavourable'. Questioned about the effects of Enid Blyton's books on reading progress, 58% felt they were generally helpful, 12% felt they were very helpful, while nobody felt that her books were very unhelpful. Only 3% of the respondents felt the books were 'generally harmful' in terms of the attitudes reflected in them, while 3% felt that they were 'very beneficial' and 48% 'generally beneficial'. Positive advantages mentioned were that the books are easy to read, that children like them and that they provide a continuing interest. The most frequently mentioned disadvantages were the 'limited vocabulary' and 'sameness of plot or character'.

Michael Woods suggests that although teachers are aware of the limitations of Enid Blyton's books, they also see their value and recognize children's interest in them as a legitimate part of children's development; he concludes that teachers do not generally subscribe to the more hostile attitudes and that in the less formal educational climate of the 1970s, children's own interests have taken on more importance.[78]

Michael Woods' survey came at the end of the period under consideration but the problem of Enid Blyton's popularity had been aired in various educational journals before this. In 1966, the teacher readers of *The Use of English* were asked, 'How does one wean 15 year old girls from a diet of Enid Blyton?' and it was indicated that this was a problem commonly posed at teachers' meetings.[79] In the selection of answers published, the generally offered solution was to persuade children to reject Enid Blyton by offering them plenty of good quality books and by getting them to criticize Enid Blyton for her deficiencies. Other teachers, however, were quick to point out her value and one teacher wrote, 'To find that fifteen year old girls are still reading Enid Blyton is perhaps not so alarming as to find that they do not read at all, or that they favour the lurid type of teenage magazine prevalent today.'[80] Just as librarians were at one time more concerned about the effects of comics and the cinema upon children, so teachers have felt that there is far worse reading material than Enid Blyton.

In a moderate article in *The School Librarian* in 1972, Colin Field suggested that while the needs of the individual child must be taken into account, the teacher's most important function is to bring new and better experiences to children and to stimulate and sustain their intellectual curiosity. Although he admits that some children have such impoverished immediate and imaginative lives that a 'Famous Five' book might stimulate them to think and feel at a new and higher level, he also questions whether, just because Enid Blyton is the most popular single author with the nine- to eleven-year-olds, teachers should base 'their reading programmes on the works of Miss Blyton'.[81]

Any attack on Enid Blyton is likely to draw forth a defence

from a member of the teaching profession. When Gillian Tindall commented critically on her work in her review of the Barbara Stoney biography in the *New Statesman*,[82] a correspondent wrote:

> Most teachers I know would concede (many reluctantly) that she could write stories of the 'can't put it down' variety. In the case of very many children she has achieved the vital transition from the mere technical ability to read into the habit of reading.[83]

When Bob Dixon published his critical article in *Children's Literature in Education*,[84] he brought forth a defensive editorial note from Kenneth Sterck, commenting that addiction is one of the conditions for the development of critical taste.[85]

It was not only teachers and librarians who became more interested in and more concerned with children's books after 1960, thus providing a market for the new books and journals on the subject. The growing interest among parents was apparent in the success of the Children's Book Group movement which began in the mid-sixties, but it was foreshadowed by the concern of the Advisory Centre for Education, mainly through its periodical *Where*, with children's books and reading. Inspired by *The Use of English* question to teachers in 1966, *Where* asked parents in 1967, 'Are your children addicted to Enid Blyton and what, if anything, do you do about it?' Edward Blishen, commenting on the replies, said:

> I myself am saddened by the number of readers who praise Miss Blyton's work as a useful step in the fostering of reading ability. My gloom is not lightened by the assertion of one of them that reading Miss Blyton's adventure stories is an effective bridge to Buchan, Stevenson and Dumas. From the Famous Five to the Three Musketeers in one step?[86]

He also commented that Enid Blyton's books were 'embraced' or 'repulsed as if they were the best in literature or the worst'. In fact the number of parents who replied to the question was relatively small. Thirteen were firmly pro-Blyton, seven were unenthusiastic but believed she did not harm while six, who included the only teachers and librarians who responded and two parents who confiscated her books on sight, were firmly anti-Blyton.[87]

In 1972 when *Where* carried out an investigation into children's favourite authors, Nicholas Tucker, reporting on the results, said that many covering letters had been sent by parents anxious to set the record straight over some uncompromising reference to Enid Blyton as their child's favourite author.[88] There are, of course, dangers in over-reacting to Enid Blyton. One of my contemporaries who banned Blyton for her two eldest children, took a more relaxed attitude in the case of the two youngest: this may have been partly due to the fact that she had occasionally been embarrassed by the older children who, on finding Enid Blyton's books on the bookshelves of their friends, had commented on the fact in hushed and shocked whispers. As well as leading to such social embarrassment, such action does give books all the attractions of forbidden fruit.

Parents have been regularly involved in the newspaper correspondence which has followed on any publicity about the lack of Blytons in the local public library. These letters are usually couched in rather emotional terms, but some useful parental contributions came in the *Times Literary Supplement* correspondence early in 1970. The most original comment came from a Mrs Wilkinson who pointed out that when no Enid Blyton books are available at the library, children tend to buy them instead, spending their book tokens on them and building up their own private libraries of Blytons, which means that the books are there to be re-read and to be borrowed by older children in the family who would probably not bother to read them if they were not so accessible.[89] This correspondence also reflected the parental feeling that although Enid Blyton's books may be second-rate, they are no worse than many of the other books which are readily available in the library. Jon Wynne-Jones suggested that Noddy is preferable to the current wave of 'salacious or near-pornographic novels blessed by the critics'.[90]

In the same correspondence the children's librarian of Brighton paid tribute to the important influence of parents,[91] and one of the most remarkable developments in the children's book world in the last fifteen years has been the growth of the Children's Book Group movement, a parent-orientated organization. The founder, Anne Wood, started a magazine, *Books for Your Children*, in December 1965. An examination of the files revealed several mentions of Enid Blyton, although an article about her promised in the editorial of March 1967[92] never materialized, and there has never been any extensive debate about her work. In both letters and articles, there seems to be a general acceptance of the fact that Enid Blyton's works are both popular and of little literary quality, although there is no attempt to examine or justify these assumptions. Parents who take an interest in what their children read seem to have been indoctrinated with the idea of Enid Blyton's low literary worth, and some have made an attempt to encourage children to read more widely while not actually banning her.

Shirley Lewis, mother of four, said her daughter went through all the accepted stages of reading, enjoying Beatrix Potter, Enid Blyton, pony and school stories. She admitted that 'while allowing her to read all through Enid Blyton, I did stipulate that of her two library books only one should be a Blyton at any one time.'[93] Another parent, Mrs A. Sharson, writing from Malaŵi, felt that her children saw Enid Blyton in perspective: she thought that children must read all kinds of books in order to develop their critical faculties but that as her children had obtained the Blyton books from school and from friends, she had never bought them for the children herself.[94] The one strong defence of Enid Blyton came from the mother of a profoundly deaf boy who had been slow to read but who eventually, at the age of twelve, had read Enid Blyton's *The Boy Next Door* and had then gone on to read through all the 'Famous Five' books. This mother said, 'He remains interested in books, although nothing has gripped him as the "Five" books did. I shall always be grateful to Enid Blyton for giving him that.'[95]

Attitudes towards Enid Blyton throughout the period from 1958 to 1974 ranged widely. With children, especially girls, of eight to twelve she was a favourite and well-loved author. Publishers and booksellers recognized and made use of her commercial success. Adults involved with children's reading argued about her and feeling ran high, but, as far as the critics and commentators were concerned, there was a general reluctance to explore the reasons for their divergence of views. Reviewing Frank Eyre's *British Children's Books in the Twentieth Century*, a revised edition of his *20th Century Children's Books*, when it came out in 1971, Nicholas Tucker wrote:

> Writers you don't really like in your period will, in almost every case, be the dreaded, profit-making and unaccountably bad Blytons . . . and their ilk, which simply merit perhaps one sniffy reference or dark aside. It doesn't matter if children like them . . .[96]

With one or two notable exceptions, this sums up the situation which existed until quite recently: only slowly over the years has a willingness even to discuss Enid Blyton's work in rational terms developed and, as will be seen, Nicholas Tucker has been one of the most helpful in this respect.

It is not suggested that the Second Golden Age came to an end during 1974 but new factors came into play which make this a convenient breaking point.

Chapter Six

Bullock and After

❁

IN 1975 the Bullock Report, *A Language for Life*, the findings of an investigation into all aspects of the teaching of English, including reading, was published. Amongst its concerns was the promotion of reading for leisure as well as general literacy standards. The need to develop reading skills and to promote reading as a source of pleasure was emphasized.[1]

By this time, more than twenty years after librarians had first expressed the view that her work was ephemeral and unlikely to last, Enid Blyton was certainly the only twentieth-century children's writer who could be described as being a household word amongst adults. Proof of this fact was not hard to find in the media. In the *Guardian* Peter Preston wrote a witty article which began, 'One dark night Noddy was driving back from watching a party political broadcast at Big Ears' when his little car coughed and fell sound asleep,' and ended with Noddy and the car seeking the help of 'Auntie Shirley'. The title, 'Blight on cereal', made the reference clear.[2] In *New Society* Reyner Banham, in an article on ice-cream vans, described 1955 prototypes as having 'a distinctly Noddy-car air',[3] and Geoffrey Parkinson reviewed a book on social work in terms of Noddy, Big Ears and Clientland.[4]

In 1974, too, various things had happened which seemed to suggest that Enid Blyton was about to be taken more seriously than before. The BBC included a programme on Enid Blyton in their series of 'Success Story' programmes, and *Island of Adventure* was serialized for 'Jackanory'. In September 1974, Hodder and Stoughton published the authorized biography by Barbara Stoney and this was widely and extensively reviewed in such periodicals and newspapers as *The Times*, by Brian Alderson,[5] the *Guardian*, by Suzanne Lowry,[6] and the *New Statesman*, by Gillian Tindall.[7]

In 1975 the interim report of the Schools Council Research

Project into children's reading interests, carried out by a team based at the University of Sheffield, demonstrated that Enid Blyton was still the most widely-read author amongst children of eight to twelve. This was the biggest project of its kind since Jenkinson's survey of the 1930s. It was based on 7800 children in a stratified random sample, representing three age groups – ten-, twelve- and fourteen-year-olds. Of the 246 titles mentioned more than ten times in the completed questionnaires, seventy were by Enid Blyton. (The authors who came nearest to her were C. S. Lewis and Anthony Buckeridge, each of whom had six titles mentioned more than ten times.) Amongst the ten-year-olds *The Secret Seven* was the third most mentioned book (mentioned less than *Black Beauty* and *Treasure Island*): amongst twelve-year-olds it was the eighth most mentioned book. Her name disappeared from the top favourites as far as fourteen-year-olds were concerned. Her books were classified by the research team as 'non-quality narrative', a term which described 36.2% of the titles listed and 33.4% of the reading done by the sample.[8]

Between the publication of the interim report in 1975 and that of the final report in 1977, there appeared a book by Margaret M. Clark, *Young Fluent Readers*, which reports a research project concerned with twenty boys and twelve girls who, shortly after beginning school, were identified as fluent readers: these children were observed over a period of years. When they were first interviewed, their reading attainment was already beyond the 'at risk' stage and all could (and did) read a variety of material with understanding. Their reading interests two or three years later are described and, although they also read Kipling, Carroll, Swift, Defoe and Stevenson, 'most of the children had an obvious love for a variety of books by Enid Blyton'. This seems to link with their love of reading a number of books by the same author in quick succession. One girl, aged seven, asked to tell a story, told an Enid Blyton story at great length, managing to capture the style of 'her favourite author' precisely. All these children were of above average intelligence and some were exceedingly gifted.[9]

The Schools Council Research Project and Margaret Clark's findings are supported by my own investigations into the remembered childhood reading of students in further and higher education. About the time that the interim report of the Schools Council team was published, at the beginning of 1975, I was marking essays written by students who had entered the librarianship degree course at Birmingham Polytechnic in the autumn of 1974. Students were asked to describe a book they had enjoyed before the age of twelve or thirteen and the picture produced by their choice of books seemed to suggest that children who go on to higher education might read at a higher level than those who did not and might be less affected by Enid Blyton. Fourteen of the sixteen students had written about authors identified as 'quality' authors by the Schools Council team and none had written about 'non-quality' authors (the remaining two were Malcolm Saville, not mentioned at all by the Schools Council report, and the *Odyssey*, which falls under the heading of traditional stories), yet half the students named authors at least one of whose books was mentioned more than ten times in the Schools Council questionnaires, thus suggesting some relationship to nationwide tastes.

In the autumn term 1975, therefore, questionnaires were completed by students entering five different courses at the Polytechnic, three courses in librarianship (the Library Association, BA and Postgraduate courses), the BA (Honours) English course and the BA (Honours) Sociology course. Although this survey and another carried out the following year amongst three groups of students entering different vocational courses both provided a considerable amount of interesting information about the reading interests of children who later achieve academic success, they also showed that these interests are very little different from the overall pattern demonstrated by the Schools Council report, although they possibly read more than the average child. Despite the fact that the students in the 1975 survey had been children of above-average ability, all of them having obtained at least two 'A' levels, were mostly from the higher socio-economic groups and had mostly been public library users from an early age, the author that they mentioned most frequently was Enid Blyton, whom very few indeed had escaped reading. The only groups with whom she had not been outstandingly successful were the postgraduate librarianship students (now more mature) and the BA Honours English students (a more developed critical ability?). Because of the high incidence of Enid Blyton reading, it was impossible to draw any conclusions about the effects, good or bad, which her books might have had. It certainly appears that children can read Enid Blyton and still achieve academic success. Most of the students felt that Enid Blyton's books were exciting and easy to read, and 38 out of 163 students (23%) said that they had felt that they were worth re-reading. This suggests that those adults who express the view that children read an Enid Blyton book once and have then exhausted it, are perhaps being too optimistic.

It was interesting, too, that the overall pattern produced by the responses to these questionnaires and the ones completed in the autumn of 1976 was very similar to that from the stratified sample used by the Schools Council team. They named a wide variety of authors, showed the special popularity of C. S. Lewis, Louisa M. Alcott, Charles Dickens and Anna Sewell's *Black Beauty*, as well as Enid Blyton, the popularity of the classics generally and the small part played by non-narrative books. Each course tended to produce a distinctive pattern of reading – this was particularly demonstrated by the classes of police cadets and pre-nursing students who completed the 1976 questionnaires and reinforced later by an investigation amongst girls taking up apprenticeships in the electrical industry,[10] and this suggests that one of the reasons for Enid Blyton's success is the fact that her stories represent so many genres. Her school stories, for example, were most popular amongst those girls who academically were high achievers.

There was also evidence of Enid Blyton's continuing popularity abroad. In 1974 Barbara Rosen in an American periodical, discussing the appeal of series books and comics for children, wrote: 'Enid Blyton, imported from England, has achieved enormous popularity locally, for all its difference of language and culture; and, despite the modish revulsion of parents, children by the million in England and America go right on reading her.'[11] The following year Dr Lucia Binder of the International Institute for Children's and Youth Literature in Vienna wrote regretfully, 'The translation of girls' books is a thriving business, but has unfortunately embraced mainly serial books, which promise to be good sellers. Enid Blyton's girls' books, for example, can be found almost anywhere in the world.'[12] In November 1977, a news item in the *Times Educational Supplement* announced that Enid Blyton was the most popular author amongst under-thirteens in France and that thirty-five million copies of translations of her work have sold since 1958.[13]

Although it has been said that Enid Blyton is banned in South Africa,[14] a letter received from a friend living in the Transvaal suggests that this is just not true. She described the setting up of a resource centre in a small and exclusive English-speaking private school and said:

> Although the stock is now *becoming* balanced, I had to deal with the *complete* works of Enid Blyton. When the kids started taking books out, I was horrified to find that twelve and thirteen year olds were still reading Blyton! – I started a 'book club' and it was fascinating to discover other authors and pass the word to the rest. Then with storytelling and drama sessions we converted even the tinies. Enid B. is really in her element in South Africa. Parents adore her, teachers encourage her. It's even on the radio *every other day*!![15]

As has been seen, Enid Blyton has never been completely banned from all British libraries. However, since 1974 there does seem to have been a certain relaxation of attitudes amongst librarians, and this has happened for two reasons, the first administrative, the second the growing concern about standards of literacy and the amount of leisure reading being done by children and young people.

On 1 April 1974, local government in England and Wales was reorganized, and new, enlarged local authorities came into existence. What had previously been small, independent, municipal and urban district library authorities merged with county and city authorities to become large metropolitan and county library authorities. Library services which had previously excluded all or most of Enid Blyton's works now found themselves merged with services which had previously supplied them. Selection policies had to be re-examined and frequently a more liberal policy was adopted.

More important, perhaps, was the concern about literacy. By the early 1970s, librarians were no longer convinced, as some had earlier been, that the provision of plenty of good quality books would remove the desire for the trivial. Although librarians might adopt a policy of promoting only the best in books talks, booklists and library activities generally, they would not exclude from stock popular authors who encouraged the reading habit.

Just before she retired from Hertfordshire in 1976, Joan Butler gave her blessing to the purchase of Enid Blyton books and thus the library service which had been one of the first to phase out Enid Blyton in the late 1940s reintroduced her into stock.[16] Other librarians were also concerned to cater for the less able and reluctant readers. One wrote to me that the 'Secret Seven' books are 'invaluable for helping children over the first hurdle of learning to read for pleasure and there is too little suitable material for that,'[17] a view which was reinforced by another who said that Enid Blyton has:

> . . . a place with 'reluctant readers' . . . Today I think we have veered too much in the opposite direction – not enough straightforward adventure stories which can be recommended as escape literature . . . Our children (in inner city areas) are not really such good readers as a survey of fiction published for them over the past years would lead us to believe.[18]

As Janet Hill points out in *Children are People*, if the bookstock is to meet community needs, then a proportionately large amount of money will have to be spent on books which are easy to read.[19] In 1974, Philip Pacey, writing about libraries generally, said that if a library is in part responsible for literacy and the raising of reading standards, then it would be reprehensible to exclude books which provide a first step in reading, 'to help people to the top, one does not saw off the bottom rungs of a ladder . . . Some "light-weight" fiction is probably essential – as may be a measure of Enid Blyton in the children's library.'[20]

Early in 1975 I attended an in-service staff training course in Shropshire and it was clear that there was an undercurrent of demand from those staff who worked with the public that there should be more concern to supply what children actually wanted to read. One discussion group suggested that 'Junior book selection is too often coloured by personal prejudice and rigid criteria of quality which are not valid to the children.' Another group, discussing the idea that it is better to read anything than nothing at all, established that there were three levels of material – quality, non-quality (including Enid Blyton) and pulp (comics and annuals). Staff felt that too many 'quality' books were being stocked, that these sat on the shelves for months and were little used and that the balance between quality and non-quality needed to be adjusted. Having made this adjustment, it should be advertised: one positive suggestion was to display a poster announcing 'Enid Blyton stocked here'.[21]

This documentation reflects what was happening in many other library authorities at about the same time, and there was a movement away from the appointment of specialist children's librarians who might cling to the earlier, rather isolationist, views about the need to maintain high qualitative standards in book selection. At another meeting of librarians in the mid-1970s Ray Carroll, speaking on the role of the public librarian, commented:

> The need for Adult Literacy Schemes is mainly a criticism of the teaching profession, but attitudes to book provision for children like banning Enid Blyton cannot have been too helpful. Lack of encouragement rather than an absolute basic inadequacy is at the root of most so-called illiteracy.[22]

At the same conference, a statement of the Hampshire County Library selection policy was provided as a working paper and this included the sentence, 'Popular light fiction for children by authors such as Blyton, Crompton and Price, should be purchased in paperback format as previously agreed at a District Librarians' meeting.'[23]

Librarians were not only prepared to stock books by Enid Blyton but actually made a positive case for doing so. In October 1976 Alan Day, a lecturer in the Department of Librarianship at Leeds Polytechnic, took the view that 'We must not allow our own professionalism to betray us into imposing a well-meaning censorship of what children should read in the way of escapist literature.' He went on to describe how, faced with the responsibility for buying children's books for a library in the early 1960s, he had ordered 'two copies of every Enid Blyton title in print'.[24] In reply to the view that public libraries exist to provide quality books rather than books which will ensure high issues, he said that it was pointless to fill the library shelves with books which no child wishes to read.[25]

The press, however, continued to publish stories of libraries censoring or banning Enid Blyton's books. In 1975, when Anthony Hugh Thompson published a book about censorship in British public libraries and included a chapter called 'The Enid Blyton affair', showing how narrow is the line between 'selection' and 'censorship', it is significant that when the book was chosen as the subject for a review article in the *Sunday Express*, reference was made to 'Enid Blyton's phenomenally successful stories' which 'have been suppressed by librarians all over the country during the past decade . . .'[26]

In 1976 the *Aldershot News and Mail* published a mocking editorial when a Hampshire librarian apparently blamed Noddy books for a drop in the reading standards of seven- to eleven-year-olds and was quoted as saying that the books have 'limited plots and limited vocabulary'. The editorial commented, 'Why a fictitious fairytale character who has been around for something over two decades should account for a 10 per cent drop in the number of children's books borrowed from Hampshire libraries during the last three months one can but wonder.'[27]

In 1977 a correspondent in the *Birmingham Evening Mail* suddenly caught up with the twenty-year-old controversy, commenting that 'It seems to have become the "in thing" recently to make some derogatory remarks about Enid Blyton's books.'[28] A fortnight later the paper reported, under the headline 'Come back Noddy, all's forgiven', that 'The City Leisure Services Committee has agreed to a request by Coun. Alan Rudge that the long-standing ban on Enid Blyton should be lifted.'[29] It is interesting, as a final footnote to the St Pancras/Camden/Birmingham saga, to report that in 1978 the present Camden librarian told a group of students in Birmingham that children's librarians in Camden could now stock Enid Blyton's books if they considered the needs of the local children warranted their inclusion in stock and because 'children like them'.

In 1977 the Library Association celebrated its centenary and to mark the occasion the Youth Libraries Group mounted an exhibition of children's books of the last hundred years at the Bethnal Green Museum of Childhood. Two of Enid Blyton's books, *Silver and Gold*, a book of verse published in 1925, and *Well Done Noddy!*, the fifth 'Noddy' book published in 1952, were included, and the press made great play of this fact. The *Nottingham Evening Post*, for example, commented, 'Noddy has won his battle with the experts'[30] while the *Guardian* report, under the headline, 'Noddy and co. come in from the cold', began with the words, 'Enid Blyton, the children's author whose work was banned by many librarians from the 1950s onwards, was rehabilitated yesterday at the opening of a major centennial exhibition of children's literature by the Library Association.'[31] This did not, however, prevent Richard Hoggart, when addressing one of the conference sessions, from condemning 'Noddy and the like for perpetuating stereotypes of class,'[32] while in 1978 the County Librarian of East Sussex was quoted as saying, ' "We know her books are popular among children but we do not actively promote them and we don't think they allow children to develop their imaginations fully." '[33]

By 1978 public librarians were very much involved in another controversial matter, the question of public lending right and how the principles should be applied. Predictably enough, under the heading of 'MPs warned of Blyton bonanza', the *Daily Telegraph* reported that 'The Public Lending Right schemes proposed so far would pay a great deal of money to writers like the late Enid Blyton, but would do little to help authors in need, a committee of MPs was told yesterday.'[34] Later in the year the *Times Educational Supplement* reported a librarian as saying, ' "And then the girls tend to go straight from Enid Blyton to Mills and Boon. We have to try to get them to look at other books." '[35]

An article by Cedric Cullingford in *New Society* in 1979 stated, 'One librarian in Cumbria, with the agreement of all the local schools, banned Enid Blyton completely.'[36] This drew forth an immediate response from the County Librarian of Cumbria, saying that he had read Mr Cullingford's article with some surprise and commenting, 'I was not aware that any of my staff had gone against county policy and "banned" this author.' He then went on to say:

> I would point out that the shelves of our children's libraries are not overflowing with books by E. Blyton. Whether we are living in a 'golden age of childen's literature' or not, the range of children's writing available is enormous, and you will not need me to underline the shallowness of the public purse in this field. If the librarian or teacher is to give children even a taste from most parts of this wide spectrum, from limited funds, the butter will be spread very thin. Large clots of Blyton on otherwise dry bread would not be good housekeeping.[37]

This is probably a very fair reflection of librarians' views in the late 1970s and early 1980s. Early in 1980, as part of a programme to mark the fourth anniversary of the opening of the library in Washington New Town, served by Sunderland Public Library, the library organized a 'Vote for your favourite author' event in the shopping centre. During two days seventeen thousand votes were recorded on a giant scoreboard, and the winner proved to be Enid Blyton, with Catherine Cookson second and James Herriot third. In the *Sunderland Echo* the headline was 'Enid Blyton is tops in New Town'. The report said, 'Enid Blyton is tops — that's the message from hundreds of book lovers in Washington who have just voted the popular author their number one bedtime read.'[38] The headline in the *Northern Echo* on the same day read 'Enid comes out top' and the news item which followed revealed that everyone expected Catherine Cookson to win, 'A spokesman at the library said they were surprised at the result. He said it was a bit embarrassing for librarians, as many think Enid Blyton books should be banned.'[39]

In 1980, as far as public libraries are concerned, the situation can only be described as confused. There is a general belief that public libraries do not stock Enid Blyton; the librarians, although perhaps in some cases faintly ashamed of the fact, claim that they do. The press comments show a certain illogicality and do not really add up to a coherent picture. For example, if few or none of her books are stocked in public libraries, how is there going to be a 'Blyton bonanza' from public lending right?

The debate about the value or otherwise of Enid Blyton has continued much less publicly amongst teachers. Some teachers actually promote Enid Blyton's books by reading them aloud. One who appeared in the 'Success Story' television programme admitted that she 'thoroughly enjoyed doing so'.[40] This was my own introduction to Enid Blyton in the 1930s and nearly thirty years later I was checking some books in a Leicestershire primary school in a room where a teacher, probably in her fifties, was reading aloud to a group of ten-year-olds. Half listening to the story, it registered in my mind as being rather banal and when it came to an end, I found that it was one of Enid Blyton's school stories.

Michael Woods found that teachers in general have a reasonably favourable view of Enid Blyton.[41] There are some teachers who feel that as long as children are reading, it does not matter much what they read, others see Enid Blyton's books as useful material on which to practise reading skills, while others believe that children should be strongly encouraged to read the well-established classics and the widely-praised contemporary fiction. The situation was well summarized by Peter Hollindale, writing in *School Bookshop News* in 1975: he suggested that teachers' views might quite legitimately vary, depending on the children with whom they are immediately concerned. Primary school teachers see diversity and enthusiasm as a necessary basis for growing critical awareness; specialist teachers of able children want to introduce them to great literature while teachers of remedial groups see reading as a crucial utilitarian skill, to be encouraged at all costs. He went on to say, 'If we, as adults, and especially as teachers, attempt to ban or ridicule Blyton, we shall *cause* her to be harmful, because children will take her into protective custody and resentfully dismiss the better things we try to offer them.'[42] He advocated a policy of promoting the best books and making sure that plenty of copies of these are easily accessible to all children.

Undoubtedly teachers are in a much better position than librarians to influence children's reading, but unfortunately not all teachers have the knowledge of contemporary children's literature which enables them to exploit their situation to advantage. The Schools Council Research Project team, emphasizing the importance of the teacher's role, wrote, 'Most junior schools need to update the narrative element in their classroom libraries, and to spend more money on children's fiction of high quality, particularly that which has been written specially for children of this age during the past quarter of a century.'[43] The continuing preoccupation with the merits of Enid Blyton amongst educationists is illustrated by the publication of articles about her by Cedric Cullingford, a college of education lecturer, in 1979, and by Peter Wright, a student on a postgraduate teacher training course, in 1980.

Some indication of the continuing concern amongst parents is reflected in a little guide published for them in 1977, including a section entitled 'The truth about Blyton' which offers reassurance, and describes Enid Blyton as the literary equivalent of 'sausages and baked beans'. Antony Kamm, the author, aims to provide reassurance for parents who are aware of the critical stances taken on the question of Enid Blyton.[44] While some parents are positively grateful to her for giving their children the reading habit, others feel that there can be little harm in her as long as other books are read, and they see it as their job to introduce alternatives. Sensibly, most parents who care probably accept that their children will grow through the Enid Blyton phase and pass on to other books.

However, by the mid-1970s it was generally accepted that Enid Blyton was a 'bad' writer; her attitudes were suspect, her characterization thought to be shallow and stereotyped, her plots unrealistic, her vocabulary repetitive and undemanding. She had come to be regarded as a touchstone for what is bad in writing for children, as the following quotations from reviews of, and comments on, other children's books show:

> There is a strong Blytonesque quality too in Tom Stacey's reissue of Frances Hodgson Burnett's *The Spring Cleaning* . . . blend of coyness, contrivance and sentimentality.

(Brian Alderson reviewing a reprint of Frances Hodgson Burnett's *The Spring Cleaning*, 1974.)[45]

Too often we are on the edge of Blytonesque easiness.

(Peter Hunt reviewing Geraldine Kaye's *Billy-Boy*, 1975.)[46]

. . . it contains an old character that I thought had died with Enid Blyton, but who obviously emigrated.

(Michael Yates reviewing Mary White's *Break-up*, 1975.)[47]

The inadequacies of the text are excellently matched by those of the illustrations, reminiscent of those accompanying Enid Blyton's 'Famous Five', where each character bore the same healthy, honest glow of anonymity.

(Gabrielle Maunder reviewing R. and D. Martin's *Katie*, 1975.)[48]

The Gumby Gang Again . . . reminds me of nothing so much as Enid Blyton, though without the weird allure that Blyton still holds over her million drowsing customers . . . Blyton and water. Helen Cresswell's *Bagthorpes Unlimited* . . . Blyton and gin. As for *The Grass beyond the Door* . . . Blyton and currant wine?

(Jane Gardam reviewing fiction for younger children, 1978.)[49]

The Enid Blyton with Tears element is at its strongest . . .

(Jan Needle reviewing books for teenagers under the heading of 'Blyton with tears', 1979.)[50]

There are often echoes of Enid Blyton's Noddy books in these stories . . . The goblin, like Big Ears in the Noddy books, has had his sting removed.

(Judith Stinton on the 'Mister Men' books, 1980.)[51]

Quite frankly, if the reviewers are right and millions of readers really do crave pap on the lines of *The Mystery of the Vanishing Gro-Bra* or *Five Go Jacking Off Together* then the time has come to say 'Come back , Enid, all is forgiven.'

(Heather Renshaw reviewing Judy Blume's *Blubber* under the heading 'Come back Enid', 1980.)[52]

If this sample is just the tip of the iceberg, as seems likely, then Enid Blyton must have featured in considerably more reviews of other people's books than she ever did in reviews of her own books, something of a phenomenon in itself for a twentieth-century writer.

The critics and commentators also showed more willingness to write about and discuss Enid Blyton's work in books and articles. Although some books about children's literature continued to ignore her existence, there were many that did not. Peter Hollindale, for example, in *Choosing Books for Children*, published in 1974, analysed the reasons for Enid Blyton's popularity. He made an interesting comparison between her and William Mayne, the latter an author who has been much admired and highly praised by the critics but who does not arouse much enthusiasm in children, largely because his style is so difficult. Hollindale suggests that although Enid Blyton's language is undemanding, it would be hard to say that her books are badly written. Although he accepts the criticisms which have been made of her work, he suggests that she is not as bad a writer as her critics claim and his views provide a useful corrective to those of most other commentators.[53]

Brian Alderson followed up his review of *The Land of Far Beyond* and his comments on Barbara Stoney's biography by suggesting in another short *Times* article that it is possible to differentiate between the kind of enjoyment derived from writers like Enid Blyton and that derived from writers like Barbara Willard, justifying his arguments by reference to the latter's 'Mantlemass' books. He commented in this same article that his reviews of Barbara Stoney's book had drawn letters defending Enid Blyton's work.[54]

In 1975 Gillian Avery's *Childhood's Pattern* appeared, followed, in 1976, by Mary Cadogan and Patricia Craig's *You're a Brick, Angela!* These are both rather individual histories of children's literature. The first, by a children's author who is also a recognized expert on nineteenth-century children's literature, covers the period from 1770 to 1950, and is concerned with what she calls mass literature; the second as the title suggests, is mainly about books for girls and the authors are concerned with the way in which the female role is portrayed in these books. All three authors, while recognizing Enid Blyton's popularity, disparage her work. She is attacked by Mary Cadogan and Patricia Craig because they feel that she really disapproves of tomboy George and because, in *Six Bad Boys*, she wrote a story in which the message that a mother's place is in the home comes over all too clearly.[55]

In *Who's Who in Children's Books*, published in 1975, Margery Fisher presented commentary in a new guise. This is an A to Z guide to characters in children's books, ranging from what is accepted as the best children's literature to the popular folk heroes. Enid Blyton is given three entries. The 'Famous Five' are described as 'impervious to emotion of any but the most superficial kind',[56] the 'Mary Mouse' books are criticized for the thinness of the narrative and characterization and the flatness of the prose,[57] while Noddy is described as a 'monstrously infantile character . . . seems to have been put together from the weakest and least desirable attributes of childhood'.[58] By comparison, Margery Fisher is quite kind in her comments on Billy Bunter, Biggles and William, and their American counterparts, the Bobbsey Twins and Nancy Drew. However, the inclusion of Enid Blyton's characters at all was a sign of the new attitudes, and Julia MacRae, a children's book editor, welcomed this, saying:

> I was glad to see Noddy included, along with Biggles, the 'Famous Five' and other such characters more often than not omitted from books about children's books . . . their influence as gateways to further reading skills is often more positive than their detractors will allow.[59]

In another A to Z, *Twentieth Century Children's Writers*, edited by D. L. Kirkpatrick and published in 1978, the essay on Enid Blyton, who was allocated one of the longer ones, was written by myself. In his review of the work, Lance Salway described this as a 'sympathetic study'.[60]

One of the most prolific commentators on popular children's writers in the last decade has been Nicholas Tucker, an educational psychologist. Having taken other critics and commentators to task for not including mention of Enid Blyton, he has repaired their omission. Although, surprisingly, he did not include any reference to Enid Blyton in *Suitable for*

Children?, a book about 'controversies in children's literature', he has written two major articles about her. One, already mentioned, appeared in the *Times Literary Supplement* in 1970, the other in *Children's Literature in Education* in 1975. Here he reviewed and commented on other people's opinions and added his own. Nicholas Tucker has consistently put forward the view that Enid Blyton serves a useful purpose. Children need Blyton for the same reasons that adults read Agatha Christie when they want to dip into something well-ordered and predictable.[61] However, although Nicholas Tucker admires her workmanship, he is also liable to refer to Enid Blyton rather frivolously in such remarks as, 'The characters are so flat one might almost be in a sexed-up Enid Blyton plot – *Five Go on an Orgy*, perhaps . . .',[62] or 'Bestiality . . . has already been exhausted by all these pony books, and of course by Enid Blyton. "Dear Timmy" murmurs the androgynous George sleepily to her dog, settling down for the night in *Five Go to Demon Rocks*.'[63] Nicholas Tucker, like the reviewers quoted earlier, uses Enid Blyton as a yardstick, assuming that the readers of his reviews will take his point when he describes a book as being 'around the level of an Enid Blyton mystery story'.[64]

In 1975, Elizabeth McQuire contributed to the *Children's Libraries Newsletter*, the journal of the School and Children's Libraries Sections of the Library Association of Australia, an article which compared the concept of home as presented in Kenneth Grahame's *The Wind in the Willows* with that in Enid Blyton's *The Magic Faraway Tree*, much to the disadvantage of the latter.[65] The choice of book was unusual here for critics tend to concern themselves mainly with the adventure stories, and particularly those which feature the 'Famous Five'. One of the most detailed examinations of an Enid Blyton adventure story appears in the final report, published in 1977, of the Schools Council Research Project, where *Five on a Treasure Island* is compared with Stevenson's *Treasure Island*.[66] In an interesting article in 1978 Peter Hunt (who had previously said that he would as much consider including Enid Blyton in a study of children's literature as he would consider 'including, say, Micky Spillane on a literature degree course'[67]), used a passage from

The Valley of Adventure to demonstrate a simple test of 'verbal quality'.[68]

Cedric Cullingford returned to the question of 'Why Children like Enid Blyton' in *New Society* in 1979, while rehabilitation continued in Peter Wright's 'Five run away together – should we let them back?' which appeared in *English in Education* in 1980. A. C. Capey and Duke Maskell also took passages from *Five Run Away Together* (as Hildick had done in 1970) and from *Five on a Treasure Island* (as the Schools Council Team, of which A. C. Capey was a member, had done in 1977) for their article in *The Haltwhistle Quarterly* in 1980. Forty years after Enid Blyton published her first full-length book, the commentators at last seem to be convinced that her work must be seriously examined in view of her popularity: it can no longer be dismissed as being of ephemeral interest.

Inevitably, Enid Blyton's books have continued to be attacked for their racism, sexism and class attitudes and these criticisms have been well publicized. Dorothy Kuya, the Senior Community Relations Officer for the Merseyside Community Relations Council, was widely reported in the national press when she spoke at a Library Association conference in November 1975, on library services in multi-racial communities and attacked both Enid Blyton and W. E. Johns for their racist attitudes. The following comment was typical, 'Ms Kuya quoting from Enid Blyton books and ordinary school text books showed that they totally ignored the history and cultures in Africa and promoted ideas of colonialist oppression towards the third world.'[69] She spoke again at a meeting of librarians in Wolverhampton the following year and drew attention in particular to *Here Comes Noddy*, which she described as the best story ever written about mugging, Noddy being mugged in a dark wood in the middle of the night by three golliwogs. Other sessions at the same conference were concerned with class and sex stereotyping in children's fiction and for these, too, examples from Enid Blyton can be quoted.[70] Inevitably, Enid Blyton's name cropped up in the series of *New Statesman* articles on 'Race, sex and class in children's books' which appeared in the *New Statesman* in the last months of 1980, although the radical Centreprise bookshop was said to 'stock Enid Blyton Famous Five stories, because of the continuous demand for them'.[71]

Commercially, Enid Blyton's success was, and is, in no doubt. Her books have continued to appear in new editions, both hardback and paperback. In the 1970s there have been at least two examples of facelifts for her books. In 1973 Methuen published a new edition of *The Land of Far Beyond*, a retelling of Bunyan's *The Pilgrim's Progress*, originally published in 1942, and gave it new illustrations by Pauline Baynes, a talented winner of the Library Association's Kate Greenaway Medal for her outstanding illustration of children's books. In this new form, the adult buyer might well be attracted to the book. Another religious book, *Before I Go to Sleep*, a collection of stories and prayers for each day of the month, with additional stories and prayers for special occasions, was reissued in 1975. The first edition, published in 1947 by Latimer House, was very much of its time in terms of production, with black and white illustrations by Grace Lodge and the prayers in a decorative script. The 1975 edition, from Brockhampton, has good, strong, colour illustrations by Grabianski and black and white illustrations by Leslie Wood, while the prefatory 'Note for the Mother', which appeared in both the 1947 and 1953 American editions, is omitted.

It is perhaps surprising that publishers have not made more attempts to redeem Enid Blyton by more aesthetically pleasing editions, particularly in the case of books and short stories which are thought to have some merit, but as there is little evidence to show that children themselves prefer well-produced books, there is little incentive for publishers to take action except in the rare case of those books, like the two mentioned, which are likely to have a special appeal for the adult rather than the child buyer. With the exception of the 'Famous Five' books, of which new paperback and hardback editions using stills from the television series have been issued, and a lavishly illustrated edition of *The Enchanted Wood*, the books which are likely to be bought by the children themselves look very much like they have always done.

During the last ten years, some specialist children's bookshops have been established in various parts of the country, often in pleasant market towns and often by people with high ideals. Reporting on one Saturday morning's sales at Longman's bookshop in Dorset, the journalist finished with the comment, 'Cynics who doubt children's ability to choose reasonable books for themselves might notice that nobody went home with an Enid Blyton.'[72] However, there are plenty of children who may be attracted to the whole idea of book-buying if they can spend their pocket money on an Enid Blyton title, and booksellers who carry a wide range of the best children's books currently available are also likely to carry a stock of Enid Blyton paperbacks as well, so that no customers go away disappointed. Her books also continue to be easily available in the majority of bookshops and in newsagents and local shops where few other children's books are likely to be in stock.

Although probably not actually promoted in the growing number of school bookshops, Enid Blyton was represented in the first selection of the Bookworm Club, launched in the autumn of 1975. The *Guardian*, commenting on the first selection of this new club, said, 'Surprising best-seller: *Down with Skool!* the St Custard's saga by Willans and Searle. Runners-up are Blyton and Kipling.'[73] However, it may be that Enid Blyton was offered as an initial inducement to children to join, for in the second issue of the magazine, there were no Enid Blytons on offer. The well-established book clubs, organized by Scholastic Publications, have never included Enid Blyton in their selections on the grounds that her books are easily available at newsagents and small local shops.

Enid Blyton's stories have also been made available through tapes and records. Early in 1980 a news item in the *Yorkshire Post* announced 'Enid Blyton tops pops' and reported that World Wide Audio Products, a small British company, had been presented with eight gold discs for their sales in excess of 250,000 copies of each of the recorded stories from the St Clare's school stories series.[74]

Noddy stories, as well as being available on records and tapes, had been used by Thames Television for many years to the extent that in an exhibition of children's books at the Victoria and Albert Museum at Christmas 1970, he was misleadingly described in the catalogue as 'the famous television puppet'.[75] The BBC did not use any of Enid Blyton's work until 1974 when *Island of Adventure* was serialized for *Jackanory*. Anna Home, the producer, explained in a lecture at the 1974 Exeter Children's Literature Conference that this was because some attention had to be paid to audience demand and that using this story would not only provide enjoyment for many children but would also provide a necessary element of roughage. This story was presented in the first week of the new season in order to attract a new audience to the programme. *Island of Adventure* is, of course, the first title in the highly regarded 'Adventure' series.

In 1978 thirteen television episodes based on ten 'Famous Five' books were shown on independent television and new 'Knight' paperback editions, using stills for the covers, were published. Much editing took place but the first episode, adapted to include all the essential background information, contained all the hallmarks of an Enid Blyton adventure story, the idealized mother, the servants and other members of the lower orders, convincing but non-existent government departments, fine weather, caves and, of course, a mystery to be solved! One of Enid Blyton's favourite words, 'queer', having by 1978 acquired a new meaning, had to be replaced by 'peculiar' and 'weird'.

Inevitably, there were differing views of the television series. Peter Fiddick, television critic, condemned it fairly thoroughly in the *Guardian*, saying, 'There is, I suppose, no point in getting particularly hoity toity if someone dramatises Enid Blyton badly . . . It was as though someone had set out to dramatise every creepy implausibility of the original . . .'[76] On the other hand, Anne Wood, writing in *Books for Your Children*, commented, 'It is thorough going, good escapist children's television just as the books are sheer entertainment for children.'[77] Enid Blyton, even ten years after her death, continued to give rise to debate. It is, however, a tribute to her fame that the televised 'Famous Five' was reviewed at all in the *Guardian*, which rarely comments on children's programmes in this way.

In an account of her experiences as a writer in residence in some Yorkshire schools (where, incidentally, she overheard one boy say to another as she went into a school one morning,

'That's Enid Blyton'), Elisabeth Mace says that thirteen-year-olds were quite happy to discuss the reading of 'Famous Five' stories as compared with watching the televised production. They preferred to read and complained that the television characters talked 'all wrong'.[78]

By 1980 Enid Blyton was still firmly established, in non-book media as well as in books. During 1976 and 1977 several librarians commented to me that her popularity was waning at last, but there is little real evidence to support this view. Adult attitudes have mellowed, reflecting perhaps the fact that the first generation of Enid Blyton readers are now in middle age and an element of nostalgia has set in.

Part II

Enid Blyton and the Children

Chapter Seven

Why Children like Enid Blyton's Books

❀

FROM THE SURVEYS of children's reading preferences which have been carried out, one can safely conclude that for over thirty years Enid Blyton has been the most popular and widely-read author amongst children of eight to twelve. Apart from the range and content of her books, two factors contribute to her popularity; first, she appeals particularly to girls, who tend to read more than boys at this age, and secondly, she writes primarily for the age at which children are most likely to read, at a point where they have acquired reasonable fluency but before the interests and pressures of adolescence begin to weigh heavily.

The main reasons for Enid Blyton's popularity with children, however, lie in the content of her books and the way in which they are written. As she showed in her interview with Adam Sykes,[1] and in the articles which she herself wrote about her methods,[2,3] Enid Blyton was well aware of the stages through which children pass in their reading; she recognized that each stage needed appropriate vocabulary and plot, characterization and presentation and, moreover, she was happy to provide what children want. John Rowe Townsend once suggested that children in 'the middle group, aged from about eight to eleven' are not 'getting their fair share of creative talent', suggesting that authors find it irksome to write for this group because the children lack both reading skills and experience of life and literature.[4] One of Enid Blyton's strengths is that she evidently did not find it irksome and therefore provided a steady supply of easy-to-read books which 'are within the scope of quite young children, and yet retain their popularity with older readers'.[5] This supply has never been successfully matched by any other author and so Enid Blyton's popularity continues.

Although it is difficult for children to explain exactly why they like certain books, because they are not sufficiently articulate or experienced enough to be able to compare and contrast, it is possible to establish their preferences from the considerable amount of research into their reading tastes, carried out in the last fifty years. These preferences seem to have changed little over the years, although the literature provided for them has changed considerably.

At the earliest stage, children are egocentric and like stories about small and weak heroes and heroines who achieve success, and stories which deal simply with a small child's problems of adjustment to the world. Normal and happy experiences are usually described realistically but potentially frightening experiences usually happen to machines, toys or animals substituting as humans so that these experiences can be safely explored at second hand through a character with whom the reader or, more likely at this stage, the listener, cannot directly identify. The attention span is likely to be limited so the story must be short and simple, in simple language, with words and situations frequently repeated. Enid Blyton meets the needs of this youngest age group with the 'Noddy' and short 'nursery' stories, which have simple plots woven around characters and situations meaningful to small children. Many of the books have colourful illustrations which constitute an important part of their appeal. Since most children are listeners rather than readers at this stage, the involvement of an interested adult is important and the average adult probably finds Enid Blyton's stories easy to read aloud.

The next stage stretches from the time when children learn to read for themselves until the time when they mature sufficiently to move on to books written for adults. As they move through this stage, they read more fluently and can therefore gradually cope with more difficult vocabulary and sentence structure, and they gain more experience of life so that they can cope with more complex ideas and subtlety of characterization. These children, however, still see the world through children's eyes and appropriate stories provide them with the means to come to terms with past and present experience and to prepare for the future through vicarious experience. The Plowden Report, emphasizing the importance and value of fiction at this stage said:

> Through story ... children grope for the meaning of the experiences that have already overtaken them, savour again their pleasures, and reconcile themselves to their own inconsistencies and those of others ... It is also through literature that children feel forward to the experiences, the hopes and fears that await them in adult life ...[6]

Although David Holbrook questioned the usefulness of 'the jaded writing of commercial hacks', amongst whom he specifically mentioned Enid Blyton, as a preparation for the experience of living,[7] she did in fact show a remarkable understanding of what children both like and need between the ages of seven and eleven or twelve.

Research shows that, after the age of six, boys begin to lose interest in fantasy stories[8] and although girls retain their interest for longer, both sexes gradually develop an interest in stories which purport to be realistic. Enid Blyton reserved fantasy for her nursery stories and for those full-length stories which she wrote, judging by the age of the central characters and the content, for children of seven to nine. Although fantasy for older children and adolescents has become fashionable in recent years, research seems to suggest that, even in the case of the successful 'Narnia' books by C. S. Lewis, it is popular mainly with only the most able children.[9]

Enid Blyton did, however, excel in the production of mystery and adventure stories and it is these which constitute her most popular and widely-read work. I. J. Leng found that mystery stories accounted for about a third of the books borrowed by both boys and girls at the age of eleven.[10] The readers of these are in the process of becoming more independent and the peer group begins to replace the family in importance. In Enid Blyton's stories, the readers see boys and girls with whom they can easily identify, involved in exciting adventures, surviving on their own without adult assistance and frequently being treated by adults as valued and important members of the community when they have solved the mystery or brought the adventure to a successful conclusion.

Enid Blyton's adventure and mystery stories are all set against a recognizable domestic background; her characters are children and even though Fatty of the 'Find-outers' and Jack in the 'Secret' books are fourteen and admired by the other children for their ability and leadership, they are portrayed as leaders of children rather than as potential leaders of men. Although it is sometimes hinted that Fatty leads a more sophisticated existence elsewhere, he is a child when he is with the rest of the Find-outers. Most boys, because of this, grow out of Enid Blyton at a fairly early age although her family and school stories appeal to girls for longer, meeting their liking for stories of the 'everyday life of a happy, loving family, or a group of congenial, interesting girls'[11] and for stories which deal with the social problems of winning friends and prestige in the community.[12] Jenkinson,[13] Carter,[14] Dunlop[15] and Leng[16] all comment on the popularity of the girls' school story, which serves these tastes well and also meets the readers' need for stories about girls rather older than themselves.

Enid Blyton therefore concentrated on the fiction genres which research shows are most popular with children; in addition her books, like most popular books, are about desirable experience rather than realistic experience. She meets the need for stories of wish fulfilment, stories which provide compensatory and escapist reading, to an extent which few other authors for children have achieved. Books at this level satisfy children, who can accept the improbabilities, the simple black or white characters and the over simplified and direct motivation. Waite suggests that not only do they satisfy, they also provide a baseline from which the majority of children can progress further.[17] Sourbut points out that the spice of danger without reality, the tomboy characters, the almost human animals all provide reassurance and that addiction to Enid Blyton is the reflection of a deep-seated human need. He concludes that, 'If ever we get to the stage where all children in school are well-fed, clothed and housed, emotionally satisfied and intellectually stimulated, doubtless Enid Blyton's books will be totally expendable.'[18]

In wish-fulfilment stories, the reader must find characters with whom he can identify and Leng goes into detail about how children set about this process; they like to identify with a character of approximately their own age although, as they grow older, boys in particular tend to look for characters somewhat older than themselves.[19] Enid Blyton, in her most popular books, provides a group of four or five children, of both sexes and ranging from seven- to fourteen-years-old so that it is easy for the reader to find a character with whom to identify. Moreover, Enid Blyton invariably retains the role of omniscient storyteller and can therefore shift the viewpoint from time to time without causing the reader any serious problems of adjustment. Although Harding suggests that identification and vicarious satisfaction are 'fancy labels' for imaginative insight into what another person is feeling, for the contemplation of possible human experience which we are not ourselves at the moment experiencing, and for formalizing what we take for granted in gossip and observation, he agrees that the reading of fiction can contribute to the search for identity, allowing the reader to try on various personalities.[20] Enid Blyton provides for this, albeit at a very simple and obvious level; it is, however, a level which is within the reach of most children.

In many of Enid Blyton's stories, the girls participate in the adventure only up to a point; the boys go on to the more dangerous and daring part of the adventure, sometimes consciously drawing attention to the need to protect the girls. Although girls sometimes comment adversely on this, research does suggest that they prefer this situation.[21, 22] It is also, presumably, satisfying for the boy readers. The character of George, however, described by Bentley as 'the outcome of true understanding of the young girl's mind',[23] reflects the last tomboy stage through which most girls pass on their way to adolescence. The tomboy character has always been popular with girls at the pre-puberty stage and there is a long line of literary examples from Louisa M. Alcott's Jo onwards. The main difference between them and George is that George never changes significantly in this respect; she is just as much a super tomboy in the last 'Famous Five' adventure as she is in the first, whereas Jo, Katy, Caddie Woodlawn and Laura all come to accept the female role and become young ladies in due course.

Enid Blyton's adult characters are, for the most part, portrayed in keeping with the normal, immature child's view of adults. They are usually included in stories only to provide home comforts (Aunt Fanny), a short cut to the winding up of an adventure (Inspector Jenks), or as a foil to the skill and cleverness of the child characters (Mr Goon, the village policeman). Although Woods suggests that Enid Blyton cannot handle adult male characters at all,[24] her adult males stand out very much more clearly than the females who are usually just super mother figures. Tucker has paid tribute to the impression made on him by the irascible Uncle Quentin;[25] there is the knowledgeable Bill Cunningham in the 'Adventure' books while Inspector Jenks might have stepped straight out of *The Flaxborough Chronicles*. These three characters represent those aspects of adult males which are probably most apparent to, and perhaps most wished for by, children – bad-tempered hostility, universal knowledge and universal power. The fact that the children are frequently praised by these powerful characters, even, at times, by Uncle Quentin, is merely part of the wish fulfilment.

There are other elements which reinforce the wish-fulfilment nature of Enid Blyton's books. For example, Terman and Lima found that children like the time and place of a story to be clearly indicated,[26] Rankin found that children prefer a familiar setting[27] and Butts commented that stories set in a foreign country (unless they are adventure stories) are unpopular.[28] Although Enid Blyton rarely gives a precise geographical location to her stories (indeed, the internal evidence is sometimes contradictory), the settings are what might be described as stylized Cornwall, Lake District, Scotland or Wales or, on occasion, 'abroad' and almost every child must be able to relate the setting to his own experience, either first hand or gained through other reading or television, and feel that the book has a firm basis in reality. It is the adult, not the child, who wants background detail to give reality to fiction; as far as the child is concerned, detailed descriptions merely hold up the action.

Enid Blyton also uses a stylized social setting, a romanticized country or village background, not unlike the world of television advertisements, a world which does not really exist but is near enough to reality to be instantly recognizable. One of the reasons for Enid Blyton's continuing popularity may well be the fact that there is little in the books to date them or to pin them to a particular locality; this also helps to explain why she is read and enjoyed by children in other countries. Every reader can assume that the time is the present and the location is just around the corner or over the hill.

In recent years there has developed a theory that one of the reasons why some children do not read is because they do not see their own life style reflected in the books they are expected to read. This may well be an an attempt to rationalize the fact that children from working-class homes are likely to have more difficulties in learning to read and, having acquired the skills, are less likely to make use of them than children from middle-class backgrounds. As Frank Whitehead and his colleagues found during the course of the Schools Council Research Project:

> ... family circumstances exert an important influence on the child's amount of reading. Thus a child with a father in a non-manual occupation is likely to possess more books and see more quality newspapers in the home, and is more likely to visit a public library regularly and to have parents who read library books ... we can also say that the child with a father in a non-manual occupation is more likely to be assessed high by his school for ability and attainment.[29]

In fact, most readers, child or adult, prefer their fiction reading to provide a window on a more affluent way of life, not a mirror reflection of their own, perhaps rather dull, life. Although Enid Blyton is quite capable of making working-class children successful achievers if it suits the needs of the plot, there is in general a superior attitude to cooks as well as to crooks,[30] and this adds to the fantasy element of the story. As research by Ellison and Williams,[31] and by Hanson[32] shows, children from all social backgrounds have very similar tastes and the same research suggests that Enid Blyton's middle-class, conventional world meets with general approval from the children.

Food is generally recognized as an important preoccupation of children, and Woods draws attention to its treatment in Enid Blyton's books, suggesting that it reflects the author's longing for her own childhood, since she frequently mentions tongues, ham, lemonade and ginger beer.[33] Although modern inventions such as fish fingers do not appear, most of the food which is mentioned is still familiar to children. Eating is given due importance and Tucker has suggested that food replaces the interest which sex provides in popular adult fiction.[34]

Many children are attracted by the idea of owning a pet and most of Enid Blyton's stories include an animal interest. In the circus stories, Jimmy Brown is shown to be a successful achiever through his skill with animals while characters like Barney in the 'Barney' books and Philip in the 'Adventure' books are given distinction by their unusual pets. The actions of the Famous Five, and of George in particular, are often affected by her fondness for Timmy, her dog. These animals and many others which appear in the pages of Enid Blyton's books are frequently attributed with human feelings by the child characters. Even in *Shadow the Sheep Dog*, where the animal is at the centre of the story, the dog's adventures are designed to point morals relevant to human children.

The kind of humour which appeals to six- to eleven-year-olds is also to be found in Enid Blyton's stories. They enjoy simple play on words, funny incidents, comic images and situations which make the reader feel superior. Bateman found that nonsense on its own produces only quiet amusement while subtle humour is noticed only by the very intelligent; he actually used extracts from Enid Blyton in his research and found that she was well within the compass of the average reader, relying heavily on word play and slapstick comedy.[35]

The reading surveys also show that children look for clearcut morality in their stories. Children tend to make moral judgments in terms of good and bad; they have a strong sense of justice and expect goodness to be rewarded and badness to be suitably punished.[36] Although preaching and moralizing must be successfully concealed,[37] the moral of the story must be clear[38] and the young reader must be certain about the author's ethical standpoint.[39] Enid Blyton herself made it clear that she appreciated these requirements, pointing out that the true children's writer cannot help communicating to her readers the values in which she believes.[40] Her stories have a simple morality at the level which appeals to children; goodness is always rewarded and arrogance and deceit are invariably punished; because she presents things clearly in black and white with no confusing intermediate shades of grey[41], she does not in fact have to preach and moralize. The moral is plainly there for all to see. However, Tucker draws attention to the fact that, as he sees it, Enid Blyton's moral judgments tend to be at a facile level; she stays at the child's level whereas a more gifted writer would prod the child on. For example, she concentrates on the finding of the treasure and the subsequent happy ending instead of showing that the winning of the treasure is only the beginning of the problem.[42]

Both Tucker, in the same article, and Harding[43] suggest that the experience of fear through stories is an important part of a child's reading; it is better to learn to face fear through books while conscious than through nightmares while unconscious. Ghost, gangster and adventure stories can be usefully demonstrate that imaginary perils can be survived and Enid Blyton provides these at a very simple, reassuring level.

Terman and Lima suggest that children look for sincerity in their reading.[44] Although Enid Blyton's writing seems to the adult eye too simple and too obviously geared to children's needs to be sincere, the fact that Enid Blyton really believed in what she was doing and never for a moment looked over her shoulder at the adult critic meant that she was perfectly sincere in every word she wrote. She was interested only in establishing a relationship with her intended readership and this she successfully did.

Enid Blyton, as well as providing all the elements which many children look for in their favourite reading, packaged these elements in a form which is easily digestible. The vocabulary is simple and undemanding, sentences are short and little effort has to be expended by the reader on lengthy descriptions which hold up the action. These are precisely the qualities which are required in books intended to encourage children to read, and it is in this area of providing children with the means of achieving reading fluency that Enid Blyton receives her greatest support from adults. Few would argue with Spalding's view that books about the 'Secret Seven' and the 'Famous Five' have 'helped many children through the stage between the little children's books and the more advanced junior novels'.[45] Although some commentators take the view that a diet of undiluted Blyton may blunt the appetite for reading, Anne James points out that it would be difficult to prove this as there is plenty of evidence to show that children who enjoy reading Enid Blyton often grow up to be adults who enjoy reading.[46] One of the reasons for the decline in reading amongst adolescents may well be the lack of an Enid Blyton equivalent who appeals to twelve- to sixteen-year-olds. In recent years attempts have been made to fill this gap and Aidan Chambers quoted a letter from a boy who wrote to him about 'Topliners', a series for reluctant adolescent readers, which said, ' "Topliners" are an excellent idea as I am sure like myself many between 12 and 18 must enjoy these books, as there are only a few good books written for us between these ages. It's rather a big step from Enid Blyton to Doetovsky (sic).'[47]

Because children lack literary experience, they need help in selecting a book which they will enjoy. An interested and enthusiastic adult can help, but children are often on their own and in this case a promising title arouses expectations.[48] Rankin established that popular books have revealing and informative titles and chapter headings which are indicative of the development of the story.[49] Most of Enid Blyton's titles provide an immediate clue to the kind of story contained in the book; *The Enchanted Wood*, *Island of Adventure*, *The Mystery of the Burnt Cottage* and *The Naughtiest Girl in the School* leave the prospective reader in very little doubt.

Children like the familar, a book by the author they already know, or, even better, another title in a series they know and enjoy. Some of Enid Blyton's popularity is undoubtedly caused by her large output, and although the evidence of the reading surveys might seem to suggest that she would be just as popular if her work had been confined to the 'Secret Seven' and 'Famous Five' series, the school stories and the books about Noddy, we have no means of knowing just how significant is the cumulative effect.

Terman and Lima, and Rankin in their American-based, pre-Blyton research, found that popular books have an attractive format similar to the conventional adult novel.[50, 51] A child picking up a book and making a decision about whether he wishes to read it forms his judgment on the basis of the format, the typography and the illustrations as well as on what he can gather of the content.[52] These help to serve as indicators that the book is within reach of his understanding.[53] The production of Enid Blyton's books is in keeping with these requirements. Although the illustrations, to the adult eye, often compare unfavourably with those in children's books praised by the critics, research shows that children prefer realistic and unstylized illustrations and although Dyer describes the illustrations in *Castle of Adventure* as execrable,[54] they do undoubedly represent the characters and the action in a way which appeals to most children. All Enid Blyton's books are plentifully illustrated, even the school stories which are likely to be read by older girls. Leng points out that although children's reliance on illustrations varies with their degree of reading skill, the fact that a book has illustrations means that it can be read by children of widely differing abilities.[55] Fenwick, concerned to discover why certain books in the school library were consistently rejected, found that those which were *accepted* had a higher than average percentage of illustrations.[56]

As Enid Blyton's popularity is now so well established amongst children, it would be interesting to see what children's reaction would be if some of her books were reprinted in small typeface, without illustrations and with dull-looking jackets or covers. A teacher-librarian's comment that 'I have found in my researches that only exceptionally popular authors, such as Blyton, are borrowed if the book is dull in appearance'[57] suggests that it might not now make much difference.

The author who appeals to children must not only use simple language but must tell the story in a straightforward way;[58] the child reader does not want leisurely explorations of character and motive.[59] The opening paragraphs must capture the reader's attention immediately, providing a direct and illuminating approach to characters and setting, and a promise of adventure and excitement.[60] The inexperienced reader needs to be put in the picture as soon as possible. As Warlow points out, the test of a mature reader is how long he is prepared to remain in an ambivalent situation.[61] An examination of almost any Enid Blyton title reveals her ability to provide a satisfactory opening paragraph. For example, the first chapter of *The Enchanted Wood* is called 'How they found the magic wood' and begins, 'There were once three children, called Jo, Bessie, and Fanny. All their lives they had lived in a town, but now their father had a job in the country, so they were all to move as soon as ever they could.'[62] The first chapter of *Five on a Treasure Island* is called 'A great surprise' and begins, ' "Mother have you heard about our summer holidays yet?" said Julian, at the breakfast table. "Can we go to Polsheath as usual?" '[63] The first paragraph of *First Term at Malory Towers* introduces the central character and indicates, with a superb economy of words, that she is off to boarding school as a new girl, 'Darrell Rivers looked at herself in the glass. It was almost time to start for the train, but there was just a minute to see how she looked in her new school uniform.'[64]

Once started, the story must move briskly and there must be plenty of action, with something happening all the time.[65, 66, 67] Enid Blyton considered herself a 'true storyteller' with a natural sense of drama[68] and her self-assessment is supported to a large extent even by her critics. Gillian Tindall referred to her as 'a tireless borrower of other people's visions', but admitted that she was 'a superb hack'.[69] Tucker described her as 'a competent storyteller',[70] while the Head of English at Didsbury College of Education suggested that she had considerable talent as an entertainer.[71] Robert Leeson has also admired her approach to her task and the way in which she built up her audience of young readers by letter, magazine column and story telling sessions.[72]

The excitement which most children look for in their reading arises not only from the plot and action, but also from the way in which the story is told. Woods points out that Enid Blyton was able to control the element of surprise in such a way that her plots are often exciting even at an adult level.[73] Much of her success in this respect probably arises from the fact that many of her long stories were written as serials for her magazines and therefore each chapter had to end in such a way that the reader wanted to read the next instalment.

Although even the most able children seem to go through a period when they find satisfaction in reading and re-reading Enid Blyton's work, adverse comments from older children are on record. One eleven-year-old was quoted as saying, 'Enid Blyton writes some good books with exciting stories but, if you read them once I find that you don't want to read them again.'[74] Ernest Roe reports Ruth, an exceptionally good reader, as criticizing Enid Blyton's books, 'Because they don't give you anything to think about . . . it's a lot of rot, life going marvellously and people being lucky all the time.'[75]

Enid Blyton, in fact, set her own limitations and, because she writes for the relatively inexperienced reader, the majority of children are likely to reject and grow out of her books quite naturally when they no longer find them satisfying, although they may well retain life-long affection for the author who brought them so much childhood pleasure.

Part III

The Work of Enid Blyton

Chapter Eight

Critical Considerations

❧

AN ACCOUNT of the Blyton phenomenon would not be complete without some consideration of Enid Blyton's work. Criticism and discussion tend to have centred on the adventure stories, particularly those about the 'Famous Five' and the 'Adventure' books, and on Noddy, with occasional forays into the books in the 'Faraway Tree' series and into stories about gollywogs. Although it is obviously impossible to cover more than a very small proportion of Enid Blyton's total output, I have tried to cast my net a little more widely than this and to look at a range representative of her most popular work.

One of the problems which faces the critic of children's books is that there is a lack of agreement about the way in which children's books should be judged. The critics of children's fiction range from those described as 'purists', who are book-centred and take the view that children's books must be judged by the same standards as adult literature, to the 'pragmatists' who believe that such criticism should be child-centred and consider that the child's viewpoint must be taken into account. For some commentators the attitudes implicit in children's books are thought to be as important as the literary quality; for others, work that has little literary merit is sometimes justified on the grounds that it provides children with easy and enjoyable reading material at a time when they need practice in order to become fluent readers.

A book that is intended to be read by children must obviously communicate with children and the author of a children's book must make allowances for a child's lack of experience and for the limitations of a child's understanding and vocabulary. Robert Leeson suggests that if the child as reader is disregarded in the effort to win recognition for children's books as literature, we shall arrive at a situation in which the children's books which are published will be admired by everyone except the children. 'The books will be praised, written about, bought, presented and finally left on the shelves while the children go out to play with Enid.'[1] How far does a need to recognize the child's limitations as a reader effect the usual considerations of plot, characterization, style and theme?

In children's fiction, a plot is essential and this must be unfolded in a way which attracts and holds the reader's interest. Ideally, the sequence of events should arise from the nature of the characters, not be imposed upon them from the outside. In a novel for children, the central characters are usually children or child-substitutes but adults who are important to the story must appear as convincing and rounded characters The quality of the characterization plays an important part in the overall quality of the work.

Although a child reader is likely to have a more limited vocabulary and less reading experience than the adult reader, it is reasonable to look for a style which avoids clichés, which incorporates original metaphors and similes, which uses challenging language structures and rhythms and in which there is a vivid immediacy of language. The creation of atmosphere, through the way in which the story is told, may well be more important than the plot itself.

The good children's story should create a credible environment and a sense of reality. If the author is skilful enough, the reader will inhabit this created world during the reading of the story and if the skill is great enough, something of that world will always remain with the reader. Themes and concepts must be appropriate to the child reader. Solutions which are offered to problems should be feasible and constructive. The novel should meet the child's need for achievement, security and acceptance, but should also open his mind to the possibility of change. The reader should be given the opportunity to make evaluative judgments and be given worthy ideals for conduct and achievement. The reading of a story should be an enriching and rewarding experience as well as an enjoyable one, increasing the reader's understanding of the world, widening his sympathies and stimulating his imagination.

Even those who defend Enid Blyton's work for its value in

providing enjoyable reading matter for the relatively inexperienced reader would hesitate to claim for it all these qualities. In the early days her work was ignored or dismissed briefly because it was judged to be lacking in quality; by the time it was discussed, the poor literary quality of her work was very much taken for granted. In his introduction to literary criticism, *An Essential Discipline*, Fred Inglis says:

> If we attempt a roll call of the mythic heroes of our literary childhood, what figures step out of the gloom? King of the Golden River, Robin Hood, Crusoe, Mole and Ratty, King Arthur, White Fang, Bagheera, Quentin Durward, Long John Silver? Perhaps, and if we are lucky. More likely, Little Noddy, the Famous Five, Biggles, Jill and her ponies, the heroes of Stalag Luft III, Colditz, Micky Spillane and Ian Fleming. I prefer the first list to the second . . . the ability to discriminate justly between the first and second list is an important and serious one.[2]

His judgment is supported by the Schools Council Research Project team who included all Enid Blyton titles cited by children amongst the 'non-quality' narrative books along with the books about Biggles and Jill, and the books by Spillane and Fleming. Peter Hunt, who takes the view that children's literature should be judged by the same standards as adult literature, stated categorically that Enid Blyton is not literature, and like Inglis, linked her work to that of Spillane, saying, 'I would as much consider including her in a study of children's literature as I would consider including, say, Micky Spillane on a literature degree course.'[3] Why is the work of Enid Blyton so readily placed on the level of comic books and sub-literature?

In his essay, 'On three ways of writing for children', C. S. Lewis described two good ways and one bad. The bad way, he thought, was to find out what children 'want and give them that, however little you like it yourself'.[4] The Schools Council team defined non-quality writing in much the same terms as work 'whose production has been essentially a commercial operation, a matter of catering for a market'.[5]

That Enid Blyton successfully identified her market, assessed its taste and catered for it is clearly demonstrated by her continuing popularity. The way in which she wrote is well documented, in the autobiography which she wrote for children, in the articles which she wrote for the *New Statesman* and *The Author*, in interviews which she gave, in Barbara Stoney's biography and by the psychologist Peter McKellar who corresponded with her between 1953 and 1958 while he was engaged in a study of the processes of imaginative thought.[6] The picture which emerges from these various accounts is a consistent one.

Enid Blyton began to write a book by knowing only what kind of a story and what length it was to be; she then made her mind a blank and the characters appeared in it, furnished with christian names (surnames, if required, were taken from a telephone directory later) and outstanding characteristics. The story then unfolded in her mind's eye almost as if she had a cinema screen there, complete with sound, smell and taste, and she merely reported what she saw. The method was only good for creative work; factual material had to be planned, drafted and polished in the normal way. In their correspondence Enid Blyton suggested to Peter McKellar that other prolific writers must have worked in the same way and mentioned Dickens in particular, but referred also to Homer, whom she admired as a good storyteller,[7] Shakespeare and Christopher Fry.[8] Although this seems to suggest a certain lack of modesty, Enid Blyton, while quick to lay claim to her undoubted gifts, was in fact charmingly modest about her skills when she discussed them in articles and letters.

McKellar took her description of her creative processes seriously and although he said they were atypical, he said that they fitted the general theory of original and creative thinking. He suggested that her functions of creativity worked in a strongly visual way, the picture owing its content to prior perceptions, often dating from long ago.[9] Enid Blyton herself realized that the images of old castles and islands which recur in her work were the result of her attraction to these on her travels and that the characters she created sometimes reminded her of people she had met. Another obvious influence, as it must be for any writer, was her childhood reading which she describes in her autobiography. Her favourite book was *The Princess and the Goblin* and she loved *The Coral Island* and *Little Women* and read every myth and legend she could find. She hated anything that was sad (*Black Beauty*) or cruel (the tales of the Grimm Brothers) and admitted skipping passages that were above her head (*The Water Babies*).[10] A first reading of her work gives the impression that this childhood reading was so absorbed that little evidence of it appeared in her own writing; everything seems to have been digested and refined to remove anything sad, cruel, boring or above the reader's head. A second look, however, reveals that something of it remains.

It is easy to mock Enid Blyton's plots, to criticize her characters as being stereotypes or made of cardboard, to dismiss her vocabulary as limited and her style as undemanding. I have tried to stand back from these generally accepted preconceptions and, in view of the affection with which her books are recalled by many of the adults who read them as children (and C. S. Lewis suggests that a book which is well and truly loved for a lifetime cannot be wholly bad[11]), to consider the possibility that there is rather more to them than easy reading material, on which young readers can practise. Do they also provide a valid literary experience which is a useful preparation for the reading and enjoyment of literature?

Chapter Nine

Noddy and the
Nursery Stories

❁

IT WOULD BE interesting to know what Enid Blyton's reputation would have been had the 'Noddy' books, against which much of the strongest criticism has been levelled, never appeared. Noddy is almost certainly her most famous creation and has featured in most of the library controversies. He is alive and well and stories about him are still appearing in new formats; for example, *The Third St Michael Book of Noddy* was published for sale in Marks and Spencers store in 1979. Some of the credit for Noddy's fame must go to the Dutchman, Harmsen Van Der Beek, who illustrated the books and created Noddy, Big-Ears, Mr Plod and the little car in colourful forms which could be reproduced as nursery toys and requisites such as soap, toothbrushes and cereal bowls.

The main criticism of the Noddy stories comes in the articles by Colin Welch and Edward Blishen, both of whom condemn them wholeheartedly. Colin Welch criticizes the books because they are written down to children and do not stretch their imagination, enlarge their experience, kindle delight in them or awaken their delight in words,[1] while Edward Blishen comments that they 'represent the reduction to surely final feebleness of all the elements of children's fantasy'.[2]

The example at which I looked was *Noddy Meets Father Christmas*, the eleventh Noddy story, published in 1955, six years after the first title, *Little Noddy Goes to Toyland*. Noddy has something in common with the heroes and heroines of many modern stories for young children; like Paddington, Pooh, Babar and Pippi Longstocking, he combines the innocence and naïvety of the child with some of the advantages of being an adult. Noddy's main advantage is that he owns and drives a car, but he also lives on his own and exercises a certain amount of independence. At the same time he is, in this particular book, scolded for being untidy and he is looked after by Mrs Tubby who lives next door and irons his clothes for him. I found Noddy's subservience to Big-Ears and, conversely, Big-Ears' condescension to Noddy the most objectionable elements in the book. In some ways it is a working out of the perennial folk tale theme of Cinderella. Father Christmas is coming to Toyland to inspect the quality of toys and is going to have supper one evening with Big-Ears' brother, Little-Ears. Big-Ears condescendingly promises to allow Noddy to drive him there and to wait outside in the car to drive him home again. Noddy is pleased to do this as he hopes for a glimpse of Father Christmas. As he is painting and polishing his car in honour of the occasion he composes a song and Big-Ears, overhearing it, arranges for it to be sung outside Little-Ears' house while Father Christmas is eating there. As a result, Noddy not only sees Father Christmas but is actually asked to drive him around Toyland. (' "It's such a nuisance too, having to find a stable each night for my four reindeer." '[3]) After visits to Bouncing Ball Village, Golliwog Town, Rocking-Horse Town, Humming-Top Village and Doll's-house Town, they set out for a small place called 'N. & B. works'. After some speculation about what this can be ('"What in the world do N. and B. stand for? I know it's something to do with perfectly new toys — but WHAT can they be? N. and B. — most peculiar!" '[4]), it proves to be the Noddy and Big-Ears works. Noddy feels a Very Important Person and goes home to a splendid party.

There is a strong plot in the folk tale tradition, although Noddy is hardly of heroic proportions and not really deserving of his good fortune, except that he falls in willingly with Big-Ears' plan. There are some imaginative ideas. The Chief Bouncer in Bouncing Ball Village is an 'enormous coloured ball, the kind that likes to be played with at the seaside', in Humming-Top Village 'all night long there was the humming of excited tops' and in Doll's-house Town Father Christmas tells the dolls they must learn how to dust and scrub and clean windows.

However, the plot and the ideas are trivialized by the vocabulary and the behaviour of the characters, who are not differentiated by their speech or actions. Father Christmas speaks as Enid Blyton, as a narrator, might speak, making such remarks such as ' "What a dear little car" ', ' "Dear me, I wish I could travel through Toyland in this instead of going in my bumpy old sleigh." '[5]

Colin Welch drew attention to the possibilities of comparison between Enid Blyton and A. A. Milne, pointing out that Noddy and Winnie-the-Pooh appeal primarily to the same age group, both with complete success.[6] Both characters are humanized toys and 'In which Piglet meets an heffalump', a story from *Winnie-the-Pooh*, makes an excellent comparison with the 'Noddy' book under discussion. In a story a quarter of the length of *Noddy Meets Father Christmas*, Milne unfolds a rather more complex plot, introduces a considerable amount of humour (humour is almost completely lacking from the Noddy story except for the probably unintentional humour of Big-Ears getting his comeuppance) and reinforces the personalities of the characters through their speech. The humour of calling elephants 'heffalumps' or acorns 'haycorns' is never drawn to the attention of the reader. The only word play in the Noddy story is on the word 'conducting'. Big-Ears tells Noddy he can conduct his friends in his song,

> 'What's conducting?' asked Noddy in fright, 'I can't conduct. That's what busmen do.'
> 'You're thinking of bus-conductors, you silly little fellow!' said Big-Ears, laughing. 'You just beat time, that's all — like this!'[7]

Neither Pooh nor Piglet, for all their modesty and timidity, would ever admit that they couldn't conduct in any sense of the word. Pooh quickly claims the he saw a heffalump even while he is wondering 'what a heffalump was like.'[8]

The main difference between *Noddy Meets Father Christmas* and 'Piglet meets a heffalump' is that the latter works at both adult and child level. The story is told economically, the vocabulary is not diluted to the level of every child, and the humour has adult as well as child appeal. If C. S. Lewis's belief that a good children's book is a book which can be enjoyed at any age is accepted, then the Noddy story is not good. It is written down to the child, and has nothing in it for the adult reader. There is little to stretch the imagination of the child or to enlarge his experience, although children may respond to the images of bouncing balls and to Noddy's modest success. There is nothing in the style which is likely to pass into family parlance as Milne's 'heffalumps' and 'haycorns' may do. Noddy's little songs, though they rhyme and scan, lack the richness of Pooh's. The plot of *Noddy Meets Father Christmas*, although tightly constructed, operates at a mundane level, lacking the depth of 'Piglet meets a heffalump', where Pooh and Piglet decide to catch a heffalump, dig a trap, bait it and return to their separate homes: Pooh returns to eat the honey bait, Piglet returns to see if they have caught a heffalump and, finding Pooh with his head stuck in the honey jar, mistakes him for the heffalump. Throughout the story the toy animals rationalize and account for their actions and the plot develops from their characters.

Despite the continuing appeal and popularity of the 'Noddy' stories, it is difficult to justify their dissemination. Children enjoy them at an age when they are most likely to have them read aloud and in this situation there is not the same need for simple reading material as there is at a later stage when children are reading the text themselves. There are plenty of attractive picture books and stories which can be read to and with the young child, which will be a much more rewarding experience than the exploits of Noddy and his friends.

The advantage of the Noddy books is that once one has been experienced, the child's expectations are aroused. He can to some extent anticipate what is going to happen; he greets Noddy, Big-Ears, Mr Plod and the other recurring characters as old friends. Enid Blyton had a number of characters whom she used regularly in stories for young children — Amelia-Jane, the doll, Betsy-May, the little girl, Mr Meddle and Mr Pinkwhistle, but she also produced countless stories of between a thousand and two thousand words, which were quite independent of each other. *Sunny Stories* and later the *Enid Blyton Magazine*, which appeared over a period of more than twenty years, used three such stories each week and others appeared in various collections and annuals. Writing stories of this length for children is not easy since more information has to be included that is necessary for the experienced adult reader and the twist at the end or open ending which is often an attractive element in the adult story is not appropriate for the inexperienced reader.

Most collections of short stories for younger children rely heavily on folk tales while collections for older children of eleven and upwards use adult stories which, because of their content or style, are within the range of the older child. Those authors who have successfully produced original short stories for children have relied heavily on the folk or fairy tale tradition. Hans Andersen, Rudyard Kipling, Eleanor Farjeon and Walter de la Mare are notable examples, the last two both being awarded the Carnegie Medal for collections. Using the style of the traditional tale provides the author with a convenient shorthand in phrases such as 'once upon a time', 'there was once a king' and 'they all lived happily ever after', which the child reader or listener understands from an early age through his experience of traditional stories. This experience is common to all societies and an understanding of the conventions does not imply any degree of sophistication.

As an example of Enid Blyton's short story collections I have chosen *Story Party at Green Hedges*, first published in 1949, partly because it includes the already mentioned, controversial story of 'The little black doll'. Fourteen stories are set into the framework of a tea party given by Enid Blyton at her home, Green Hedges. The reader is invited to fill in his or her name on an invitation at the beginning of the book; the other thirteen children are all named and described, and each story is told for a particular child. The tea table and the arrival of the guests are described and between the stories there are linking passages in which the children show their appreciation of the last story and a child issues specifications for the next. Halfway through there is a description of the tea and at the end all the children go home looking forward to the 'next exciting story party'. The stories themselves provide a balanced diet, being about dolls, animals and various supernatural creatures; there are some realistic stories about children and some provide a mixture of all these elements. The stories are told economically and most have a moral. Even the much criticized story of the little black doll puts over the message that it is not important what people look like. A rabbit learns that rudeness doesn't pay and Fred learns the importance of having a memory rather than a 'forgettery' the hard way when he forgets all about an invitation to the circus which he has been asked to deliver to his headmaster. Elsewhere characters achieve success. Tinker, the mongrel dog, is despised by the other dogs and cats in the road but succeeds in making friends with the new arrival, a Manx cat with no tail.

> The dogs and cats of Cherry Road talked to one another about the new cat.
> 'She's grey,' said Scamper the terrier.
> 'She's small,' said Smut and Soot.
> 'She's got a very tiny mew,' said Tiddles the tabby.
> 'Her eyes are green,' said Scottie.
> 'She's the only animal in that house,' said Ginger, the orange-coloured cat.
> 'I'd like to chase her,' said Tinker the mongrel.
> The cats turned to stare at him, looking down their noses scornfully.
> 'You *would*!' they said. 'You have no manners. You are a common little mongrel.'
> 'Mongrels should be seen and not heard,' said the dogs.[9]

This section of the story is well told although other sections lack the vigour of this particular passage.

The story which comes nearest to the folk tale in style and content is the tale of Timothy, 'the cheeky boy'. Timothy likes to be cheeky and examples of his rudeness to his mother and her friends are quoted. One night he wakes up, finds a brownie in the bedroom and is cheeky to him too. (' "Hop off, funny-face." ') The brownie says:

> 'You can be CHEEKY – CHEEKY – CHEEKY!'
> And as he spoke, he vanished in a most peculiar way. Timmy could just hear his voice saying 'CHEEKY' over and over again, and then it stopped, and there was nobody and nothing there.[10]

The next morning Timothy's cheeks are swollen up and eventually he realizes that when he is cheeky they swell a little more but when he is polite they subside a little. He realizes that he must cure himself and the story ends with him well on his way to becoming polite and well mannered. The true traditional tale is more likely to end in the rude or unkind character being killed rather than cured but there is the same kind of approach. It makes an interesting comparison with a story by Mrs Molesworth, 'Con and the little people', first published in 1875 and recently reprinted in *The Hamish Hamilton Book of Other Worlds*, edited by Roger Lancelyn Green. This is a much longer story, but compare the openings. Enid Blyton begins:

> There was once a little boy who loved to be cheeky. He spoke rudely to his mother and father, and he was cheeky even to his teacher.[11]

Mrs Molesworth begins her story:

> There was once a boy who was a very good sort of boy, except for two things; or perhaps I should say one thing. I am not really sure whether they were two things, or only two sides of the same thing; perhaps, children, you can decide.[12]

The endings to the two stories also follow a similar pattern. Enid Blyton ends:

> Well, the last time I saw Timothy, he had one cheek just a little bit swollen, but he was hoping nobody would notice. It was harder to get out of the habit of being cheeky than he thought! Poor Timothy. He had a dreadful time, hadn't he, but if it taught him to be polite and well-mannered, it was worth it.[13]

The story of Con, whose fault is that he does not like lessons and whose head is '*always* running on fairies', ends:

> What Con's mother really came to think about this story in the end, I cannot say; nor do I know if she ever told his father. I fancy Con seldom, if ever, spoke about it again. But as all who knew him when he grew up to be a man could testify, his taste of the land of 'all play and no work' never did him any harm.[14]

It was once pointed out by I. A. Richards that 'We take a hint for our response from the poet's reputation.'[15] Enid Blyton sometimes suffers from the critic's prejudice and because we know she is the author of 'The Cheeky Boy' we think we can detect a lack of literary style in her story, while Mrs Molesworth benefits from her status as a major, nineteenth-century children's writer. Enid Blyton's short stories for younger children should be looked at more carefully; some might well deserve a place in an anthology in the year 2050.

Chapter Ten

The Fantasy World

❁

IN THE FIELD of fantasy, British writers have made a major contribution to children's literature. The creatures of fantasy, elves, fairies, gnomes and giants, are to be found in many of Enid Blyton's short stories where, apart from their magical powers, they tend to behave in a rather human way. As well as numerous short stories, Enid Blyton also wrote two series of fantasy stories; there are two books about the travels of the wishing chair and three about the Faraway Tree.

Adventures of the Wishing Chair, published in 1937, constituted my introduction to Enid Blyton and I was enthralled when it was read aloud in my primary school. A re-reading many years later proved disappointing but the first title in the other fantasy series, *The Enchanted Wood*, published two years later, has worn rather better. The stories about the Faraway Tree are amongst Enid Blyton's most highly praised work. Diana Norman claimed *The Enchanted Wood* as Enid Blyton's best book,[1] Brian Doyle mentioned the trilogy as his own personal favourite,[2] Gillian Tindall quoted them as examples of her 'most imaginative and least derivative stories',[3] while Babara Stoney stated that 'her best books are the Adventure stories and the early fairy tales such as *The Faraway Tree*'.[4]

In both these sequences the central, human characters move from the real world into a succession of fantasy worlds, a not uncommon happening in the most popular and most accessible of fantasy stories. Most modern fantasy stories have their roots in traditional myths, legends and folk tales. C. S. Lewis, in his 'Narnia' books, draws on Christian myth and Norse legend, Tolkien uses Norse and Anglo-Saxon legends, Alan Garner Norse and Welsh legends, while the Arthurian story has been a source of inspiration for many recent writers such as Penelope Lively, William Mayne and Susan Cooper.

E. Nesbit, in her stories about the Psammead and the five children, and Hilda Lewis, in *The Ship that Flew*, books which can be usefully compared with those about the wishing chair, both owe something of their quality to their use of myth and legend.

Peter and Mollie acquire the wishing chair when they go to buy a present for their mother. It takes them on a series of adventures, not to the geographical, historical or legendary locations visited by the Nesbit and Hilda Lewis children, but to a giant's castle, to the Grabbit gnomes, to the land of dreams and so on. The idea of the wishing chair is simple and attractive, but does not seem to link directly to any traditional story, although Enid Blyton may have known Frances Browne's book, *Granny's Wonderful Chair*. It is not, however, difficult to see a link between the Faraway Tree and the Norse world tree, Yggdrasil. Maureen and Hugh Crago have suggested that the Faraway Tree goes back to Yggdrasil via Mrs Molesworth's *Christmas Tree Land*,[5] but it seems more likely that Enid Blyton was drawing directly on her memory of Norse stories. In her account of her childhood reading, she says,

> I read every single old myth and legend I could get hold of – the old Norse myths, the old Greek myths which I thought were beautiful, but rather cruel, I still think that . . . I couldn't bear most of Grimm's fairy tales, and I don't like them now, I thought some of them were cruel and frightening,[6]

and she comments that some of the Hans Anderson stories were 'too sad'.[7]

Looking at the description of Yggdrasil in one of the currently available versions of the Norse legends, one finds the following:

> For the evil ones strive continually to destroy the World Tree: down in Nifelheim, where one root grew, the evil Nid Hog was for ever gnawing at it, while serpents twined and bit. Higher up four harts ran upon its branches and nibbled at the leaves, while at the top sat a wise eagle watching all that was done, and Ratatosk the mischievous red squirrel scampered up and down it, carrying news and gossip between Nid Hog and the Eagle.[8]

Whereas the roots of Yggdrasil reach down into other worlds, the upper branches of the Faraway Tree lead into a succession of strange worlds. However, a red squirrel plays an important part in the life of the Faraway Tree just as he does in the life of Yggdrasil: it is his job to ease travel up and down the tree.

> (Jo) set off. He ran through the Enchanted Wood and came to the Faraway Tree. It was a hot afternoon and not many little folk were about.
>
> It seemed almost too hot to climb the tree. Jo whistled. The little red squirrel popped down the tree and looked at him. 'Leap up to the top of the tree and ask old Moon-Face if he'll drop me down a rope with a cushion on the end, and haul me up, squirrel,' said Jo.
>
> The squirrel bounded lightly up the tree.[9]

With all the cruel, frightening and sad elements of the legendary Norse tree removed, and with all the difficult names omitted, one can see that this is what might be left. Surprisingly Enid Blyton's use of a tree as a gateway to fantasy worlds seems to be unique.

Children reading the Hilda Lewis or Nesbit books have a good chance of acquiring some general knowledge. Both authors make references to literature, E. Nesbit to Kipling[10] and Hilda Lewis to *Hereward the Wake*,[11] for example, or to historical figures, such as William the Conqueror.[12] Enid Blyton makes few demands of this kind on her readers. There are no allusions at all in *Adventures of the Wishing Chair* while literary allusion in *The Enchanted Wood* stretches only to Goldilocks and the Three Bears, whom Fanny and Bessie seek out to help rescue Jo from the Land of Ice and Snow. Father Bear tells the girls that Goldilocks has 'gone to see if she can buy some porridge cheap',[13] which is something of a trivialization, but the reader's responses are likely to be stimulated when he goes on to say, ' "But she likes the baby bear's bed best, because it's so soft and warm" ' and Fanny comments, ' "She did in the story." '

' "What story?" asked the mother bear.

"Well – the story of the three bears," said Fanny.

"Never heard of it," said the three bears, all together, which really seemed rather extraordinary to Bessie and Fanny.'[14]

This incident provides a simple introduction to the idea of using traditional stories within the context of contemporary fiction, and is thus a preparation for the appreciation of deeper meaning. The references to the Goldilocks story add an extra dimension, albeit small, to the adventures of Fanny, Bessie and Jo.

The Nesbit and Hilda Lewis children all have a fair amount of general knowledge which is revealed not only during their adventures but also in their conversation and play between adventures. School and home are mentioned too and this helps to heighten the effect of the fantasy. As Margery Fisher has said, 'Nobody can fail to believe in E. Nesbit's fantasies, for they are so firmly rooted in character and circumstance.'[15] Peter and Mollie, on the other hand, when they are not having adventures, pass their time squabbling or playing ludo, tiddleywinks or snakes and ladders. Typically, during one brief interlude, they visit a farm with 'Uncle Jack and chose a lovely black puppy with him'.[16] This incident although brief, provides a contrast to the magical adventures, but matches so well to most children's daydreams that, in a way, it is merely an extension of the fantasy.

When *Adventures of the Wishing Chair* has reached the required length, an ending has to be contrived, and Peter and Mollie are suddenly dispatched to boarding school, whereas the Nesbit and Hilda Lewis books move to a graceful and natural conclusion. At the beginning of the last chapter, Peter announces that

> 'Mother has just told us some bad news.'
> 'What?' cried Chinky.
> 'She has told us that Mollie and I are to go away to school,' said Peter.
> 'But you go to school now,' said Chinky, puzzled. 'You like school.'
> 'Yes, but this is a new school, it is called a boarding-school,' said Mollie.[17]

Compared with the dialogue of the Nesbit and Hilda Lewis children, this seems both artificial and condescending, and it seems strange that children can read at both levels during a relatively short period of their lives and apparently be satisfied with all that they read.

The characters of human children in fantasy stories tend to be relatively undeveloped. In the books considered here, precise ages are not usually given, although the age relationship of one child to another may be indicated. Noel Streatfeild suggests that the Nesbit children were deliberately drawn faintly so as to point up the character of the Phoenix.[18] The Nesbit and Hilda Lewis children do have specific character traits: Sandy, in *The Ship that Flew*, is fond of food; Nesbit's Anthea has a somewhat more developed conscience than her siblings, and these characteristics sometimes affect the development of the plot. However, although the children are convincing, they are in every case subordinate to the fantasy element. Enid Blyton, on the other hand, provides a group of clearly distinguished children in *The Enchanted Wood* and a student recently commented to me how clearly Fanny, Bessie and Jo stayed in her mind as compared with the children in C. S. Lewis's 'Narnia' books. This seems, on closer examination, to be due to Enid Blyton's differentiation of the girl role and the boy role and the fact that the two girls are distinguished by hair colour (Bessie is dark, Fanny fair), a distinction emphasized by the simple illustrations, and by age (Fanny is always quite obviously the baby of the family, while Bessie, it must be admitted, always seems far older than the eight years which she celebrates in the Land of Birthdays). Some of the marked deterioration in the second book of this series, *The Magic Faraway Tree*, is due to the introduction of a fourth human child, Dick, whose behaviour seems largely dictated by the needs of the plot and who is, therefore, rather less convincing.

In fantasy stories of the type in which human children are given access to magic, it is usually necessary to provide a guide who can explain the rules. On their first adventure in the wishing chair, Peter and Mollie rescue Chinky who remains with them as a courier to the strange lands they subsequently visit and gets them out of trouble on various occasions. As a character Chinky, for all his pointed face and pixie ears, is too much like the children themselves to be a memorable character: he completely lacks the humorous potential of Nesbit's Phoenix or Psammead.

Although Enid Blyton's humour is mainly of the slapstick variety, she does, in *The Enchanted Wood*, create some successful comic characters. Dame Washalot, who pours her dirty washing water away down the Tree regardless of who is coming up, and Mister Watzisname, who spends most of his time asleep and is angry if woken up, provide regular humorous hazards. The cheerful Moon-Face and fairylike Silkie act as guide to the magic elements. The most striking character, however, is undoubtedly the Saucepan Man who provides a different kind of humour; he is hung all over with saucepans and kettles and is invariably deafened by the continual clashing of the pots and pans. Jo says:

> 'We've just come to ask you out to tea.'
> 'Ask me for a bee?' said the Saucepan Man, looking surprised. 'I'm so sorry, but I don't keep bees, only saucepans.'
> 'Not bees,' said Jo. 'To ask you out to TEA.'
> 'But I don't want to go to sea,' said the Saucepan Man. 'I don't like the water at all. Never did. Very kind of you, I'm sure, but I hate the sea.'
> 'Not the sea, but TEA, TEA, TEA!' cried Jo.[19]

This kind of humour is introduced with every appearance of the Saucepan Man.

In Enid Blyton, both the slapstick humour and the verbal humour are at an elementary level. Nesbit's humour is at a very much more adult level, with the Phoenix or the Psammead acting in an adult role.

> 'Autre temps, autre moeurs,' said (the Psammead).
> 'Is that the Ninevite language?' asked Anthea, who had learned no foreign language at school except French.[20]

Such a joke is likely to be lost on the majority of child readers but it is the kind of humour which helps to give Nesbit's books appeal for the adult reader.

The vocabulary used by both Hilda Lewis and Nesbit is varied and demanding, but the story carries the reader along. By comparison, Enid Blyton's vocabulary is undemanding: as is frequently the case in her work, 'horrid', 'peculiar', 'queer' and 'exciting' are used over and over again. At one point in *Adventures of the Wishing Chair*, in the chapter called 'The horrid quarrel' the word 'horrid' is used six times in the space of 420 words.[21]

One problem which the author of fantasy has to solve is that of involving the child characters in magic without the adult characters becoming aware of this involvement. It is a problem which would intrigue many child readers, but Enid Blyton ignores it completely. Peter and Mollie have a convenient playroom, a shed at the bottom of the garden, where they can hide both the chair and Chinky; they contrive to have all their adventures at times when they will not be missed. On one occasion Chinky does suggest that mother will be worried because they are not in time for tea, but the chapter ends before the reader has to be told whether mother is worried or not. The mother in *The Enchanted Wood* accepted the strange Faraway Tree Folk without question when they turn up at the children's house. Both E. Nesbit and Hilda Lewis go to some trouble to establish credibility in this respect. Nesbit's adult characters are well developed and their reactions and behaviour, although simplified for the young reader, are in character. Hilda Lewis shows considerable ingenuity in accounting for people who come from the past to the present. In one adventure, the children rescue and bring back to their own time a young man from the England of Robin Hood, who conveniently and convincingly slips into the job of the new gardener.

The Nesbit and Hilda Lewis books have clear geographical settings: *The Ship that Flew* is set firmly on the south coast, *Five Children and It* in Kent, *The Phoenix and the Carpet* in London. Enid Blyton's books could be located almost anywhere. *Five Children and It* and *The Enchanted Wood* both start in the same way with the children moving to the country. As I read both stories about the same time as a child, I was long under the impression that this was the correct way, if not the only way, for fantasy stories to begin. In both cases, the new house is a long way from the station. For the Nesbit children, it is three miles by carriage, the Blyton children have five miles to walk, but in both cases the feeling of being a long way from civilization where anything might happen is created.

In both books town and country are contrasted and the country is seen as a place where unusual things happen. On the first page of *The Enchanted Wood*, Fanny speculates, ' "We might see fairies" ', while on the fourth page of *Five Children and It*, 'before Anthea and Cyril and the others had been a week in the country they had found a fairy'.

The contrast comes in the difference between the two houses. Blyton's is a stereotyped dream cottage, described as 'sweet. Roses hung from the walls – red and white and pink – and honeysuckle was all round the front door. It was lovely.'[22] No indication is given of its location. Nesbit's 'was not really a pretty house at all, it was quite ordinary' but it is placed geologically in the first paragraph, between a chalk quarry and a gravel pit, and we later learn that it is in Kent and that Rochester is the nearest town.

In *The Enchanted Wood*, the magic is introduced gradually although the children are not taken by surprise because they are quite clearly prepared for fairies and magic happenings. Almost as soon as they see the wood, Fanny is convinced that it is magic. As the youngest child, she has already been allowed to speculate on the possibility of meeting fairies. Both the child characters and the child reader are well prepared, therefore, by the time the fantasy folk appear and one of the brownies explains about the Faraway Tree. The Nesbit children are taken by surprise, but even here, 'It is wonderful how quickly you get used to things, even the most astonishing. Five minutes before, the children had had no more idea than you that there was such a thing as a sand-fairy in the world, and now they were talking to it as though they had known it all their lives.'[23]

Enid Blyton makes good use of what might be considered popular childhood fantasies. Jo builds an igloo in the Land of Ice and Snow, and he has a chance to fly an aeroplane, Fanny acquires a walking and talking doll, but both E. Nesbit and Enid Blyton make use of what must be the commonest childhood fantasy of all, flying. It is interesting to compare the passages which describe the wings and the feeling of flying. Bessie, in *The Enchanted Wood*, wishes that the wings which accompany her fairy fancy dress could fly:

And at once her silver wings spread themselves out, and she rose into the air like a big butterfly, flying beautifully. Oh, it was the loveliest feeling in the world.[24]

Compare this with E. Nesbit's description:

. . . they were soft and smooth, and every feather lay neatly in its place. And the feathers were of the most lovely mixed changing colours, like the rainbow, or iridescent glass . . . Of course you all know what flying feels like, because everyone has dreamed about flying, and it seems so beautifully easy . . . they had to fly quite a long way apart so as not to get in each other's way. But little things like this are easily learned.[25]

E. Nesbit's description is far more detailed than Enid Blyton's; the latter provides the bare bones for the child reader to flesh out in so far as he can.

Other images and incidents can be compared. Nesbit, in her creation of the Phoenix, uses the Phoenix legend and develops him into a convincing, humorous character. Instead of using a fabulous creature already known to legend and literature, thus expanding the reader's knowledge, Enid Blyton introduces a creature entirely from her own imagination – the Snoogle, who is described as the 'funniest-looking creature' the children have ever seen. He has the body of a dragon, the tail of a cat and the head of a yellow duck.[26] The Snoogle, apart from the occasional 'quack', speaks in a manner very similar to that used by the children and Chinky. He has no distinctive style of his own and his appearance does not enrich the reader's experience in the same way that that of the Phoenix does.

The acquisition of the chair, the carpet and the ship all involve visits to shops. Those in the Blyton and Lewis books are very similar. The Blyton children, looking for a present for their mother, search for an antique shop and find one in a narrow back street. There are some strange happenings while they are in the shop and the children finally sit down in an old chair, with their legs tucked up to avoid being bitten by a red fox which has jumped out of a box. When Peter says, ' "I do wish we were safely at home!" ', the chair grows little wings and takes them there.[27]

In *The Ship that Flew* Peter has to go to the dentist and afterwards, when he goes to spend the shilling which he has been given by his father, he finds a little shop in the window of which is a 'tiny ship, not longer than six inches, carved in some old dark wood'. There is a detailed description of the little Viking ship,[28] whereas we are told little about the wishing chair. Peter buys the ship for 'all the money he has in the world – and a bit over' and on the way home, cut off by the tide, he says ' "I wish, I *wish* I could get home" ' whereupon the ship grows until it is big enough to carry him safely home.[29]

In *The Phoenix and the Carpet*, the nursery carpet is ruined when the children try out some fireworks and mother buys a replacement secondhand. When it is delivered, an egg rolls out and mother insists that it is taken back to the shop from which she has bought the carpet. The shopkeeper believes the children have come to complain and refuses to listen to their explanations about the egg.

> The children fled, and they think, and their father thinks, that they couldn't have done anything else. Mother has her own opinion. But father said they might keep the egg.[30]

It is this egg, of course, which produces the Phoenix.

Although few children are likely to read the three books in the order suggested here, the books do show a natural progression in style and complexity of ideas, appropriate to a child's natural reading development. Enid Blyton provides an introduction to the ideas and images which are used by Hilda Lewis and E. Nesbit. In each case the children try to return goods to the shop. The chair refuses to obey Peter and Mollie, Lewis's Peter cannot even find *his* shop, the shopkeeper refuses to listen to the Nesbit children. All the children have a strong moral sense but when Peter and Mollie tell the chair to go back and it refuses, they accept the situation. Lewis's Peter goes one stage further; he looks for the shop but cannot find it (it is only when he is older and decides that the time has come to return the ship for good that the shop reappears). The Nesbit children find themselves in a very adult situation, facing the shopkeeper who thinks they have come to complain about his goods. Each book marks a further stage in understanding.

A similar kind of development can be seen in the 'tower' situation which occurs in each of the three books. When Peter and Mollie try to rescue Chinky from a tower which has no windows, no chimneys and no door, they need the help of an elf, a mouse and two magic pills, plus a great deal of luck.[31] The Lewis children find themselves prisoners in a tower when they go back to Norman times. Although the style is simple, suspense is cleverly built up until at last one of the boys finds that he can just reach the tip of the ship through a narrow slit window, and wish it small enough to pass through the slit so that they can escape from the topless tower.[32] The whole incident is carefully structured and no new magic is required, whereas Blyton creates a problem which has to be solved by the introduction of new characters and additional magic spells. It is only when the Nesbit children find themselves at the bottom of a doorless and topless tower in France that they learn from the Phoenix that they are limited to three wishes a day, which they have already used, and they have to call upon the powers of the Psammead, met in a previous book, in order to escape.[33] Although this adventure ends typically (few of the adventures in any of the books are without their snags and Mollie is moved to remark at one point, when an adventure has been successful throughout, 'I wish *all* our wishing-chair adventures were like that'), it is one of the least satisfactory incidents in the Nesbit book. It evidently had its roots in a childhood experience which she describes in her autobiography[34] and she comments that it was an idea to which she often returned. The tower image seems to be attractive to children and it is not surprising that it appears in all three books, being used in the chapter headings – 'The strange tower' (Blyton), 'The topless tower' (Nesbit) and 'Matilda's tower' (Lewis) – for good measure.

Nesbit and Hilda Lewis, having created their magic agents and laid down rules, operate within these rules. One of the points frequently made by Nesbit in her fantasy books is the misfortune which can arise from making accidental wishes. In the middle of a particularly successful Faraway Tree adventure, the Blyton children find themselves whisked away to a strange island because of the Saucepan Man's hearing problems when he mistakes wish for fish. The Blyton children escape rather more easily from the Little Lost Island than the Nesbit children do from the consequences of their inadvertent wishes, for Fanny still has a piece of wishing cake in her hand and can wish them all safely back in the Land of Birthdays.[35]

Although *The Enchanted Wood* contains some of the best of Enid Blyton's writing, the two sequels are not as good. Whereas E. Nesbit introduces a new idea in each of the books which make up her trilogy, the Enid Blyton sequels merely offer more of the same. Although some indication of the orginal inspiration can occasionally be found, the later books seem to be merely exploiting the success of the first book. Particularly noticeable is the increasingly high degree of tolerance with which the children's mother accepts the strange happenings when they impinge on her own life.

However, the very fact that the Blyton fantasies can be compared to fantasies by authors such as Nesbit and Hilda Lewis does suggest that her books provide useful reading experiences for children whose reading skills are relatively undeveloped. Ideally the wishing-chair and Faraway Tree books should be read at a rather earlier age than the other books considered here. Some children, of course, may never achieve the fluency needed to enjoy the books by E. Nesbit and Hilda Lewis and in this case Enid Blyton's stories have served a purpose in presenting to children the imaginative possibilities of journeys to strange places through magical forms of transport.

Chapter Eleven

Holiday Adventure Stories

❀

SOME OF Enid Blyton's most popular books and series can be described as holiday adventure stories. This kind of story became very popular in the 1930s after the publication of Arthur Ransome's *Swallows and Amazons*. By 1938, when Enid Blyton made her first contribution to the genre with *The Secret Island*, the pattern was well established: there was a mixed group of boys and girls (parents and other adults were invariably removed to the fringe of the action) and the events took place during the course of one holiday, given shape by the regional setting and by an interest in a hobby or sport such as birdwatching or sailing, or an adventure involving the finding of treasure or the tracking down of criminals.

Holiday adventure stories have a very early ancestor in Defoe's *Robinson Crusoe*, one of the most influential books ever written in terms of the number of books in which its influence can be detected. It inspired Johann Wyss's *Swiss Family Robinson*, which in turn inspired innumerable boys' adventure stories in the nineteenth century, including R. M. Ballantyne's *The Coral Island*, published in 1958. Of this Enid Blyton wrote, 'And I also loved *The Coral Island* by Ballantyne. It set me off dreaming of adventures of all kinds.'[1] This was the first notable book in which a group of young people were shipwrecked on an island without adult support and it influenced not only Enid Blyton but William Golding when he wrote his modern fable, *The Lord of the Flies*.

The development of the desert island story was also influenced by Rousseau, whose theories of education placed great reliance on *Robinson Crusoe*, which was to be the only book given to his model pupil, Emile. This gave added respectability to Defoe's book and pointed its relevance to children. In 1883 Robert Louis Stevenson introduced the idea of even more exotic island adventures in *Treasure Island*, one of the most famous and widely read children's classics. These facts provide a framework within which to look at Enid Blyton's stories of holiday adventure.

The Secret Island (1938) is the first book in the 'Secret' series: it was Enid Blyton's first full-length adventure story and first appeared as a serial in *Sunny Stories*. It is affectionately remembered by adults perhaps because, in addition to the survival theme, it also uses the Cinderella theme. Peggy, Mike and Nora, whose parents have disappeared on a flight to Australia, are ill-treated by the aunt and uncle with whom they have been left. They are helped to run away by Jack who lives nearby with his grandfather and who becomes a convenient adult substitute. Jack not only knows how to catch rabbits and fish, and where the best nuts and blackberries are to be found, but is also an optimist who never grumbles and makes a joke of everything, encouraging the other children. In view of the way in which Enid Blyton is criticized for her snobbery, it is worth noting that Jack, despite his working-class background, is soon established as the leader and is always in a position of practical superiority throughout the adventure. Although he makes mistakes, they are never serious. For example, he manages to bring a cow to the island but it is only when he needs to milk it, that he realizes that he has not brought a bucket.

Peggy's role is that of substitute mother, organizing the cooking and doing the mending. Mike and Nora are twins: Mike's role is small, acting as male support for Jack, while Nora is the only character who is apparently changed by their experiences. When the children first run away, Nora is lazy, babyish and silly; when she fails to check the fences round the hens, Jack tells her that she is a 'fairweather person', but towards the end of the story the reader is told that Nora is 'no longer the careless little girl she had been'.[2] However, this change is described to, rather than felt by, the reader and throughout the rest of the series Nora remains very much the baby of the group.

The geographical setting of the story appears to be the Lake District and the story could be read on this assumption: it is not until the second book in the series that the reader learns that the island is only about forty miles from Spiggy Holes, which is precisely placed in Cornwall. The island is an archetypal English one with perfect features: the landing place is a natural little cove, there are caves for hiding in and for storing things and there is a spring to supply water. It has blackberries, hazlenuts, wild raspberries and strawberries and mushrooms for the picking and there are fish to be caught. Since the children are still on the island as Christmas approaches, two holly bushes are also provided. None of this is impossible but the ideal is provided in unlikely abundance.

The children quickly set about creating a paradise, improving on nature. They are not unaware of the Robinson Crusoe element: one of them comments, ' "An adventure! A real proper adventure, almost like Robinson Crusoe . . ." ' and later, when Jack buys a copy of the book to help pass the dark winter evenings, Peggy comments, ' "It will be fun to read about Robinson Crusoe because he was alone on an island, just as we are. I guess we could teach him a few things, though!" ' Jack immediately assumes his adult substitute role to reply, ' "He could teach *us* a few things, too!" '[3]

The survival theme dominates the book. The children go to the island in June when the weather is good and there are plenty of wild fruits; once their paradise is established, they are threatened with discovery and when they have found ways of concealing their existence, their survival is threatened by the onset of winter. The plot is skilfully constructed around this theme: the children survive a series of crises and manage to look after themselves. With the approach of Christmas, Jack goes on a shopping expedition and hears that the children's parents have turned up and the family is safely reunited in time for the holiday.

The book reflects many childhood fantasies: the children manage to build a willow house, they are preoccupied with the acquisition of food, they overhear flattering remarks about themselves. Parallels to these incidents can be found in other children's books such as Marryat's *The Children of the New Forest* (the interest in food) and Twain's *Tom Sawyer* (Tom arriving back just in time to hear his own funeral service). The one piece of fantasy which seems unjustified in *The Secret Island* is the fact that the children's parents buy the island for them at the end of the story: although this comes in useful in the second book of the series, it seems an unnecessary bonus.

The morality of the book is very much at child level. The children do not run away from loving and caring parents: Peggy, Nora and Mike are ill-treated by their aunt and uncle while Jack is unwanted. The children make it clear that they feel they are entitled to take food supplies in return for all the hard work they have done for the uncaring adults in their lives.

The reader requires little literary experience to enjoy the story but, apart from the references to *Robinson Crusoe*, the building of the willow house provides interesting literary echoes. How many children later recall this idyllic home when they come across, 'Make me a willow cabin at your gate' in Shakespeare's *Twelfth Night* or, since Jack explains that the gaps between the willow must be filled with clay, Yeats' 'And a small cabin build there, of clay and wattles made' in *The Lake Isle of Innisfree*?

For a child reading the book in the 1980s, there is little to date it. The children don't have a transistor and the trippers bring a portable gramophone to the island, but these small details are more than compensated for by the topical concern about the litter which the trippers leave behind.

The book is easy to read in terms of vocabulary and style. Peggy's cry of ' "Look here, boys! . . . Look, Nora! How those trippers have spoilt our beach!" ' has overtones of the reading scheme. There is little description: even the building of the willow house is described mainly through conversation even to the extent of Jack saying, ' "I'm up the third tree now – look, here come the top branches bending over with my weight – catch them and hold them!" '[4] Explanations are offered of any expressions which might puzzle the reader. For example, 'Jack had been busy. He had chopped down some willow saplings –young willow-trees – with his axe, and had cut off the longer branches.'[5] The sentences are short, the vocabulary is simple, the overall length is only about forty-eight thousand words, compared with the hundred and forty thousand words of *Swallows and Amazons*, but it nevertheless conveys accurate, if over idealized information about plants, trees and birds. The plot is well constructed, there is some degree of characterization and there are points of reference to provide a basis for the reading of more demanding literature.

Unfortunately, such a plot can only be used once: although the island motif appears in the first book of Enid Blyton's main adventure stories' series, it could not be used again as the basis of a simple running away and surviving story. *The Adventurous Four* (1941) is one of the few Enid Blyton books firmly set in time and space. Here the four children are on holiday in a fishing village on the northeast coast of Scotland, father is in the Air Force and mother is 'knitting hard all day long'. For children reading the story when it was first published, this was a realistic contemporary setting and this fact, linked to a fairly precise place and time, may be the reason why only one further book about this set of characters appeared and that not until 1947.

There are four children, two boys and two girls. Andy is the son of a local fisherman, at fourteen has just left school (this also dates the book to pre-1945), and, like Jack in *The Secret Island*, is the adult substitute character in the tradition of Masterman Ready and Papa Robinson. The experience acquired in helping his father has given him a maturity and the kind of knowledge which are invaluable in the ensuing adventure. He can handle the boat when a storm blows up, can make sensible decisions and organize the building of a shelter and, later, a raft. Tom, aged twelve, and his sisters, Mary and Jill, twins of ten, are apparently from a different social background but Andy is the natural leader, not only because of his age but because he is competent in ways that the others are not. The fact that Mary and Jill are twins is unimportant: they are almost indistinguishable (although Jill talks rather more than Mary) and they play the usual female role. Tom is the supporting male character and his main characteristic is that he is always hungry: his appetite is frequently commented on and this gives point to his anxiety when he leaves his camera behind, 'For once in a way, Tom had no appetite at all. He couldn't eat a thing.'[6] In going off on his own to recover it, without telling the others, he is discovered and taken prisoner by the Germans.

The children are allowed to take out one of Andy's father's

boats to camp out overnight on an offshore island. A storm blows up, they lose their way and although they ride out the storm safely, the boat runs onto some rocks and they are shipwrecked. These children are, therefore, in the classic desert island situation. They are able to take anything they want from their own boat, on the island they find potato plants and a wooden shack which Andy thinks they can patch up and, on the nearby island, accessible at low tide, they find a cave full of tinned food. However, a greater danger looms. A third island, which can be reached by swimming (only by the boys – ' "I don't believe the girls could swim so far, though" ' says Andy, and Jill is only too ready to agree), turns out to be a German submarine base. After various encounters with the Germans, the two boys manage to escape on a raft and are spotted by a British seaplane which happily includes Tom's father amongst the crew.

The plot, despite its basic unlikelihood, is well constructed. The camera and field glasses which have been brought for birdwatching prove useful in gathering information about the enemy: the way is carefully prepared for the children to escape from awkward situations, and the awkward situations are themselves given credibility. The lack of an anchor, which would have prevented them from drifting onto the rocks, is accounted for (and this incident also shows that even Andy is not infallible), and the reader is prepared for the finding of the potato plants and the ruined farm because he has already been told that, 'Far to the north lay other islands, desolate now, but once owned by a few farmers, who tried to get a hard living from the rocky soil.'[7] The northerly situation of the islands is never overlooked. There is not the fertile profusion of the Secret Island; a few bilberries are all that the children find growing. There are no trees, only stunted bushes, so there is no possibility of building a willow cabin here.

The children take with them a gramophone and some records, which are put safely in the cabin. In the storm, however,

There was a crash as the packet of records fell down.
'Blow!' said Jill, 'They'll all be broken.'
So they were – all but one. It was very sad. The girls carefully put

the one whole record into a safe place and wondered what the boys would say when they knew.[8]

Later, when Tom is a prisoner in one of the caves and the other children are wondering how to rescue him, Andy puts this one record on the gramophone.

> There was only one record that was not broken, and that was the one with the lullaby on one side and nursery rhymes on the other. The girls listened, rather bored, for they had heard that record scores of times since they had come to the island.[9]

However, the record is used to fool the Germans into believing Tom is still a prisoner in the cave when in fact he has escaped through an airhole which Andy has discovered, and has climbed down the cliff. The details of the escape are carefully given and although the boys are lucky in that the rather complex scheme actually works, it is nevertheless quite convincing.

> Andy knew it was time to pull the string that was tied to the gramophone! He jerked it. The switch slid to one side and the record began to go round . . .
> The sentry heard it and thought it was Tom singing. He felt satisfied that his prisoner was still in the cave . . .[10]

The successful escape is also dependent on the discovery of the airhole and this too is carefully prepared. Although the style is simple, there is no skimping of vital details in the description of how Tom is rescued. The children are lucky, perhaps, but enough detail is given to make credible the fact that the plan works.

The story first appeared as a serial in *Sunny Stories* and provides a good example of Enid Blyton's technique in this respect. Each chapter ends on a note of promising suspense, for example, 'But she didn't know what an extraordinary adventure it was going to be!', 'No sail! Whatever were they going to do?', ' "I do wonder what we'll find!" ', and '. . . what a surprise they got when at last they reached the hollow and looked down at it!' Even in a continuous reading, the rise to a peak of suspense at the end of nearly every short chapter carries the reader along. One strange feature of the book which I accepted as a child but which must strike any adult reading the book is the way in which the Germans are treated. Neither Germans nor swastikas are ever mentioned. The first indication of the enemy's presence is when a seaplane flies over the island, and Tom notices, 'The sign of the crooked cross . . . painted on each wing – the sign of the enemy, the fear of half the world.'[11] Later Jill actually refers to the submarines as being marked with ' "the crooked cross" '. The Germans are always referred to as 'the enemy', although they are given what are clearly intended to be German accents, saying 'something that sounded like "Yah, yah!" ' and ' "So! There are four of you – and all children! This is the boy who escaped – ah, you thought you were very clever, didn't you!" '[12] Children reading the story when it was first published must have been well aware who the enemy was and must have been quite familiar with the word swastika.

Like many other children's books of the same period, there is a strong patriotic note. Tom is determined not to show his fear, 'he was British, and these men shouldn't think they could scare him!', 'That would show the enemy how brave British children could be.' Patriotic feeling supports Jill when she and Mary have to stay behind when Tom and Andy leave on the raft, and she says, ' "So, for the sake of our country, Mary and I will stay behind without any fuss . . ." ' The final chapter is full of patriotic sentiments but these were entirely appropriate in writing for children in 1940–1. Just why Enid Blyton saw fit not to call the enemy the Germans and why she referred to the swastika as 'the crooked cross' is difficult to explain. Interestingly, she showed a sympathy with Scottish nationalism which was rare in the 1940s, when she allowed Andy to say, ' "You think you can beat a Scots boy, but you can't . . . I'll beat you yet! You and your submarines!" '[13]

The kind of moral that was apparent in *The Secret Island* is also found here. The children are careful to bury their rubbish –'they could not bear to make (the island) ugly by leaving empty tins about.'[14] When they find the caves full of tinned food, and before they know that it has been put there by the Germans, Tom decides that they will keep a careful account of what they take and pay for it when they find the owner.

Both the Germans and the Scots (Andy and his father) are given appropriate, but not difficult to read, styles of speech. Some of the description is good, albeit at a simple level. For example, this is the passage which describes the children in the wrecked boat:

> So they waited, clinging uncomfortably to the slanting sides of the ship. Dawn was not far off. It silvered the eastern sky as they waited. The light grew stronger, and then a gold edge appeared on the horizon. The sun was about to rise.
>
> And in the golden light of the early sun they saw something not far off that made them shout for joy.
>
> 'Land ho!' they yelled, and would have danced in delight if only the deck had not been so slanting. And land ho there certainly was!
>
> A sandy shore stretched to a rocky cliff. Stunted trees grew further inland, touched with gold by the rising sun. It was an island of some sort, desolate, rocky and lonely – but it was at least land! Somewhere where they could light a fire and boil water to make themselves warm. Somewhere where other people might be to give them a helping hand.[15]

This passage has many characteristics typical of Enid Blyton's style, such as the 'yelled', the exclamation marks, the clichés of silver and gold, but for a child of nine or ten it is a piece of imaginative writing, made comprehensible by the short sentences, the interjection of 'Land ho!', the action (if negative) of dancing in delight, and the final promise of comforts to contrast with the discomfort of the first sentence.

Many children's books published in the 1940–44 period had plots similar to that of *The Adventurous Four*, with themes and sentiments guaranteed to boost morale, but few have survived to the present day. Two books which have survived are Mary Treadgold's *We Couldn't Leave Dinah* (1941), which was awarded the Carnegie Medal, and Noel Streatfeild's *The Children of Primrose Lane*, also published in 1941. Although both these books are longer than *The Adventurous Four*, their plots are no more credible: in the first, children carry valuable German secrets from an occupied Channel Island, in the second they capture a German spy. Both books seem concerned with boosting morale. ' "At any rate, we're English children, and if six English children aren't as good and better than one German man, we might as well give up fighting the war," '[16] says one of Noel Streatfeild's characters and this expresses the attitudes of both these authors as well as that of Enid Blyton.

With *Five on a Treasure Island* (1942), we come to the book which introduced the Famous Five, another group of four children, the fifth being Timmy, the dog. The 'Famous Five' series is, apart from the Noddy books, the most criticized of Enid Blyton's work. Ironically, the 'Adventure' books, which share many of the same features, are the most generally approved. In both series adults play a rather more important part, and there is less sense of place than in the books already discussed, two possible reasons for their comparative weakness.

Five on a Treasure Island is not only given no geographical location: it is almost impossible to find one for it. The children's parents decide to go to Scotland on their own, the children are told they cannot go to Polseath, which sounds as if it is in Cornwall, as usual, and this suggests that Kirrin Bay, to which the children are eventually sent, is in neither, yet to get there the children start from London by car soon after breakfast and don't arrive until six in the evening.

Although the events in *The Secret Island* and *The Adventurous Four* are unlikely, they are given a certain amount of credibility. In *Five on a Treasure Island* we find the kind of incredibility which gave Enid Blyton her poor reputation. No explanation is given for the parents' sudden decision not to accompany Julian, Dick and Anne on holiday as usual: no plans seem to have been made for the children and it is only when Julian asks about holiday plans that father thinks of his brother Quentin, whom the children have seen only once before. Father has recently met Aunt Fanny in town and has gathered that things are not going too well financially and that she 'would be quite glad if she could hear of one or two people to live with her for a while, to bring a little money in.'[17] He goes off to telephone her and returns about ten minutes later,

'The children knew at once that he had fixed up everything.'[18]

In less than the two thousand words of which the first chapter consists, the holiday plans have been made, the journey to Kirrin bay completed and two of the important characters, Uncle Quentin and his daughter, Georgina, have been introduced by name. Uncle Quentin has been established as 'a very tall, frowning man, a clever scientist' who spends all his time studying, not very good-tempered when he is 'disturbed', while Julian comments on Georgina, ' "Funny name isn't it? More like a boy's than a girl's." ' The whole point about Georgina, or George, as she prefers to be called, is that she wants to be a boy. To her are transferred the qualities which belong, more convincingly, to Jack and Andy in the earlier books. The local fourteen-year-old boy, Alf, is relegated to calling George 'Master George' and to playing a minor role since George herself can handle a boat like a man, is a much better swimmer than Julian and Dick and also a good climber. She can also serve as the knowledgeable character in this book because the demands are not too great; here it is not a question of survival, but of finding a treasure. George does develop to the extent that she learns that 'sharing pleasures doubled their joy' and she becomes a rather more pleasant person, but throughout the series her tomboy qualities persist and dominate. Anne, by contrast is a very girlish girl. Julian, as the elder boy, takes the lead to some extent and is allowed to have some good ideas, while Dick fills the supporting male role, showing initiative only when the plot demands it.

The adult characters are rather stereotyped. The only one who stands out is the formidable Uncle Quentin whose reputation as a bad-tempered scientist, established in the first chapter, is continually emphasized. He greets the children when they arrive with a 'fierce frown', later he comes in with 'an angry, frowning face' and, later still, frowns 'till his glasses nearly fell off'. Nicholas Tucker has said that for him, as a child, the most exciting part of *Five on a Treasure Island* was Uncle Quentin's character.[19] Uncle Quentin is memorable, largely because he has been stripped of any characteristics which might soften or counteract the state of perpetual fury in which he seems to exist. In this first book of the series, his uncompromising attitudes are an important part of the plot since he takes the box which the children have found and sells it; later, he is on the point of accepting an offer for Kirrin Island before the children have managed to find the treasure and this causes the children to pit their wits against the prospective buyers.

It is not surprising that the children do not consult adults; in this book and in many subsequent ones, the adults are seen wholly from the children's viewpoint, the author identifying completely with them and with the child reader. 'Julian thought she didn't understand grown-ups very well. It wasn't a bit of good fighting grown-ups. They could do exactly as they liked. If they wanted to take away George's island and castle, they could!'[20] Later, when Uncle Quentin asks why they didn't tell him what was going on, 'The four children stared at him and didn't answer. They couldn't very well say, '"Well, firstly you wouldn't have believed us. Secondly, you are bad-tempered and unjust and we are frightened of you. Thirdly, we didn't trust you enough to do the right thing." '[21] Although Uncle Quentin's character perhaps provides some reason for the children's lack of confidence the fourth reason, that it would spoil the story, is of course not mentioned.

The fifth member of the Famous Five, Timmy, the dog, has almost human understanding and converses in a series of barks which are interpreted for the reader by one or other of the children; he also plays a part in the plot, rescuing the map when it falls in the water, and provides a sub-plot because George's ownership of him is against her parents' wishes and he has to be looked after by Alf, the fisher-boy.

The plot, despite its incredibility, is well constructed. Kirrin Island at the mouth of Kirrin Bay belongs to George's mother and will one day belong to George; it is a perfect island with a natural harbour, smooth yellow sand, blackberries, rabbits and a ruined castle. In a storm an off-shore wreck is washed up and can now be explored. The children find a box containing a map which appears to indicate the whereabouts of a treasure. Overcoming the difficulties caused by Uncle Quentin and the men who wish to buy the island, the children find the treasure.

There is no theme as there was in the books discussed earlier. It is taken for granted that the finding of the treasure will solve all the problems and there is no suggestion that this is merely the beginning of problems. Although it is significant that the most likely explanation of the wreck, that it is a Spanish Armada ship, is never mentioned, there are some credit points. For example, printed on the map is the word 'ingots'.

> 'Ingots!' said Anne, puzzled. 'What does that mean? I've never heard that word before.'
> But the two boys had. 'Ingots!' cried Dick. 'Why — that must be bars of gold. They were called ingots.'
> 'Most bars of metal are called ingots,' said Julian, going red with excitement.[22]

'Ingots' is probably the only word used in the book which a child reader may, like Anne, not have met before: it is treated as a word to be rolled on the tongue, a word full of promise and excitement. At the same time, the characters involved in the explanation all speak very much in character. Anne, the youngest and rather naïve, doesn't know the word and doesn't mind saying so. Dick and Julian have heard of it and Julian, the elder, can expand on Dick's explanation. The fact that George does not participate in this conversation is also true to character: if she had never come across the word before, she would certainly never admit it. As a story to encourage the young reader, *Five on a Treasure Island* can be recommended but, as a preparation for reading literature, it lacks the qualities of *The Secret Island*.

The 'Adventure' series, in which *The Island of Adventure* (1944) is the first title, has been the series most acceptable to librarians. After examining *The Island of Adventure*, one can only assume that this approval arises from the fact that it is longer and therefore judged to be a more demanding book than the others. In the three books already discussed the scene is set quickly. In *The Secret Island* Peggy, Mike and Nora have already met Jack when the story begins, in *The Adventurous Four* Mary, Jill and Tom have already met Andy, and in *Five on a Treasure Island*, although there is a little more build-up to the point of departure, all the important characters, apart from Timmy, are introduced, at least by name, on the first two pages. In *The Island of Adventure*, however, the bringing together of the four children (two sets of two this time) and the setting up of the adventure situation takes much longer. The book begins with Philip Mannering on his own; through Kiki, the parrot (and this puzzling encounter goes on for five pages before explanations are forthcoming from Lucy-Ann), he meets Lucy-Ann, who is anonymously 'the girl' for four pages before her name is mentioned by her brother Jack. Dinah, Philip's sister, does not appear in person until the fourth chapter in which the other three at last arrive at Craggy Tops, the scene of the adventure, after a quite complex series of events. This slow start is untypical of Enid Blyton.

The two sets of children are nicely contrasted. Jack and Lucy-Ann think the world of each other, while Dinah and Philip are always quarrelling. However, the plot of this and the other 'Adventure' books is no better, and made no more credible, than that of most of the 'Famous Five' stories, as the children successively – and successfully – track down forgers, spies, robbers, gun-runners and other assorted criminals.

The series of stories about Barney, which began with *The Rockingdown Mystery* (1949), is perhaps the most sophisticated of Enid Blyton's series and seems intended for an older audience than the others. These six books, despite the appearance of 'mystery' in each of the titles, are holiday stories about Diana, Roger, their young and precocious cousin, Snubby, Snubby's dog, Loony, and Barney the mysterious boy with a pet monkey who lives the life of a loner, capable and independent. The plot of *The Rockingdown Mystery* has much in common with those of the adventure stories already discussed. Diana, Roger and Snubby are spending the holidays in the country with Miss Pepper, their mother's old governess. Her name provides plenty of opportunities for jokes, but the children appreciate her for her understanding of the fact that they are always hungry. She and the tutor, who arrives to coach them, place an element of restriction on the children's activities but the latter's main purpose is to serve as a suspect until the children discover that he is in fact a detective investigating a crime. Loony, the spaniel, has many of Timmy's characteristics, his actions interpreted by the children.

How, then, does the book differ from the other adventure

stories? Roger and Diana are fourteen and thirteen respectively and Snubby, eleven, is always regarded as a 'little' boy and his behaviour and speech viewed through the eyes of the older children. Although unusual words are explained – for example, Miss Pepper explains that a 'dower' house is 'a house set aside for the mistress of the big mansion when her husband died and her son and his wife came to take over the mansion . . .'[23] – the book also contains some of the most sophisticated dialogue to be found in Enid Blyton. Barney's father, who had left his wife before Barney's birth, was a Shakespearean actor and Barney, searching for his father after his mother's death, is very keen to read Shakespeare's plays.

> 'What I want to do is to get hold of some of Shakespeare's plays and read them. I suppose you can't lend me any?'
> Snubby couldn't imagine why anyone should want to borrow Shakespeare's plays. Diana tumbled to it at once.
> 'You want to know the plays your father acts in – or used to act in!' she said. 'You want to know the things he liked and the parts he could play!'
> 'That's right,' said Barney, pleased. 'I've only read one of them – about a storm and a shipwreck, it was. It's where I got Miranda's name from.'
> 'Oh, yes – *The Tempest*,' said Roger. 'That's quite a good one to start off with.'[24]

There is also a much more adult approach to the things which adults usually regard as important. Barney is eager to seize the opportunites offered by the fact that the children are being given lessons by the tutor, and the advantages of the warmth and comfort of a real home are pointedly contrasted with advantages of the freedom of Barney's rough and ready existence. It is significant that this series is the adventure series least frequently mentioned by either adults or children and it seems probable that most children have graduated from Enid Blyton before they can cope readily with the very slightly more sophisticated approach. The 'Barney' books, with their Gothic novel element, are evidently not required as a stepping-stone to adult literature.

Although there was only one follow-up book to *The Adventurous Four*, each of the other books discussed here marked the start of a series. The most popular is undoubtedly that concerned with the doings of the Famous Five; in this the characters not only do not develop, they do not actually age at all through twenty-one volumes, the last, *Five are Together Again* (1963), published twenty-one years after the first. Any child trying to provide the series with a convincing chronology would be somewhat at a loss. Although the 'Famous Five' books are criticized for being the same book over and over again, in fact there is an amazing variation in the plots and in the manipulation of the characters. The romantic circumstances in which the Five find themselves on the occasions when they are not having adventures away from Kirrin Bay demonstrate quite a lot of ingenuity and, at a superficial level at least, are geographically convincing.

The 'Barney', 'Adventure' and 'Secret' books follow each other in a logical sequence. In the first book in which he appears, Barney is motherless and searching for his father, whom he has never known and who does not know of Barney's existence. In the third book in the series, *The Rubadub Mystery*, father and son are reunited. In *The Island of Adventure* the children meet Bill Cunningham who is investigating the mystery in which they become involved, and Mrs Mannering, a widow, appears briefly at the end of the story. In the second book, *The Castle of Adventure*, Bill and Mrs Mannering are still on surname terms, by the time of the events in *The Valley of Adventure* she is calling him 'Bill' and the friendship continues to develop until, by *The Mountain of Adventure*, he is calling her 'Aunt Allie'. In *The Ship of Adventure*, they decide to marry. At the age of thirteen-and-a-half my niece, looking back at the series, was able to trace this developing relationship and commented,

> Mrs Mannering says that she can't trust Bill because he puts the children into so much danger. Lucy-Ann follows this up by having an idea. Bill and Mrs Mannering should marry, then neither the children nor Bill could be led astray. Bill raises his eyebrows to Mrs Mannering and she says 'Why not?' (most unromantic).

In a foreward to the seventh book, *The Circus of Adventure*, Enid Blyton explains that she had meant to close the series with *The Ship of Adventure*, in which Bill and Mrs Mannering decided to marry, but that she had continued because of readers' pleas and that now, of course, Mrs Mannering is Mrs Cunningham. The romance, the proposal and the explanation are all conducted at a very simple, unsophisticated level.

Overall, the 'Secret' series is perhaps the best although even here the last two books do not rise to the level of the first three. The children are frequently left by their parents. In *The Secret Island* the parents, Captain and Mrs Arnold, have set off two years previously to fly to Australia and have disappeared. This book of course, was written and published in the 1930s, not long after Amy Johnson's record-breaking solo flight to Australia. The second book, *The Secret of Spiggy Holes*, draws on the traditions of the Ruritanian story when the four children are involved in rescuing a kidnapped boy who proves to be the heir to a Ruritanian kingdom. This type of story was very popular with writers of children's books in the period up to 1950 and Geoffrey Trease was moved to quote a letter which he had received from the principals of a London school:

> In one (story) a party of girls were allowed to go for a picnic some miles from the school without any mistress. Among them was a 'Ruritanian' princess with a gang of international crooks after her. She had been sent to the school for safety and was naturally kidnapped on the picnic.[25]

Noel Streatfeild's *The House in Cornwall*, which has a plot very similar to that of *The Secret of Spiggy Holes*, is, if anything, even less credible. The two books, both published in 1940 after having run as magazine serials, have many interesting parallels. Both stories are set in Cornwall, both sets of parents are absent, Enid Blyton's Peggy and Noel Streatfeild's Sorrel are domesticated girls, the English children feel great sympathy for the kidnapped boys, aeroplanes land on convenient lawns and fields at the climax of both stories, when each party has rescued its own Ruritanian prince or, in Noel Streatfeild's case, king.

The Secret Mountain (1941) owes its inspiration to another nineteenth-century adventure story, Rider Haggard's *King Solomon's Mines*, a fact particularly obvious when the Arnold family manage to escape a native tribe in central Africa by claiming an eclipse of the sun as 'white man's magic' in the same way that Alan Quartermain and his friends use the eclipse of the moon. The differences between these two books reflect the changes which had taken place in writing for young people between the 1880s and 1940s. Rider Haggard's heroes are men but by 1941 books for children were generally expected to be about children. Enid Blyton was therefore at something of a disadvantage in that she had to get four children out to Africa and into a situation where they could find a lost civilization. To have them going out in search of treasure was impossible, so Rider Haggard's other reason is used – the missing relative. To go in search of their missing parents, the children are conveniently able to make use of an aeroplane, complete with pilot, which has been given to Prince Paul, now at school with the boys, for his birthday. Rider Haggard had actually been to Africa and his setting is a world away from the rather cosy Africa created by Enid Blyton. However, it is interesting to compare two parallel incidents –the eclipse used to escape and the moment when the central characters are trapped. Enid Blyton's description of how the Arnolds discover a convenient eclipse is due is, on the whole, rather more convincing than Haggard's description of the similar discovery made by Captain Good.

When the Arnold family is united again, they are trapped by the mountain people:

> . . . the door completely closed. There it rose above him, a tall, shining door, as wide as a great gate – fast shut.
> 'They've tricked us!' shouted the Captain angrily, and he hammered on the door. But there was no handle, no latch, nothing to get hold of or to loosen. There was no getting through that enormous door it was plain![26]

Rider Haggard's description is rather different:

> The ponderous mass of rock had closed, probably for ever, for the only brain which knew its secret was crushed to powder beneath it.[27]

C. S. Lewis has told of the great impression which this scene and Rider Haggard's description made on him, 'The trap I remember for ever: how they got out I have long since forgotten.'[28] However, Enid Blyton's style does reflect the awefulness of the occasion.

The Secret of Killimooin (1943) is the weakest of the five 'Secret' stories. The children go to Baronia, which is pure Ruritania, for a summer holiday: this book has overtones of the German robber romances with mountain robbers and Blind Beowald, the goatherd who plays a wooden flute, and a Secret Forest. The atmosphere is remarkably good and the book's weakness is probably due to the fact that the adventure seems of little import to the children who are never in the real danger they experience in the other books.

The final book, *The Secret of Moon Castle*, appeared ten years later and owes something to Jules Verne or H. G. Wells. Certainly the 'priceless' metal called 'Stellatephemy', which is being secretly mined in the grounds of Moon Castle, is almost as convincing as Wells' cavorite.

It is a pity that neither the books about Barney nor the 'Secret' books have enjoyed the wide readership and popularity of the other adventure stories and perhaps if librarians and teachers had taken the trouble to identify these as being of higher quality than the rest and had exploited them, some Enid Blyton titles at least could have provided a useful bridge to more demanding reading.

Chapter Twelve

Detective Fiction

❀

ONE OF Enid Blyton's most popular series is undoubtedly the one concerned with the adventures of the 'Secret Seven'. The books about the 'Five Find-Outers' are also quite well known, featuring the down-trodden village policeman, Mr Goon. These two series show children playing at being detectives and the events rely heavily on the collection of clues and some exercise of the powers of observation and deduction. 'Mystery' stories are much in demand amongst children and it is not easy to write good ones since the child as detective is at an obvious disadvantage, limited by the restrictions of childhood and lack of resources, physical strength, knowledge and experience. In the adult detective story, much of the interest lies in the intellectual processes of deduction, so that such a story is likely to be lacking in incident and action. Those stories about child detectives which are generally admired by the critics usually show the children solving a mystery as a by-product of their own concerns. To represent Enid Blyton's work in this field, I have examined *The Secret Seven* (1949) and *The Mystery of the Burnt Cottage* (1943), each of them the first title in a series.

The Secret Seven, one of the very simplest full-length stories which Enid Blyton ever wrote, can be read by children from the age of seven or eight. The seven children are almost indistinguishable one from another, and it is appropriate that Janet and Peter, the two children at whose house the Secret Seven meet, have names which might have been taken straight from a reading scheme book. The others are George, Pam, Barbara, Colin and Jack. The dog, Scamper, who has the same quality of almost human intelligence possessed by Timmy, belongs to Janet and Peter. A recurring figure in the series, Susie, Jack's younger sister, appears only briefly in this first book but even here comes over as a sympathetic character, despite the best efforts of the author. Susie is a good example of one of the weaker aspects of Enid Blyton's characterization. The reader is continually being told that Susie is 'annoying', 'horrid', 'interfering' and 'mean' but her behaviour does not bear this description out; the discerning reader who can go beyond what the author actually says about a character is likely to see Susie in a rather different light.

The vocabulary of *The Secret Seven* is exceptionally simple; even the word 'ambulance' is explained as, ' "You know, the van that ill people are taken to hospital in?" '[1] There is nothing to enrich a child's language except a discussion of 'delumptious' and 'scrumplicious' as mixtures of delicious and scrumptious. Nevertheless there is the occasional piece of dialogue which rises above the average:

> The blackcurrant tea really was good, and went very well with the oatmeal biscuits. 'It's good for colds, too,' said Janet, crunching up the skinny blackcurrants from her mug. 'So if anyone's getting a cold they probably won't.'
> Everyone understood this peculiar statement and nodded.[2]

The Secret Seven do not fall into adventure without effort. They hold a meeting at which George says, ' "Can't we solve a mystery, or something like that?" ' and, fortunately, that night a mystery presents itself. Jack goes out after dark to look for his 'Secret Seven' badge which he has lost, and sees a van arrive at a house which is known to be empty except for an old, deaf caretaker, and hears mysterious noises. Informed of this, the other children realize that someone is up to no good and set out to solve the mystery. It transpires that two men are hiding a stolen racehorse in the cellar of the house and are in the process of dyeing its coat so that it can be raced under another name. The problems of getting a frightened horse down cellar steps are glossed over lightly. When Peter and Jack are put in the cellar themselves, Peter goes up to the horse (Jack comments on its 'rolling eyes'), ignores the fact that it squeals and shies, rubs its nose and immediately 'the horse stood absolutely still'. Peter's skill is accounted for by the fact that he has been brought up on a farm and is accustomed to the horses there. The least credible part of the story, however, is the reaction of the parents when they learn that the boys at least have been out at night tangling with criminals: the dangers are never mentioned and parents express only pride and admiration in the achievements of their children. The 'Secret Seven' books do not really stand up to close examination: their only value is as fast moving, simple, escapist stories which provide reading practice for children of seven to nine.

The Mystery of the Burnt Cottage comes nearer to the classic detective story. Allowing for the fact that the Find-Outers cannot be called in to solve a mystery in the way that Hercule Poirot or Sherlock Holmes might be, they do adopt some of the same techniques. The story starts in a promising way:

> It was at half-past nine on a dark April night that all the excitement began.
>
> The village of Peterswood was perfectly quiet and peaceful, except for a dog barking somewhere. Then suddenly, to the west of the village, a great light flared up.
>
> Larry Daykin was just getting into bed when he saw it. He had pulled back his curtains so that the daylight would wake him, and he suddenly saw the flare to the west.[3]

The following morning the children hear rumours that the fire which destroyed Mr Hick's cottage was not an accident and decide to find out who was responsible. They look for clues, assemble a list of suspects and gradually eliminate them: at the end Fatty deduces from something that Mr Hick says that he is the culprit and the children then manage to work out how he did it and yet establish a watertight alibi.

In this book the five children are clearly distinguished as characters although Larry (thirteen) and Pip (twelve) are almost interchangeable. Daisy (twelve) is treated almost as an equal but Bets, who is only eight, is portrayed as a very much younger child. She is an embryonic Watson character, someone to whom elementary but necessary explanations (about insurance, for example) can be made, although even after the word 'clue' has been explained to her, she continues to talk about 'glues'. The fifth member of the gang is Fatty or Frederick Algernon Trotteville, who has just arrived in the village and is staying at the hotel with his parents. He is fat, boastful and opinionated but he is also kind, especially to Bets, whom the others tend to push around, and he does emerge as a quite complex and interesting character who assumes the leading role in the later books in the series.

The parents remain very much in the background but some of the other adult characters are quite convincing, particularly Mr Hick's cook, Mrs Minns, and Mr Smellie, one of the suspects. The most regrettable lapse of taste comes in the character of Mr Goon, the village policeman, and there is some justification for all the criticism made of this particular character portrayal. The children's attitude to Mr Goon is quite deplorable and seems totally unnecessary to the unfolding of the plot except possibly to give slightly more urgency to their detective activities. Mr Goon is portrayed as a thoroughly unpleasant character: on his first appearance he kicks out at Fatty's dog and this is apparently supposed to justify the children's subsequent behaviour and attitude. When Bets admits that she is rather frightened of him, Fatty responds with, ' "Pooh! Frightened of that old stick-in-the-mud with his froggy eyes? . . . You want to be like Larry, sail down a hill on your bike, and knock him off, crash, round the corner." '4

Most of the time the children operate within the restrictions imposed on them as children, and the final sequence of events which enables them to solve the mystery arises from Bets' naïvety which causes her to tell the whole story to Mr Hick, making him react in such a fashion that he gives himself away. As a very junior detective story, providing a preparation for the reading of Conan Doyle or Agatha Christie at a later stage, *The Mystery of the Burnt Cottage* merits some attention.

Where does it fail when compared with C. Day Lewis's highly praised *The Otterbury Incident*, written in the same decade and described by Margery Fisher as 'a jewel among children's stories'?5 Conversely, where does it succeed? Although *The Otterbury Incident* is enjoyed by children, it has not had the same extensive readership as the Enid Blyton title; this can be accounted for by the fact that it is written in the first person, a style which does not appeal to many children (it is significant that Enid Blyton never used it), it is illustrated by Edward Ardizzone who, although an illustrator deservedly praised by adults, has the knack of making all boys, even Richard Hannay in *The Thirty-Nine Steps*, look like his character, Little Tim, and it is a book on its own, not part of a series. In addition, it is primarily a book about boys: girls are very much on the sidelines and are not involved in the central action, a fact which might lessen its appeal to the girl reader.

There are three points of comparison – the creation of the setting for the story, the involvement of the children in the mystery and the involvement of the police. Although *The Mystery of the Burnt Cottage* is one of the rare Enid Blyton books where reference is made to a real place, when the chidren decide to have a picnic at Burnham Beeches, the village of Peterswood where the children live lacks a sense of reality. As characters and households only a stone's throw from where most of the children have lived all their lives are brought into the story, there is no suggestion that they already knew the children or that the children knew them. The use of 'Tempests' as a name for a type of aeroplane seems less likely to convince children than adults. C. Day Lewis, on the other hand, creates a very convincing old cathedral city somewhere on the line to the west (since the Devon Belle goes over the level crossing) and, without deliberately describing them, provides a normal background of home and school for the boys.

In *The Mystery of the Burnt Cottage* the children have nothing better to do so they decide to find out who started the fire; in later books they are actually sitting around on the front page waiting for a mystery to turn up (but then so, presumably, was Sherlock Homes). In *The Otterbury Incident* the boys decide to raise money to pay for a broken window, the money is stolen and in getting it back the boys happen to track down some Black Market criminals, who are erstwhile forgers. Their involvement in solving the crime is both credible and legitimate, although the way in which, and the reason why, the money is stolen does not stand up to very close examination. The author recognizes this:

> Why should a chap like Johnny Sharp, who flashed wads of notes in one's face, go to such trouble to pinch a few pounds from a gang of 'kids'? Somehow it didn't ring true to me. Peter Butts, who is a cynical type, said that if you were a natural crook like Sharp you'd

bump off your grandmother for 6d.; big money, small cash, it didn't matter, it was all grist to your mill. Well, honestly, I don't believe it.[6]

Even the other explanation put forward, that it is a trick to make Ted's sister, Rose, grateful to Johnny Sharp, seems no more reasonable and, as a crime, Mr Hick burning down his own cottage for the sake of the insurance money seems much more convincing.

In any book of this kind there has to be a moment when the police are called in. The unpleasant rivalry between the Find-Outers and Mr Goon has already been mentioned. About halfway through the book, Larry suggests that they should go to ' "Inspector Jenks, he's head of all the police in this district. Daddy knows him quite well. He's a very, very clever man, and he lives in the next town." '[7] but the children decide to solve the mystery first. By the time they do so, Mr Goon has been to complain of their behaviour to their parents, so they are in disgrace and they feel that their story would not be listened to, let alone believed. Fortunately, Inspector Jenks happens to be fishing on the river bank, overhears them discussing what has happened and is able to sort things out. He has nothing but praise and thanks for the children and even expresses the hope that they will work together on other mysteries in the future. In *The Otterbury Incident* the boys decide not to call in the police at the stage when the desirability of doing so first becomes obvious, because one of themselves is under suspicion and they feel the police might not be so convinced of Ted's innocence as they are. Later, when the boys are making the final moves on the criminals, George, the storyteller, goes for the police. Inspector Brook, in the last chapter, behaves very differently from Inspector Jenks; although he praises the boys, he also points out the dangers of their behaviour and leaves them (and the reader) feeling that they have been treated leniently for their misdoings. He makes it clear that the boys should call in the police as soon as they suspect criminal activity and not take the law into their own hands, and the career of the King's School boys as detectives is nipped in the bud.

Finally, although it is only slightly longer, by about six

thousand words, than *The Mystery of the Burnt Cottage*, the style of *The Otterbury Incident* is rather more sophisticated, using a much wider range of vocabulary, simile and metaphor, ironic humour and literary allusion. For example, breaking into the room where the forging of coins has taken place, Toppy and Ted discover that everything is covered with dust and cobwebs, ' "Miss Havisham's wedding-cake!" whispered Ted.'[8]

By comparison, Enid Blyton's story contains nothing that would not be fairly readily understood by the child likely to be reading it. It reflects a child's wish to be regarded as a useful member of society, valued by adults. It undoubtedly provides the kind of reading which children enjoy, and perhaps need, at a certain period of their development.

Chapter Thirteen

The Circus Stories

❀

THE CIRCUS seems to have had a special attraction for Enid Blyton for the word 'circus' appears in the title of twelve of her books and she also used visits to the circus or circus backgrounds in her other stories. For example, the girls of St Clare's go to see Galliano's Circus and Carlotta, one of the pupils at the school, comes from a circus background and is capable of doing 'marvellous tricks'. To some extent, this probably reflects the importance of the circus as a source of children's entertainment in the 1930s, when a small touring circus was still a viable economic possibility and before the audience's expectations were raised too high by television presentations. However, the circus also contained elements which were intrinsically appealing to Enid Blyton, such as the animals, the spectacular successes, the excitement, the romance and the unusual characters.

Enid Blyton was by no means the only children's writer to use a circus background and two notable circus stories survive from the 1930s, Howard Spring's much praised *Sampson's Circus* (1936) and Noel Streatfeild's Carnegie Medal-winning *The Circus is Coming* (1938), which make a useful comparison with Enid Blyton's books from the same period.

Her first full-length circus story was *Mr Galliano's Circus* which, like *The Circus is Coming*, was published in 1938. This originated as a serial in *Sunny Stories* and to some extent this fact accounts for its episodic construction. Jimmy Brown is very keen on animals and hangs about the circus when it arrives in his town, although he cannot afford a ticket to see the performance because his father is out of work. He is allowed to help, makes friends with a circus girl, Lotta, who is a bareback rider and when the circus carpenter disappears with the takings he manages to get the job for his father, and the Brown family join the circus. Jimmy then has a succession of adventures, rescuing animals who have strayed, curing a sick dog and, in between times, learning to walk the tightrope and teaching his own dog, which he has been given as a reward, to perform tricks. The story ends at the point at which Lotta's parents are leaving the circus to perform elsewhere, and it looks as if Lotta will have to go too, until kind Mrs Brown invites her to stay with them.

Basically the plot is not unrealistic. It is far more credible than the plot of *Sampson's Circus*, which revolves around the lost inheritance of one of the central characters, and slightly more credible than that of *The Circus is Coming*, in which Santa and Peter run away to find their uncle who works in a circus after the death of their aunt, when it seems likely that they will be sent to live in different orphanages. Because it is not pinned in time at all as *Sampson's Circus* (the plot has its roots in the First World War) and *The Circus is Coming* (one of the sealions is called Hitler) are, Enid Blyton's book has worn quite well, particularly for the uncritical young reader. The fact that Jimmy's father is unemployed but has the skills appropriate to a circus carpenter and can instantly uproot his family and join the circus, rings as true in the 1980s as it did in the 1930s.

Sampson's Circus is the most sophisticated book of the three and perhaps for this reason has never been particularly popular with children. The plot is complex and much of the characterization is at an adult level. Mr Sampson, Charley Chaffinch and the Princess Samsonia are all presented satirically in a way which will pass over the heads of many young readers since the reader is left to observe for himself the fact that, for example, Charley Chaffinch's claims to be both a great boxer and a hard worker are totally false. The story is told in the first person by one of the two central characters, eleven-year-old boys, who are a confusing mixture of sophistication and unbelievable naïvety.

Noel Streatfeild's circus was based on real life experience. She was asked to write the story and she spent six months travelling with a circus to collect material. Against an authentic background, she shows how Santa and Peter develop as people as their circus experiences affect the rather prim upbringing which they had had in the years before they joined the circus. Everything that happens and all the characters they meet contribute to this development. Their experience is widened by meeting adults and children from different cultures: there is some stereotyping in Fritzi's German stolidity, Fifi's French chic, Russian Alexsis' poor sense of time, but there is a wealth of interesting detail about foreign food. The adult characters are rounded out and develop as real people during the course of the book.

Both Howard Spring and Noel Streatfeild recognize the need for wish fulfilment. Howard Spring, although he describes the boys as 'no great shakes as horsemen' one day, allows them to be mounted on horseback, drawing the cage of a newly acquired tiger through the streets of Harcombe, the next. Noel Streatfeild's Peter, like Enid Blyton's Jimmy, has a gift for working with animals. When a performing poodle is ill, he has the idea that the poodle is missing the elephant. When he is proved to be right , he accepts philosophically the fact that he doesn't get any credit for suggesting it. His developing skill with horses is accounted for by the fact that his father was a groom, so that he may well have inherited this gift. Santa proves to have some talent for acrobatics, but in both cases it is made clear that the children will only succeed if they work hard. The story ends on a note of triumph when, on a night of gales, there is a fire and Peter and Santa rescue the horses and then manage to put the fire out. However, this is the only dramatic incident in the book and the reader's interest is maintained up to this point by the way in which circus life itself is made to seem interesting and exciting.

Enid Blyton's book, despite the basic plot, is much closer to pure fantasy. Whereas Noel Streatfeild's circus is motorized and visits real places that can be found on the map, such as Blackpool and Bridlington, Enid Blyton's is horsedrawn: there seems to have been some confusion in her mind between gipsies and circuses since the circus caravans are described as clip-clopping down country lanes with smoke coming out of their chimneys, in a very romantic way. Noel Streatfeild, as in all her books, is careful to set out the regulations concerning child performers and every time the circus arrives at a new town, all the children report at the local school, carrying cards to show what standard they have reached. Enid Blyton ignores the requirements of compulsory education completely, and both Lotta and Jimmy perform in the circus ring without a hint that they require special permission from the authorities as they are clearly both under the age at which they may legally do so. Lotta lives out a common young female fantasy. Dressed like a fairy from the top of the Christmas tree, she rides into the circus ring on the back of a horse and performs a succession of wonderful tricks for the admiring and applauding audience.

All three authors recognize the importance not only of showing their child characters as successful, but also of showing them to be admired by the observers of their success. Howard Spring's Jo describes how, riding through the streets of Harcombe, 'We certainly made a good show, and were, I think, the hit of the afternoon. Everyone cheered.'[1] Noel Streatfeild's Peter and Santa feel that it is 'lovely to see other children wishing they were them'.[2] Enid Blyton, however, carried this a stage further. Jimmy finds the straying elephant and returns with him to the circus. He vows to teach the new chimpanzee, Sammy, to brush his teeth and, through a simple trick, succeeds. When Sammy disappears, Jimmy is able to find him and returns in triumph to the circus once again. Jimmy can imitate birds, he learns to walk the tightrope, he trains his own dog and all these talents and successes are appreciated by the adults round him. His skill with the tigers is compared favourably with that of Mr Galliano; Mr Wally, Sammy's owner, tells him, 'You have one of the greatest gifts in the world, young Jimmy . . . one of these days you will be famous, for you will be able to do anything you like with animals.'[3] Jimmy is deserving of all this in so far as he is brave, good natured, philosophical, kind and polite: he is, perhaps, what all children yearn to be. Neither he nor Lotta is ever made to look foolish.

The adult characters are stereotypes and exist solely in relation to the children. The fact that Mr Galliano's moods are immediately detectable from the position of his top hat – the further it is on the side of his head, the happier he is – is a fair indication of the level of adult characterization. When two new trapeze artistes join the circus, the reader knows immediately, from the fact that their dog is thin and that one of the men surreptitiously kicks the dog, that they are bad characters and will not last long.

Most striking, however, is the difference between the ways in which the same situations at the end of *The Circus is Coming* and *Mr Galliano's Circus* are handled. In Noel Streatfeild's book, when Peter and Santa are promised a future with the circus, they are almost too happy to speak, although a vista of the delights to come opens up before them. When it is agreed that Lotta will stay with the Browns while her parents are abroad, however, Enid Blyton describes the children shouting and jumping about in order to express their pleasure. She conveys the sense of pleasure and excitement by brief, factual statements rather than by the creation of atmosphere. Earlier in the book, similarly, we are told that, 'Jimmy was never tired of hearing all the tales of circus folk,'[4] although these are only briefly described, especially when compared with the similar tales told by Noel Streatfeild's circus folk.

Mr Galliano's Circus provides a simple and entertaining read. Although it makes few demands on the reader – even the word 'cart-wheel' is carefully explained – it would enable the child to progress with confidence to *The Circus is Coming* and *Sampson's Circus*. The quality of this particular Enid Blyton title becomes more apparent when one looks at one of her later circus stories, *Come to the Circus* (1948). From the child's viewpoint, this contains many of the same attractive elements such as a variety of interesting characters, a strong animal interest and success for the two central child characters, but they are not assembled with the skill that, by comparison, distinguishes *Mr Galliano's Circus*. The characters are less convincing, the incidents seem hackneyed and the story is less effectively told. Undoubtedly with the idea of ringing changes on the circus theme, here it is the heroine who joins the circus. Fenella, a ten-year-old orphan living with her aunt, is suddenly informed that as the latter is getting married, she must go to live with Uncle Ursie and Aunt Lou, who work in a circus. Fenella is timid, but kindhearted, hardworking and very good at sewing. She is not welcomed by Aunt Lou but, like the Cinderella character she is, she wins the hearts of all whom she meets including, ultimately, that of Aunt Lou. To provide some relief to all her goodness and virtue she carelessly and uncharacteristically leaves open the bears' cage on one occasion.

The Cinderella aspect of Fenella's character is emphasized when, during the circus procession through a village, she sits 'like a princess' in 'the golden carriage' and,

> 'Look at her! She's like Cinderella!' shouted a boy.
> 'Cinderella had a golden carriage, didn't she? My, isn't she grand!'[5]

On her arrival at the circus, Fenella is befriended by Willie Winkie the Whistler, who is twelve and performs in the ring with his pet goose, Cackles, and also does bird imitations. Willie's act and Fenella's eventual involvement in it do not come over as convincingly as Jimmy's training of Lucky, his dog, and Lotta's feats on horseback. Fenella has to overcome her timidity to the extent of training a bearcub to do tricks. There are some other wish-fulfilment items, such as Fenella's splendid doll, Rosebud, who makes a rather unconvincing belated appearance on the scene, and lessons with Mr Presto, the conjuror, which are hardly integrated into the development of the story. The appropriate naming of Uncle Ursie, who performs with his bears, is not even mentioned.

Circuses are used incidentally in *Five Go Off in a Caravan* (1946) and *The Circus of Adventure* (1955) to provide additional colour and a new twist to the plot. In the 'Famous Five' title, the confusion between circuses and gipsies seems complete even though the owner of the circus is called 'Mr Gorgio', Romany for non-gipsy. The two villains whom the Famous Five are, of course, instrumental in capturing are Tiger Dan, the chief clown, and Lou, the acrobat, who travel and work with the circus merely as a convenient cover for a series of brilliant thefts as they move around the country. The children make friends with Tiger Dan's ill-treated nephew, Nobby, and thus have access to the delights of the circus camp. In *The Circus of Adventure*, Jack, separated from the other children, falls in with a travelling circus and persuades two acrobats to help him rescue the children from the Ruritanian castle, where they are being held prisoner, by means of a tightrope and trapeze swing. Here the circus is essential to the plot and Jack can use Philip's skill with animals as a bargaining point for help in the rescue. It is easy to see why Enid Blyton was so attracted to the idea of circuses: they contain the elements which fit her stories to perfection.

Chapter Fourteen

Family Stories

❀

THE FAMILY or domestic story for children is a clearly defined category of children's fiction, read mainly by girls. At its simplest, it is concerned with personal relationships, between brothers and sisters, children and parents, or between the family and the local community. It is often episodic, with a series of incidents happening to one or to various individuals, but some kind of framework is usually imposed on these, and the final incident may well provide a climax which brings the story to a satisfactory end. The most widely-read children's story of this kind is probably Louisa M. Alcott's *Little Women*, a book read at some time by the majority of girls in English-speaking countries. Here, the framework is provided by father's absence at the American Civil War, the climax by his return and by Meg's engagement, and the story consists of a series of events which, interesting and attention holding in themselves, also reveal the characters of the four sisters, their relationship to their mother and to the various people in the local community. Nothing happens which is not completely credible in the circumstances but everyday life is descibed in a way that makes it exciting so that the reader wants to go on reading to find out what happens next. The action and interest arise from the characters who learn and develop through their experiences. To illustrate Enid Blyton's treatment of the family story, I have selected four books, *The Children of Cherry Tree Farm* (1940), *The Family at Red-Roofs* (1945), *The Put-em-Rights* (1946) and *Six Bad Boys* (1951).

The Children of Cherry Tree Farm is perhaps the weakest of the four although it has been said to have adult appeal,[1] and the two sequels have been said to deserve 'almost unqualified praise'.[2] The incidents are set within a clear framework: at the beginning of the story the parents depart for America, where father has business, and the children go to stay with an aunt and uncle in the country; the story comes to an end when the parents arrive back in time for Christmas. The children have enjoyed their experience of country life and are delighted when father makes the rather surprising decision to give up his business (unspecified, but for which he has just spent nine months abroad) and take up farming instead. This is yet another example of Enid Blyton's inability to avoid the gilding of the lily in order to provide a happy ending and, in this case, two sequels.

There are four children, Rory (thirteen), Sheila (twelve), Benjy (ten) and Penny (seven). The two youngest are the most developed characters, probably reflecting the intended readership. Benjy's love of nature is established early both through conversation when Sheila teases him and Benjy says, ' "Wouldn't I just love to see all the spring flowers coming out and to watch for frog spawn in the ponds," ' and through the comment that he spends 'all his spare time reading about animals and birds'.[3] Penny has the typical good fortune of the youngest, being the first to hear the news of their visit to Cherry Tree Farm and the one who, after she has deliberately been left behind at the farm by the elder children because of her short legs, finds Tammylan, the scholar gipsy character who teaches them about wild life.

Tammylan is introduced in the third chapter when he is described by Uncle Tim as 'the wild man' who knows about birds and animals, and the children determine to find him. He is a good answer to the criticism that Enid Blyton is intolerantly middle class and prejudiced. Tammylan is a dropout if ever there was one, ' "He looks queer – long hair and long beard, and funny clothes, you know" '[4] but once the children have established contact with him and Uncle Tim has been along to meet him, the friendship is allowed to proceed; he is never explained but evidently comes from a good background because although the farm labourers speak differently from the children and address them as 'Miss' and 'Master', Tammylan talks to them as equals. In fact, the concept would be quite familiar to many children in the 1940s, because of the popular nature study programmes which formed part of Children's Hour, in which Romany was the leading character.

The book seems to have a strong didactic purpose; for example, on their first picnic expedition to find Tammylan, they carelessly throw the paper away and are reproved for this. The idea of children developing through contact with nature, guided by a knowledgeable person, was not a new one in 1940 (it is, after all, the basis of Frances Hodgson Burnett's *The Secret Garden* of 1911), and it is still being used today. Alison Morgan's *Ruth Crane* (1973) makes an interesting comparison with Enid Blyton's book. It is firmly set in a Welsh village, whereas the location of Cherry Tree Farm is never revealed: all we know is that it takes all day to get there from London. Ruth has lost her father in a car accident, her sister and mother are seriously ill in hospital and she and her younger brother are staying with an aunt and uncle where, being American, academically gifted and with no housewifely skills, she is sadly out of place. In this situation she is helped by 'Old Mossy' who lives rough in the hills and who, at their second meeting, shows her a nest of baby hedgehogs, explaining that the mother has been killed on the road, 'Ruth put her hand nervously into the hollow, and to her surprise the spikes were soft, like the green fuzz on unripe sweet chestnuts.'[5] The children who go to Cherry Tree Farm are merely recovering from a series of childhood ailments, but a hedgehog is also important for Penny, who longs for a pet. One hedgehog rescued from the netting round the tennis court escapes, but Tammylan knows where there are five babies with their mother and he takes one of these for Penny, 'Tammylan put his hand into the hole and felt about. He brought it out again and in it Penny saw a very small hedgehog indeed!' Penny exclaims, ' "Oh, its prickles are quite soft and pale!" '[6] The concepts and the style are at a very much simpler level in Enid Blyton's book. Penny takes the hedgehog home, the others are 'half-jealous' but rally round to make a homely nest for it.

For Enid Blyton the relationship between the children and Tammylan constitutes the essence of the story; in Alison Morgan's book Mossy is an essential part of the plot but also affects the way in which Ruth's relationship to her brother, her cousin and to the whole Welsh community changes as she matures through her experiences. Enid Blyton's children do not mature through their contact with Tammylan; the characteristics that they are given at the beginning of the book, smallness and silliness in the case of Penny, a love of animals and success with them in the case of Benjy, are exactly the same at the end; all that Enid Blyton's children acquire are fat legs and rosy cheeks.

This book, however, demonstrates Enid Blyton's story-telling skills, since what appears, on examination, to be nothing more than a series of natural history anecdotes undoubtedly possesses the quality of making the reader want to go on reading.

Of the four Enid Blyton books considered in this chapter, *The Family at Red-Roofs* comes nearest to the pattern of family story established by *Little Women*. The story begins with the Jacksons moving to a new house after father has been promoted, a prospect of new prosperity ahead. Father goes abroad on business, his ship is wrecked and he is apparently drowned; meanwhile Mrs Jackson is taken ill. The family survives the various disasters and the story ends happily when father returns. This is one of the few Enid Blyton books dated by domestic detail; the new five-bedroomed house is rented for £2.10s a week on a three-year lease and the family plan to add to this 'expensive' arrangement by employing a man for the garden and a maid to help with the housework. Molly, the eldest daughter, proposes to train as a kindergarten teacher at the High School where she is a pupil, the method Enid Blyton herself had followed in the 1920s.

Constance Martin has suggested that, compared with *Little Women*, this book is 'milk-and-water' and that seventeen-year-old Molly seems more like a child of ten.[7] Certainly Enid Blyton's anxiety to point a moral seems to prevent her from allowing her characters to develop and mature through their experiences. There is one episode in particular which parallels similar events in both Louisa Alcott's sequel to *Little Women*, *Good Wives*, and Susan Coolidge's *What Katy Did*. Molly invites Prudence, a school friend, to visit them; the younger children see through the affected and snobbish Prudence immediately but the normally sensible Molly seems incapable of doing so until her mother talks to her after Prudence's departure. She comments to Molly:

'Has Prudence any real friends, dear? She knows the meaning of riches and good food, a car, servants and things of that kind, but does she know the meaning of kindness, loyalty, humility and charity? I don't think so. Those are the real things, the things to be desired.'[8]

In contrast, Louisa Alcott's Amy and Susan Coolidge's Katy are quite clearly shown to mature as the result of similar experiences and whereas both Amy and Katy get themselves into this situation as a result of their already well-established characters, the situation seems to be superimposed on Molly in order to make a point.

However, *The Family at Red-Roofs* is perhaps not as worthless as Constance Martin suggests. It was forward looking in that one of the characters says, ' "I think every girl ought to have some kind of work to do." '[9] It provides a useful introduction to the formula and characteristics of the domestic story and as it is easy to read it could provide a bridge to the girls' classic stories for the younger or less able girl.

The Put-em-Rights invites comparison with a number of children's stories such as E. Nesbit's *The Wouldbegoods* or Helen Cresswell's *Jumbo Spencer*. The framework is provided by a summer holiday, at the beginning of which a group of six children hear the 'Tramping Preacher' who comes to the village of Under-Ridge and gives them the motto of 'Watch – pray and work'. This inspires the children to form themselves into a band to run the village and help people.

One of the weaknesses of this book is that it lacks an anchor figure. One of the children should be a totally sympathetic character with whom the readers can identify as they can with Oswald or Jumbo. In her anxiety to exploit the moral possibilities of the story, Enid Blyton has given each of the six children some unattractive trait. In the opening paragraph we are introduced to Sally and, by the laws of children's literature, she should therefore be the central character, not necessarily perfect but at least a character whom the reader can like and something of a leader. In many ways, however, she is the least attractive character of the six and her bossiness is resented both by her peers and by adults. She obviously takes after her mother, the headmistress of the village school, who is described as 'always running this, that and the other'.[10] Sally sets off to see the rector's children, Micky, who is 'mean', and Amanda, who is 'lazy'. There are two other children there, Podge a 'bit fat' and careless, and his cousin Yolande, who is scared of everything. The sixth member of the group is Bobby Jones whose mother is a snob and has taught him to despise the other children at the village school to which he, alone of the six, goes. He is proud of his friendship with Sally and the others and agrees with everything they say: they instinctively dislike him but are not openly rude to him.

Each child in turn has a job to do. As the children hear of things which need 'putting right', the job is allocated to one of the group, at first by drawing lots. Micky's task of stopping the odd-job man Fellin's ill-treatment of his dog continues throughout the book. Micky tries a little simple psychology, praising and showing affection for the dog and ends by buying the dog; fortunately, since Micky is not quite sure how he'll manage once school starts again, Fellin, now a reformed character, wants to buy him back. Micky's meanness is cured when he has to pay for a collar, a licence and, finally, the dog itself.

In many ways Amanda's project and conversion are the most interesting and convincing. She is given the task of reforming the sluttish Rene Potts whose cottage and baby are both filthy. Rene, who is in fact ill, is taken to hospital and her younger sister, Francie (later referred to as a niece – an unusual slip for Enid Blyton, although certain inconsistencies appear from one title to another in, for example, the 'Famous Five' series), is sent to clean up the cottage. Amanda and Francie spur each other on and end by becoming good friends and getting real enjoyment and satisfaction out of their job. This growing friendship, with a breaking down of class barriers, is perhaps the most attractive element in the story.

Podge and Yolande become involved in the same project when the children hear that the Tupp family is to be turned out of its cottage. Podge is given the task of preventing this and decides to talk to the landlord, receiving a shock when he discovers that the landlord is his father and that the Tupps are being turned out, not because they haven't paid their rent (which Podge grandly offers to pay), but because Mr Tupp has stolen things, including Podge's bike which he has carelessly left lying around. It transpires that the thief is really the eldest Tupp boy who was dropped on his head as a baby and is therefore subnormal. Yolande manages to overcome her babyish fears, talks to her father, who happens to be a brain surgeon, and of course, he is able to achieve a miraculous cure.

Bobby's mother hears that Mr Pepper is in prison and Bobby is sent to console the Peppers. Mrs Pepper resents his interference and throws the soup, which he kindly takes round, over him. The tables are neatly turned on Bobby and his mother since Mr Pepper is not in prison at all whereas Bobby's father is, a fact concealed by his mother, who poses as a widow. Mrs Pepper knows the whole story and Sally takes on the job of persuading her not to spread the story round the village and of comforting Bobby and his mother. Her lack of genuine sympathy antagonizes both parties and very nearly exacerbates the situation.

Despite its improbabilities, this story makes compelling reading. Some of the writing is really good, for example the chapter where Sally tries to sort things out with Mrs Pepper. Her approach to the latter is made quite credible, in keeping with her character as already established. Most readers must find Mrs Pepper's reaction to Sally most enjoyable and we are given a convincing and sympathetic insight into Mrs Pepper's thoughts as she tells Sally what she thinks of her. Mrs Pepper continues to develop as a character, one of the most convincing adult characters in the whole of Enid Blyton's work, although still to some extent handicapped by the requirement that she should speak her thoughts aloud if they are to be known to the reader. The strength of Mrs Pepper tends to emphasize the fact that most of the other characters, apart from Amanda, are cardboard stereotypes. There are jobs which are clearly girls' jobs (cleaning up Rene Potts) and boy's jobs (' "The boys think that if landlords have to be tackled, it is better for them to do it, not us girls." ').[11] Sally, who says this, is not, however, a complete female stereotype. 'Privately she thought she could do it a great deal better than the boys.'[12] The attitudes throughout are somewhat class conscious. Although Bobby and his mother get their comeuppance for snobbishness, the children are referred to as 'Missy' and

'Master' by some of the less affluent villagers. The weakest feature of the book, however, is the almost complete lack of humour.

Six Bad Boys has been described by Michael Woods as a rare, for Enid Blyton, but unsuccessful attempt at social realism.[13] The first edition, however, contained a foreword by Basil Henriques, the legendary Juvenile Court Chairman, who praised the book for its 'brilliant' description of the working of the minds of Bob and Tom and added, 'the gradual deterioration of both boys is told in a manner which I have never seen surpassed.'[14] Which verdict is the right one?

Even in the 1980s there are comparatively few children's books about children with social problems which may cause them to commit petty crimes. In 1951 Enid Blyton was breaking new ground, writing, as she explains in a prefatory note to *Six Bad Boys*, a story to entertain 'as all stories are written', but also 'to explain some of the wrong things there are in the world, and to help put them right.'[15]

Enid Blyton's skill in producing a readable story well within most children's comprehension is clearly demonstrated when *Six Bad Boys* is compared with Sheila Haigh's *Watch for the Ghost* and Bernard Ashley's *Terry on the Fence*, both published in 1975. Enid Blyton's book is episodic, with two of the boys sneaking into the cinema without paying and then becoming involved with the 'Four Terrors' and going from bad to worse. Through the six boys Enid Blyton can show different reasons for boys getting into trouble although in each case the root cause is adverse home conditions. In Enid Blyton there is a variety of approach, whereas in Sheila Haigh and Bernard Ashley, there is only one central character.

Enid Blyton explains the reason for the behaviour of her characters very clearly. The child reader can sympathize with Tom's discontent with his quarrelsome family, Bob's resentment at having to return to an empty house and to help with the housework when his mother decides to go out to work, the fact that the fatherless Fred and Len are out of control, that Patrick is regularly beaten by his father and that Jack lives with his parents, two brothers and three sisters in two 'dirty and smelly and untidy' rooms. The reader can easily understand why these six boys should escape to the refuge of their headquarters, set up in the cellar of a half ruined old terrace house, and subsequently become involved in a life of crime. Although Enid Blyton manipulates her characters for the sake of her message (she could quite well have shown Bob enjoying being on his own and helping his mother instead), the young reader has no difficulty in seeing why the boys behave as they do. It is not so easy for him to understand why Bernard Ashley's Terry embarks on his career of crime merely because he comes across a gang of boys from a slightly lower social class and is 'prepared to do anything to narrow any gap which these boys felt existed between them'.[16] A character even more difficult for the child reader to comprehend is Sheila Haigh's Dan, whose problem is that he cannot read, a situation which the child who has just successfully learnt to read himself would probably find difficult to appreciate.

Watch for the Ghost is only slightly more than half the length of *Six Bad Boys* and is included in the 'Pied Piper' series of books for children of about seven to nine. It is, however, quite demanding in terms of the emotional experience which it offers to the reader. Dan wears glasses, does not like football and has difficulty in making friends; his parents quarrel about him and his mother in particular makes a fuss of Janet, his clever and attractive twin. The adult reader will be disturbed by the lack of understanding at Dan's school and even more horrified by his father's approach to the problem which is to take Dan to the bookshop, buy an obviously unsuitable book on the advice of the shop assistant and then to sit down with him to read it without any knowledge of how to teach reading. Dan does, of course, eventually learn to read, taught by an old lady whom he meets, and plans to surprise his parents. Blyton parents would have been gratifyingly astonished and con-gratulatory, but Dan's have lost interest and the resulting scene is agonizing. Dad wants only to read the paper, mum says she is too busy and Dan goes to bed to cry. In the final chapter the old lady dies and although the ending is satisfying, with Dan hopeful for the future, it is satisfying at a very adult level. Enid Blyton shows her understanding of the need to provide a satisfying ending at child level in *Six Bad Boys* where the fate of all the boys is described in a final chapter, set a year after they have been in court. Only one boy's future is left in doubt and even for him some hope is expressed, 'He might learn to be honest and to go straight – or it might be too late.'[17]

What perhaps makes *Six Bad Boys* most acceptable to a child, however, is the fact that at the centre of the story are two normal children, a boy and a girl, with whom the reader can identify and can therefore look objectively at the misfortunes of the six boys; he is not compelled to identify with any one of them as he has to do with Terry or Dan.

Watch for the Ghost makes emotional demands on the young reader, *Terry on the Fence* makes literary demands as well. It is considerably longer (77,000 words) than *Six Bad Boys* (45,000 words) and the reader is shown the viewpoint of the various adults involved in Terry's story; he is, for example, told about the German wife of the caretaker, 'his war bride with the Teutonic temper', a phrase rich in associations for the adult reader but not so meaningful for the majority of eleven-year-olds. *Terry on the Fence* is an interesting documentary story but children may well be defeated in the opening chapters unless they receive some adult encouragement. *Six Bad Boys*, on the other hand, is compulsive reading; the psychology may be oversimplified, the action unrealistically swift and the situations clichéd, but they add up to a book which children can and are likely to read. Viewed objectively, *Terry on the Fence* and *Watch for the Ghost* are better books in terms of literary quality. In terms of child appeal, Enid Blyton knew exactly what she was doing. A ten-year-old, asked to compare *Watch for the Ghost* and *Six Bad Boys* (although of above average intelligence and a good reader, *Terry on the Fence* was beyond him at this age), put his finger on an important point when he wrote, 'The main difference is that *Watch for the Ghost* is all one adventure and *Six Bad Boys* is lots of different ones.' He preferred *Six Bad Boys* which, for him, was more realistic.

In looking at each of these four books, I found that the words which came to mind in each case were 'compelling reading'. In writing stories about domestic adventure and families, Enid Blyton had got the measure of her readers.

Chapter Fifteen

Enid Blyton's World
of School

❁

ENID BLYTON wrote three major series of school stories, all of which are still in print. There are three titles in the 'Naughtiest Girl' series, which were published in 1940, 1942 and 1945, after having been serialized in *Sunny Stories*. The six books about St Clare's were published in the period 1941 to 1945 while the six books about Malory Towers followed in the next six years, 1946 to 1951.

When Enid Blyton published her first school story in 1940, school stories were at the height of their popularity amongst girls. A survey carried out in Sheffield Public Library in 1938 showed that during the ten days of the survey, girls borrowed 454 school stories as compared with 286 fairy stories, the next most popular genre. The popularity of girls' school stories was recognized but deplored by many teachers and librarians. The views of headmistresses in the 1930s on this subject and their attempts to ban them have already been mentioned, while Constance Stern writing in the *Library Association Record* in 1936 criticized the 'thousands of bad school stories added annually to the libraries' for their snobbery and sentimentality.[1]

The school story as a genre has never had a high literary reputation, perhaps because a child's view of school is so far removed from that of an adult that it is impossible to write a novel set against the background of school which is equally valid at both levels. Certainly, by 1940 the school story had been somewhat debased. For boys it was represented by the knockabout humour of Frank Richards' 'Greyfriars' stories, while for girls the stories had come to rely heavily on secret passages, the detection of crime, the restoration of rightful heiresses and dramatic rescues from fire and drowning. In

1949, Geoffrey Trease began his chapter on school stories in *Tales Out of School* with the following paragraph:

> For sale: Large desirable residence on remote part of Cornish coast; smugglers' caves, secret passage, treacherous tides, suitable school or institution . . .
> Penblethering Priory: qualified staff, incl. resident enemy agent. Inspected by Min. of Edn. and C.I.D. Farm produce, gravel subsoil . . . If advertisements like this are rare in our newspapers it is possibly because school stories bear little relation to reality.[2]

Enid Blyton's school stories not only constitute some of her best work, they also represent a final peak of achievement for the genre.

The heroine's first sight of Malory Towers suggests that it is ideally suited for the kind of plot criticized by Trease:

> Darrell looked. She saw a big, square-looking building of soft grey stone standing high up on a hill. The hill was really a cliff, that fell deeply down to the sea. At each end of the gracious building stood rounded towers . . .
> The windows shone. The green creeper that covered parts of the wall climbed almost to the roof in places. It looked like an old-time castle.[3]

Enid Blyton, however, made no use of what by 1940 were common elements in school stories. Her plots were constructed around the characters; the girls are what their families, their upbringings, their circumstances and their special gifts have made them, and for the most part the action arises from their characters. Much of the interest and appeal of the stories lie in the very simple but comprehensible psychology of these characters. Admittedly, there are sometimes unusual pupils, such as Carlotta, the girl who has been brought up in a circus, but on the whole the range of backgrounds represented amongst the girls is very credible. Although there is a dramatic rescue scene in *Last Term at Malory Towers*, this is introduced as a means of restoring a working partnership between two of the girls; it is not, as is often the case in this type of story, a means of compensating a deprived or misunderstood heroine.

At the time when they were first published Enid Blyton's stories catered for a somewhat younger girl than most of the school stories then available; her characters seem younger and less mature and she does not include the wealth of cultural information which filled the pages of Angela Brazil's books. In this she reflected, probably quite fortuitously, the fact that girls were beginning to mature and grow beyond school stories at an earlier age. She was also much more up to date in that her plots did not depend on what to modern readers must seem quite incredible restrictions. For example, in *Fifth Formers of St Clare's* (1945), Antoinetta gets the better of Angela by using the latter's expensive face cream to clean the latter's shoes; at a not much earlier date, the story would have been about Angela being in dire trouble because she had face cream in her possession. The school stories have worn well and are still read and enjoyed by many girls of eleven and twelve.

In her three series of school stories it is possible to see Enid Blyton developing as a writer, although she uses the basic formula of a boarding school as a world in which children and young people are important and where the drama arises from incidents and conflicts which might seem insignificant in the world outside.

There are few stories set in co-educational boarding schools so Enid Blyton was something of a pioneer when she set her first school story, *The Naughtiest Girl in the School*, in one. The reason for this setting was probably because the story first appeared as a serial in the magazine intended for both boys and girls. Elizabeth is sent to Whyteleafe School because she is unmanageable, and she is determined to behave so badly that she will be sent home. The school is run on progressive lines; those who criticize Enid Blyton for her sexism ignore the fact that the school is run by two women, with supporting male teachers. Apart from the interest of the school's organization (it is organized by a council of the children themselves, with the teachers sitting on the sidelines), the story is concerned with Elizabeth's gradual acceptance of school and her friendship with Joan, who suffers from parental neglect. Despite a rather dramatic ending, the story is neatly and simply worked out. The other two books about her show Elizabeth developing, accepting more responsibility and finally becoming a monitor.

Possibly Enid Blyton felt that the co-educational setting did not find favour with her readers. At any rate St Clare's and Malory Towers are for girls only. Having made Elizabeth only ten when she goes to Whyteleafe, Enid Blyton went to the other extreme in *The Twins at St Clare's* (1941) and the twins are over fourteen when they arrive at the school, also determined to dislike it. They are given Irish names, Patricia and Isabel O'Sullivan and are described in the first book as having an 'Irish lilt' in their voices but their Irishness is never exploited nor even mentioned in later books and it seems probable that it was merely an echo of the popular stereotype, the rebellious Irish girl, who is eventually forced or persuaded to conform to the conventional pattern (for example, Honor Fitzgerald in Angela Brazil's *The New Girl at St Chad's*). Again, the action arises largely from the characters: some of the situations are rather stereotyped, but are worked convincingly into the plot. In her school stories Enid Blyton intended to show mental and moral growth as well as physical growth, and certainly her treatment of characters seems likely to give even her least mature readers some idea of why people behave and develop in the way that they do.

Elizabeth seems rather older than her ten years, the twins much younger than their fourteen, but for her third series of school stories Enid Blyton conceived what is probably her most successful and convincing heroine, Darrell Rivers. The choice of name is significant since there is an obvious link to that of Kenneth Darrell Waters whom Enid Blyton had married in 1943 after divorcing her first husband. Kenneth Darrell Waters, like the fictional Darrell's father, was a surgeon and had performed an emergency operation on one of the Blyton children in the sitting room at home.[4] This event is used in *First Term at Malory Towers* (1946), in which Darrell's father performs an emergency operation on one of the girls: interestingly, it comes over as one of the least convincing episodes in the book.

Darrell is a very attractive heroine. Unlike Elizabeth and the twins, she is keen to go to school but does not, like the typical keen and eager schoolgirl heroine, imagine that it is going to be like it is 'in books'. She has a fiery temper, like her father, and, during the course of the six books, learns to control it. The final book, *Last Term at Malory Towers*, maintains the standards of the earlier titles. Various strands are woven into the plot, the fate of the snobbish Gwendolen, of Jo whose unacceptable behaviour is encouraged by her father, the relationship between Amanda, outstanding at sport, and June, in whom Amanda sees promise and whom she offers to coach. The bargain struck by Amanda and June completely lacks the sentimentality to be found in many girls' school stories, and they embark on a most convincing love-hate relationship, intolerant of each other in many respects but both determined to achieve their joint objective and in the process developing into much more admirable characters.

This final book in the series is also concerned with the need to accept responsibility as one grows up. It is probably Enid Blyton's most mature work, showing the characters seriously looking forward to adulthood. Darrell and three of her friends plan to go on to St Andrew's University, this overwhelming popularity of a Scottish university amongst Cornish school-girls being accounted for by the fact that it was the university chosen by Enid Blyton's younger daughter.[5]

One feature for which Enid Blyton's school stories have been criticized is the use of the French teacher, the Mam'zelle, as a butt for practical jokes. This comic relief character appears in all three series: in the 'Malory Towers' books there are two, one fat and one thin. Enid Blyton is quite ruthless in the way in which she allows these characters and their nieces, who arrive as pupils at both St Clare's and Malory Towers, to maltreat the English language for the humorous effect. The French girls are also shown to be lacking the 'English sense of honour', but the Mam'zelles are usually shown to be quite capable of looking after themselves and the one who teaches at St Clare's is at the centre of one of the best comic episodes in the whole of Enid Blyton's work. This occurs in *Fifth Formers of St Clare's* where, one night, when there is a midnight feast, one genuine sleepwalking and one faked sleepwalking, Mam'zelle, believing herself to be on the track of burglars, manages to lock two girls in cupboards and a third in a bathroom and then goes to inform the headmistress. This episode is beautifully told; all the various elements have been well prepared throughout the story and the style of telling extracts every ounce of humour from the situation.

Although the school stories represent something of a peak of achievement, they are still written at a very simple level. Considerable use is made of tricks and practical jokes to hold the reader's interest. The vocabulary and style are undemanding and terms commonly found in school stories are either not used or are carefully explained. For example, the term 'fagging' is not used in *The Twins at St Clare's* although part of the plot revolves around this, while 'sending to Coventry' is carefully explained in *Last Term at Malory Towers*. June says:

'From this moment Jo is in Coventry!'
Jo hadn't heard of being sent to Coventry before. It was new to her. It meant that not a single person spoke to her, answered her, or even looked at her.[6]

However, the school stories do not have many of the weaknesses, or the sentimentality and snobbishness, of earlier school stories by other authors, and in their plot construction and particularly in the way in which the plots develop from the characters, they rank high amongst the best of Enid Blyton's work.

Chapter Sixteen

Critical Conclusions

ALTHOUGH SHEER QUANTITY, and therefore accessibility, must be one of the factors in Enid Blyton's popularity, the works surveyed in the preceding chapters are those which contributed most to her fame amongst children. This survey, therefore, provides a basis for a consideration of the adverse criticism and consequent defence of her work.

When the decision of certain library authorities not to buy the works of Enid Blyton was questioned, it was necessary to provide reasons for this decision. The reasons fell into two categories – those linked to literary quality and those linked to the values and attitudes reflected in her work. As far as the latter are concerned, they are essentially the values of the middle class prevalent in the 1930s; some are still relevant today (for example, the insistence on not leaving litter around the countryside), while others are quite inappropriate to a multi-cultural society and a society that we like to think is committed to equality of opportunity. The same criticism, however, might be made about writers of accepted literary quality.

Most of the criticisms that relate to literary quality also relate to Enid Blyton's simplicity. Her books are simple even when compared with many of the other books written for children, and read by them at about the same age that they are reading Enid Blyton. Her plots are well constructed and undoubtedly exciting, but the simplicity of the writing and of the characterization lays them open to criticism because, to an adult reader, they are often incredible.

Although the characterization is described as poor, this is an oversimplification of the matter. In creating characters, Enid Blyton tells her reader everything that it is necessary to know and tends to make the characters wholly good or wholly bad, or to give them, and to emphasize continually, one outstanding feature. This works well for the most part, but it must be admitted that sometimes what is said about a character contradicts the evidence provided by what that character says or how that character behaves. This is most likely to happen in the case of minor characters, such as Susie in *The Secret Seven* or Mafumu, the little native boy, in *The Secret Mountain*. Similarly Enid Blyton is careful to inform the reader that something is good, exciting, queer, creepy or horrid, instead of letting events speak for themselves.

There is a lack of depth in Enid Blyton's work which to some extent arises from the way in which she wrote, which did not allow for any research or checking of facts. She made some use of her own experiences, but for the most part she was content to invent, whether it was the name of a government department or some proprietary or technical name, in a way which convinces the more immature reader, but fails to satisfy at a more sophisticated level.

The strongest criticism which can be made of Enid Blyton, however, relates to her vocabulary. She makes use of a very limited number of words and seems at times to have an almost pathological fear of using a word which might not be understood by all her readers. Words such as lovely, nice, dear, little, cosy, peculiar, horrid, dreadful and, most unfortunate of all, queer, fill her pages. There is little use of metaphor or simile, and exclamation marks are constantly used to lend emphasis to comments and remarks. Thus a circle is created: her very simplicity is a major attraction as far as children are concerned, but it is the simplicity which condemns it in the eyes of many adults.

No one can deny that there was and still is a market for Enid Blyton's work. She was well aware of this market and of the needs of the various age groups for which she wrote. In this sense her writing can be seen as a commercial operation, catering for a clearly defined market, a fact which caused the Schools Council Research Project team to categorize all her work as 'non-quality'. However, she was also very sincere in her writing, evidently liking what she wrote because her only concern was to write the kind of story which she believed, quite accurately, children wanted.

In view of the enthusiasm and affection with which adults frequently recall their childhood reading of Enid Blyton, she perhaps cannot be regarded as 'wholly bad', even in the literary sense.

No other writer has succeeded to the same extent in meeting the evident need which there is amongst children for books of this kind. As Elaine Moss wrote in 1974:

> . . . children could do with more new straight undemanding adventure stories properly written – books that would oust forever the Blyton series now being reissued, which Margery Fisher, in a recent number of *Growing Point*, condemned as 'slow poison'. Enid Blyton demonstrated that children are so hungry for *stories* that they will read the same story over and over, slightly disguised.[1]

However, this is more easily said than done. Enid Blyton almost certainly had an advantage in embarking on her career as a children's writer when she did but she also possessed skills which have not been combined so successfully by any other writer. She varied her plots so that although the outcome might be predictable, there were plenty of elements to hold the reader's attention.

Enid Blyton's work caters for two kinds of children's needs. There are those children who, as Joyce Stranger pointed out, may 'never gravitate beyond Blyton'[2] and there are those who will, but who need plenty of practice in order to acquire fluency. Joyce Stranger again:

> Reading is an adventure, not a chore to be fostered as a sort of daily do your stint. What if children do move from Blyton to comics to books that you perhaps consider also rans? Do you always read for the good of your soul?[3]

Even her sternest critics admit that Enid Blyton provides children with easy and enjoyable reading material at a time when they need plenty of practice in order to become fluent readers: by her keenest defenders, this is seen as the main justification for her work. It is interesting to observe that in recent years, in order to encourage Welsh children to read Welsh language books, a series of stories called 'Cyfres y

Llewod' ('Lions Series') has been modelled on the 'Famous Five'.

Writers for children must write within the framework of the reader's understanding. As K. M. Peyton has said:

> . . . this is as wide or as narrow as the writer cares to make it (as wide, for example, as set by Alan Garner in *The Owl Service* or as narrow as the view of Enid Blyton in the Famous Five or Secret Seven series) . . .[4]

Before children reach the stage when they can read and enjoy *The Owl Service*, however, they not only need fluent reading skills, they also need an understanding of literary conventions. The appreciation of fiction is a sophisticated achievement which is acquired through reading stories and thus becoming capable of perceiving more complex patterns of events and of picking up more widely separated and diverse clues. The child who is just beginning to read stories has limited experience of life, a limited attention span, a limited vocabulary and limited comprehension. Adults talking to children about books they have read and apparently enjoyed sometimes find that even 'good' readers have missed the main point of the book. A group of adults talking about books they remember reading as children often find that each of them remembers different things about the same book. Children's responses to what they read are complex and we know comparatively little about them. Does it matter if they do not understand what they read? Is it better for them to read a book of recognized literary quality of which they understand little? One thing is certain: each child's threshold of tolerance varies according to ability and personality. Some children quickly abandon a book if they do not understand it: others finish a book once started even if they find it difficult, and may well gain something from the experience.

The fear is expressed that the reading of too much Enid Blyton may make a child reader lazy. Is it not possible that for some, perhaps most, children, it provides preparation for more demanding and more enriching literary experiences? There is much in Enid Blyton's work which could be usefully exploited in the development of an appreciation of literature.

The majority of children grow out of Enid Blyton naturally and the very fact that her work caters so well for the immature is a contributory factor in this. Although examples can be found of young people who are mentally retarded or who fail to develop emotionally, continuing to read Enid Blyton's books in their middle and late teens, there is nothing to suggest that they would fare any better if her work did not exist.

Adverse or favourable comments are made by those who care, but does it really matter what children read? Just as we know little about the way in which individual children respond to fiction, we know little about the long-term effects of poorly written, boring, immoral or frightening books, although it is generally agreed that some of those stories that we read and hear as children do stay with us and in some way furnish our minds. Books, however, are only one of many influences which affect children's attitudes and behaviour, and it is impossible to isolate cause and effect.

There seems little doubt that enjoyment of Enid Blyton's books encourages the reading habit and the research which I carried out amongst students in higher education showed that those who had, as children, read a lot of Enid Blyton had also read a lot of other authors as well, and that reading and enjoying her when young is not a handicap to academic achievement.

The attitudes of adults towards Enid Blyton are influenced by the circumstances in which they are involved with children's reading. Publishers and booksellers are likely to be affected by commercial pressures, teachers and parents by their concern that children should acquire the reading habit and critics by the convention that literature which they consider to have little merit is not worthy of their attention. What attitude should librarians adopt? It is hoped that this examination of the more popular series and titles will help librarians to become more aware of the issues involved but, as will be seen in the final chapter, it may well be that the Blyton phenomenon, although a continuing one, has ceased to be a problem for librarians.

Chapter Seventeen

A Continuing Phenomenon . . .

❀

AT THE BEGINNING of the 1980s it is clear that interest in Enid Blyton continues. She is phenomenal in that she has come to occupy an unassailable position in the history of books for children. Evidence of the fascination which she continues to have for those involved with children and their reading can be seen in an earlier chapter where the articles published in 1980 by Peter Wright, and by A. C. Capey and Duke Maskell are mentioned. In October 1980, the book page of the *Birmingham Post* included a short article in which Jean Richardson paid tribute to the fascination of Enid Blyton and to her phenomenal sales.[1]

Enid Blyton's status as a household name was also demonstrated in 1980 when, in his play *Liberty Hall*, Michael Frayn included her as a character who, along with Warwick Deeping, Godfrey Winn and Hugh Walpole, finds herself at a Balmoral converted into a 'sort of workhouse for writers' in a Stalinist Britain of 1937.[2]

One can go on collecting and recording Blyton references indefinitely and one must obviously call a halt at some point, but it is perhaps worth mentioning two which appeared in December 1980, just as the manuscript of this book was being finalized. One was to be found in the *New Statesman* 'Weekend Competition', which began, 'Recent weeks have seen Mrs Thatcher described as the Enid Blyton of politics . . .' and asked for more 'such illuminating comparisons for contemporary British figures . . .'[3] The other was to be found in 'Comment' in the *Library Association Record*, where Professor Keith Harris criticizing librarians for their ostrich-like attitudes to new developments in information studies, suggested that they have become 'immersed in their Enid Blytons in full leather (to meet both public and academic library needs) . . .'[4]

Amongst some adults Enid Blyton's work continues to be a byword for worthlessness. Anne Corbett referred to '. . . the "bad book" pulp fiction of Enid Blyton-Walt Disney genres,'[5] and David Holloway to her books as 'rubbish'.[6]

However, nothing can erase the effect which Enid Blyton has had on the reading of several generations of British children and in some cases these effects have been far reaching. Writing about the popular BBC *Blue Peter* programme, Biddy Baxter recalled how her disappointment in receiving two identical letters from Enid Blyton in her own childhood made her determined that no child who wrote to *Blue Peter* should have the same experience.[7] Paul Bethell, one of the winners of the *Guardian* 1979 Student Journalist Awards, wrote of his early days in secondary school, 'I had begun to have inklings that school wasn't in practice going to be all that Enid Blyton had promised . . .'[8]

Amongst the consumers, Enid Blyton retains her place. Reporting on a survey he carried out amongst boys in two London comprehensive schools, John Richmond commented, 'Roald Dahl and Enid Blyton maintain an impressive supremacy in both first-year classes. Between them, they have as many readers from the two lists as all the other authors put together.'[9] In paperbacks published in 1980, Enid Blyton was claimed to be 'Granada's bestselling author', and in a letter dated the 30 December 1980, my cousin wrote that her seven-year-old daughter was 'wanting, more than anything else at the moment, a copy of *The Faraway Tree* and *The Enchanted Wood* by Enid Blyton. The teacher has been reading it to them at school.' The consumer's view is clear.

Amongst future generations, Enid Blyton's work may well enjoy classic status. In fact, a few years ago *Five on a Treasure Island* was included by Longman in their 'Squirrels' series which a publicity leaflet described as consisting of the 'best and most popular children's classics rewritten and simplified for young readers' and thus Enid Blyton, almost alone amongst modern children's writers, found herself in the distinguished company of Chaucer, Washington Irving, Mark Twain and Jonathan Swift.

As far as most parents and other adults who buy books as presents for children are concerned, other factors may affect the situation. Towards the end of 1980, just before Christmas, I carried out an informal survey in bookshops and bookselling outlets. At a small out-of-town shopping centre, children's books were available only at the one newsagent's shop: of the dozen children's titles in paperback (there were no hardbacks at all), seven were by Enid Blyton. In the city centre the main chartered bookseller had on display *Enid Blyton's Bedtime Annual 1981*, the *Famous Five Annual*, three 'Noddy' titles in hardback and over a hundred titles in paperback. Marks and Spencers store had on sale the third (1979) and fourth (1980) St Michael Books of *Noddy Favourites*. Displayed in the window of W. H. Smith's shop was the *Famous Five Annual*, which is an interesting development from the television series with *Five Go to Mystery Moor*, first published in 1954, running through the volume, some of the chapters retold in comic strip form, interspersed with articles on compasses, fog, moors, gipsy tales and other subjects relating to the main story, and various puzzles and quizzes. It is illustrated by stills from the television film and line drawings in the same style. Inside W. H. Smith's shop, in the children's book department, there were some 'Noddy' books, at least seven different 'gift boxes', a fairly new pictorial edition of *The Enchanted Wood*, which has full colour illustrations by Janet and Anne Grahame Johnstone, *The Enid Blyton Goodnight Story Book*, *Enid Blyton's Treasury of Verse*, an interesting 1979 publication which brings together much of Enid Blyton's verse, with a preface by her daughter, Gillian Baverstock, the forty-eight titles in the hardback 'Enid Blyton Rewards' series and well over fifty different titles in paperback, mostly in multiple copies.

In the shops where the number of children's books was small, a relatively high percentage of the titles on display was accounted for by Enid Blyton, while in those where the range was very wide, it would not be surprising if many buyers, overwhelmed by the sea of unfamiliar authors and titles, seized thankfully on the familiar name of Enid Blyton.

The supply of Blyton titles to bookshops is unlikely to dry up while the demand continues. The Knight Book catalogue for 1981 advertised 'two titles in a new series of adventures about Julian, Dick, George and Anne...', *The*

Famous Five and the Mystery of the Emeralds and *The Famous Five and the Stately Homes Gang.*

So how can librarians deal with what seems likely to be a continuing phenomenon? It is difficult for them to use Enid Blyton's work as a stepping stone to more difficult or demanding books as parents and teachers can. In fact, so far as stocking her books in public libraries is concerned, the situation has become manageable. *British Books in Print,* 1979, lists nearly 250 Blyton titles but of these less than a quarter are available in the kind of hardback editions normally bought by public libraries. While all the 'Adventure' and 'Malory Towers' titles were available in hardback editions suitable for the library, those librarians wishing to stock complete sets of the 'Famous Five' and 'Secret Seven' would have to make do with paperbacks of some of the titles. Titles that are reprinted are usually in paperback format – as Arrows, Beavers or Knights in 1980 – or in the glossy 'reward' or 'annual' presentation volumes which would sit oddly on library shelves. Perhaps because of the years of controversy, the business of publishing Enid Blyton has geared itself to the private buyer.

Librarians can now afford to adopt a positive attitude, to recognize that Enid Blyton has points of contact with authors who offer more complex ideas treated in a more complex way, and that her work can be used as a means of helping children to progress in literary experience. Some children will move forward without much external assistance; others will need help if they are not to drift on to adult equivalents or to abandon reading altogether.

Until recently, the only other easily accessible source of general satisfaction in the field of reading material has been comics. With the growth of children's paperbacks, it is possible that other equally popular reading material may emerge. Meanwhile the Blyton phenomenon continues . . .

References

❊

Full bibliographical details, when not given, may be traced through
the bibliography.

I   ENID BLYTON AND THE LIBRARIANS

Chapter 1: Introduction
  1 Colwell, E. *Library Association Record* 54 (3) 1952, pp. 78–80.
  2 Eyre, F. *20th Century Children's Books*, p. 49.
  3 Stoney, B. *Enid Blyton*, pp. 233–5.
  4 *Guardian* 28 January 1976, p. 5.
  5 *Sunday Times* 2 October 1977, p. 16.
  6 Dobson, R. B. *and* Taylor, J. *Rymes of Robin Hood.*
       Heinemann, 1976, p. 319.
  7 Thwaite, M. F. *From Primer to Pleasure in Reading*, p. 19.
  8 Norman, D. *Daily Mail* 14 September 1968.
  9 Tucker, N. *New Society* 12 March 1970, p. 446.
 10 Tucker, N. *New Society* 20 August 1970, p. 337.
 11 Greenfield, G. *Books* 2 1970, pp. 24–5.
 12 Inglis, R. *A Time to Learn.* Owen, 1974, p. 223.
 13 *New Society* 28 August 1975, p. 459.
 14 Avery, G. *Childhood's Pattern*, p. 226.
 15 *Nottingham Evening Post* 29 September 1977, p. 6.
 16 *Guardian* 29 September 1977, p. 2.
 17 Cullingford, C. *New Society* 9 August 1979, pp. 290–1.
 18 Larner, C. *New Society* 20/27 December 1979, p. iv.
 19 *Unesco Statistical Yearbook* 1978–79, p. 1099.
 20 Kamm, A. *Bookseller* 20 September 1975, pp. 1752–4.
 21 *Books* 356, 1964, pp. 194–5.
 22 Tucker, N.*New Society* 12 March 1970, p. 446.
 23 Woods, M. *New Society* 19 September 1974, pp. 731–3.

Chapter 2: The Early Years
  1 Fyleman, R. *The Fairies have never a penny to spend. Oxford
       Book of Children's Verse*, edited by I. *and* P. Opie, p. 321.
  2 De la Mare, W. 'The Buckle.' *Poems for Children*, 1930, p. 11.
  3 Trease, G. *Books and Bookmen* 14 (8) 1969, p. 24.

4 Walker, J. *Some Things for the Children*. Duckworth, 1974, pp. 10–14.
5 Norman, D. *Daily Mail* 29 November 1968.
6 Freeman, G. *The Schoolgirl Ethic*. Allen Lane, 1976, pp. 19–20.
7 Colwell, E. *Signal* 13, 1974, p. 36.
8 Crouch, M. *Readings about Children's Literature*, p. 187.
9 Stern, C. *Library Association Record* 38 (6) 1936, p. 245.
10 Graham, E. *Signal* 9, 1972, p. 105.
11 Trease, G. *The Thorny Paradise*, p. 13.
12 *The Junior Bookshelf* 1 (2) 1937, p. 36.
13 *The Junior Bookshelf* 5 (4) 1941, p. 145.

Chapter 3: The War Years 1939–45
1 Stoney, B. *Enid Blyton*, pp. 221–44.
2 Attenborough, J. *A Living Memory*, pp. 143, 257.
3 Ibid., p. 230.
4 Ibid., p. 230.
5 Graham, E. *Signal* 12, 1973, p. 122.
6 Lock, M. *Library World* 45 (520) 1943, p. 153.
7 Lewis, L. *Wilson Library Bulletin* 19 (8) 1945, p. 553.
8 Stoney, B. *Enid Blyton*, pp. 225–8.
9 Bethnal Green Public Libraries. *What are Children Reading Today?*, p. 3.
10 *The Junior Bookshelf* 11 (4) 1947, p. 160.
11 Lock, M. *Library World* 45 (520) 1943, p. 154.
12 Bethnal Green Public Libraries. *What are Children Reading Today?*
13 *The Junior Bookshelf* 9 (1) 1945, p. 14.
14 Lewis, L. *Wilson Library Bulletin* 19 (8) 1945, p. 553.
15 Bethnal Green Public Libraries. *What are Children Reading Today?*
16 Beer, P. *Mrs Beer's House*. Macmillan, 1968.
17 Ellis, A. *Books for Your Children* 3 (3) 1968, pp. 10–12.
18 *Times Literary Supplement* 6 December 1974, p. 1370.
19 Raphael, Frederick, *editor. Bookmarks*. Cape, 1975.
20 Stoney, B. *Enid Blyton*, p. 120.
21 Bourne, R. *Books for Keeps* 2, 1980, p. 4.

Chapter 4: The Period of Recovery 1946–58
1 Library Association, Youth Libraries Section. *Public Library Service for Children: a Survey*, 1958–9, 1960.
2 Savage, Ernest A. *A Librarian Looks at Readers*. Library Association, 1947, p. 68.
3 *Librarian and the Book World* 36 (5) 1947, pp. 99–100.
4 Colwell, E. *Library Association Conference Proceedings* 1947, p. 58.

5 Ibid., p. 55.
6 Carter, G. A. *Library Association Record* 49 (9) 1947, pp. 217–21.
7 McGill, H. *Library Association Record* 51 (8) 1949, pp. 236–40.
8 Thompson, A. H. *Censorship in Public Libraries*, pp. 137–57.
9 Trease, G. *Tales Out of School*, p. 7.
10 Ibid., p. 117.
11 Dedman, S. C. *Library Association Conference Proceedings 1949*, p. 45.
12 Ibid., p. 41.
13 Ibid., p. 41.
14 Blyton, E. *Library Association Record* 51 (9) 1949, p. 285.
15 Thompson, A. H. *Censorship in Public Libraries*, p. 145.
16 Colwell, E. *Library Association Record* 54 (3) 1952, p. 79.
17 Ibid., pp. 79–80.
18 Ibid., p. 80.
19 *Spotlight* 1 (2) 1955, pp. 3–4.
20 *Spotlight* 1 (5) 1956, p. 6.
21 *Spotlight* 1 (9) 1957, p. 4.
22 *Daily Mail* 14 September 1968.
23 Smith, B. Oliph. 'Books in Action: The County Library in the Community.' *Library Association Conference Proceedings 1955*, p. 25.
24 Hill, J. *Children are People*, p. 119.
25 Marsh, G. *Life and Letters* 47 (99) November 1945, p. 78.
26 Dunlop, D. C. *Scottish Council for Research in Education Studies in Reading II*, 1950, pp. 81–105.
27 Geary, B. *and* Haywood, M. E. *The Reading of Primary School Children in Brighton.*
28 Carsley, J. D. *British Journal of Educational Psychology* 27 (1) 1957, pp. 13–23.
29 Smith, W. H. and Sons Ltd. *Survey of Boys' and Girls' Reading Habits*, 1957.
30 Black, E. L. *and* Schofield, A. *Times Educational Supplement* 13 June 1958, p. 986.
31 Trease, G. *Tales Out of School*, p. 118.
32 Woods, M. S. *New Society* 19 September 1974, pp. 731–3.
33 Cutforth, J. A. *Library Association Conference Proceedings 1956*, p. 73.
34 Eyre, F. *20th Century Children's Books*, p. 53.
35 British Research Bureau and Market Information Services. *Child Readership Survey (8–15 Years).*
36 Library Association. *Books for Young People*, 'Introduction' to Group I, 1952, p. 3, *and* Group II, 1953, p. 5.
37 Library Association. *Books for Young People* Group I, 1952, p. 12.

38 Library Association. *Books for Young People* Group I, 1955, p. 13.
39 Library Association. *Books for Young People* Group II, 1960, p. 19.
40 Lines, K. M., *comp. Four to Fourteen* 1950, p. 54.
41 Lines, K. M., *comp. Four to Fourteen* 1956, pp. xi, 172.
42 *The Junior Bookshelf* 13 (3) 1949, pp. 117–18.
43 *The Junior Bookshelf* 10 (4) 1946, p. 151.
44 *The Junior Bookshelf* 10 (1) 1946, p. 36.
45 *The Junior Bookshelf* 12 (2) 1948, p. 75.
46 Bewick, E. *School Library Review* 6 (1) 1952, p. 7.
47 Southwell, P. A. G. *The School Librarian* 3 (12) 1947, pp. 351–6.
48 *The School Librarian* 3 (12) 1947, p. 370.
49 *The School Librarian* 4 (5) 1949, p. 252.
50 *The School Librarian* 4 (5) 1949, p. 298.
51 *The School Librarian* 5 (3) 1950, p. 172.
52 *The School Librarian* 5 (3) 1950, p. 178.
53 *Times Literary Supplement* 21 October 1949, p. vii.
54 *Times Literary Supplement* 17 November 1950, p. xviii.
55 *Times Literary Supplement* 28 May 1954, p. iii.
56 Smith, L. H. *The Unreluctant Years*, p. 190.
57 White, D. N. *About Books for Children*, p. 10.
58 *Library Association Record* 62 (10) 1960, p. 80.
59 Meigs, C., *editor. A Critical History of Children's Literature*, p. xxi.
60 Ibid., p. 580.
61 Eyre, F. *20th Century Children's Books*, p. 53.
62 Marsh, G. *Life and Letters* 47 (99) 1945, p. 79.
63 Dohm, J. *Journal of Education* 87 (1033) 1955, pp. 358–61.
64 Woods, F. *Journal of Education* 87 (1034) 1955, p. 404.
65 Welch, C. *Encounter* 10 (1) 1958, p. 18.
66 Ibid., pp. 19–20.
67 Ibid., p. 22.
68 *Library Association Record* 62 (10) 1960, p. 80.
69 *New Zealand Libraries* 22 (8) 1959, pp. 179–85.

Chapter 5: The Second Golden Age 1958–74
1 Townsend, J. R. *Written for Children* (1965), p. 151.
2 Townsend, J. R. *Children's Book News* 4 (4) 1967, pp. 189–91.
3 Trease, G. *Books and Bookmen* 14 (8) 1969, p. 23.
4 Fisher, M. *Intent Upon Reading*, p. 28.
5 *Books* 356, 1964, pp. 194–5.
6 *Growing Point* 1 (4) 1962, p. 62.
7 *Growing Point* 11 (9) 1973, pp. 2133–7.
8 *Growing Point* 12 (4) 1973, pp. 2230–1.

9 *Growing Point* 4 (6) 1965, pp. 620–1.
10 *Children's Book Review* 5 (2) 1975, p. 68.
11 Townsend, J. R. *Written for Children*, p. 331.
12 Ibid., p. 331.
13 Holbrook, D. *English for Maturity*, p. 204.
14 Chambers, A. *The Reluctant Reader*, p. 67.
15 Chambers, A. *Introducing Books to Children*, p. 123.
16 Green, R. L. *Tellers of Tales*, 1969, p. 265.
17 Crouch, M. *Treasure Seekers and Borrowers*, p. 99.
18 Ellis, A. *How to Find Out about Children's Literature*, p. 127.
19 Ellis, A. *The Family Story in the 1960s*, p. 13.
20 Hobson, H. *and others. The Pearl of Days*. Hamilton, 1972, p. 372.
21 Doyle, B. *The Who's Who of Children's Literature*, p. 32.
22 Doyle, B. *Books and Bookmen* 14 (8) 1969, p. 26.
23 Ibid., p. 26.
24 Ray, S. G. *Children's Fiction*, pp. 81, 85, 49.
25 Williams, G. *Children and Their Books*.
26 Hildick, W. *Children and Fiction*, pp. 134–5.
27 Tucker, N. *Times Literary Supplement* 16 April 1970, p. 422.
28 Alderson, B. *The Times* 2 May 1973, p. 13.
29 Orwell, G. 'Boys' Weeklies', *Horizon* 3, 1940, Reprinted in *Inside The Whale and Other Essays*. Penguin, 1957.
30 Jeger, L. *The Guardian* 24 May 1966, p. 8.
31 *Books for Your Children* 11 (4) 1976, p. 1.
32 Freeman, G. *The Undergrowth of Literature*. Nelson, 1967; Panther, 1969, pp. 94–6.
33 *English* 13 (74) 1960, pp. 55–8.
34 West Riding County Library. *Children's Questionnaire: Otley Branch Library*, 1962.
35 Butts, D. *Use of English* 15 (2) 1963, pp. 87–90.
36 Percival, A. *National Froebel Foundation Bulletin* 143, 1963, pp. 1–10.
37 Lawrence, E. *National Froebel Foundation Bulletin* 147, 1964, pp. 2–11.
38 Middlemiss, S. H. *Books and Libraries (unpublished thesis)*, 1966.
39 Lane, M. and Furness-Lane, K. A. *Books Girls Read*, 1967.
40 Leng, I. J. *Children in the Library*, 1968.
41 Ellis, J. I. *English in Education* 3 (1) 1969, pp. 31–6.
42 Yarlott, C. and Harpin, W. S. *Educational Research* 13 (1) 1970, pp. 3–11 *and* 13 (2) 1971, pp. 87–97.
43 Buchanan, E. *New Library World* 72 (857) 1971, pp. 127–9.
44 *Observer Magazine* 4 July 1971, p. 38.
45 Nottinghamshire County Library *and* County Youth Service, *The Reading Habits of Young People Aged 13–19*, 1971.

46 Roddick, J. *Children's Reading* (unpublished), 1971.
47 Petrie, G. *The Child's Choice* (unpublished thesis), 1972.
48 Tucker, N. *Where* 73, 1972, pp. 275–8 and *Where* 74, 1972, pp. 317–9.
49 Taylor, J. J. *Use of English* 25, 1973, p. 10.
50 Eyre, F. *British Children's Books in the Twentieth Century*, p. 34.
51 Blishen, E. *The Guardian* 9 December 1971.
52 Garner, L. *Sunday Times Magazine* 6 February 1976, p. 18.
53 Karl, J. *Top of the News* 34 (1) 1977, p. 66.
54 Thompson, A. H. *Censorship in Public Libraries*, p. 145.
55 *Daily Herald* 6 April 1963.
56 *Guardian Journal* 5 February 1964.
57 *Evening Post and News* 7 February 1964.
58 *Manchester Evening News* 7 February 1964.
59 *Yorkshire Post* 7 February 1964.
60 *Daily Mail* 7 February 1964.
61 *The Teacher* 14 February 1964.
62 *Daily Express* 7 February 1964.
63 *Birmingham Evening Mail* 24 October 1964.
64 *Birmingham Evening Mail* 27 October 1964.
65 *Birmingham Evening Mail* 27 October 1964.
66 *Birmingham Post* 3 November 1964.
67 *Birmingham Evening Mail* 3 November 1964.
68 *Birmingham Evening Mail* 12 April 1969.
69 *Birmingham Evening Mail* 17 August 1971.
70 Yemeni, B. H. 'Public Libraries' *Censorship* 3 (1) 1967, pp. 20–27.
71 Norman, D. *Daily Mail* 14 September 1968.
72 *Times Literary Supplement* 11 December 1969; 22, 29 January, 12 February 1970.
73 *Worcester Evening News* 31 October 1970, p. 6.
74 *Coleraine Chronicle* 18 November 1972, p. 1.
75 Payne, M. *Books* 356, 1964, pp. 209–13.
76 Greenfield, G. *Books* 2, 1970, pp. 24–5.
77 Martin, C. *Books* 2, 1970, p. 26.
78 Woods, M. *New Society* 19 September 1974, pp. 731–3.
79 *Use of English* 17 (3) 1966, p. 199.
80 *Use of English* 18 (1) 1966, p. 38.
81 Field, C. *The School Librarian* 20 (3) 1972, pp. 204–6.
82 Tindall, G. *New Statesman* 27 September 1974, p. 434.
83 *New Statesman* 4 October 1974, p. 470.
84 Dixon, B. *Children's Literature in Education* 15, 1974, pp. 43–61.
85 Sterck, K. *Children's Literature in Education* 15, 1974, pp. 59–61.

86 Blishen, E. *Where* 32, 1967, p. 29.
87 Ibid., p. 29.
88 Tucker, N. *Where* 73, 1972, p. 275.
89 *Times Literary Supplement* 29 January 1970, p. 111.
90 *Times Literary Supplement* 12 February 1970, p. 169.
91 *Times Literary Supplement* 11 December 1969, p. 1426.
92 *Books for Your Children* 2 (3) 1967, p. 3.
93 *Books for Your Children* 7 (3) 1972, p. 14.
94 *Books for Your Children* 9 (1) 1973, p. 23.
95 Billam, J. *Books for Your Children* 4 (3) 1969, p. 7.
96 Tucker, N. *New Society* 2 December 1971, p. 1104.

Chapter 6: Bullock and After
 1 Department of Education and Science. Committee of Inquiry
    into Reading and the Use of English. *A Language for Life.*
    HMSO, 1975. (Bullock Report).
 2 *The Guardian* 20 February 1974, p. 10.
 3 *New Society* 11 April 1974, pp. 82–3.
 4 *New Society* 26 December 1974, pp. 830–1.
 5 Alderson, B. *The Times* 18 September 1974.
 6 Lowry, S. *The Guardian* 12 September 1974, p. 11.
 7 Tindall, G. *New Statesman* 27 September 1974, p. 434.
 8 Whitehead, F. *and others.* Children's Reading Interests, 1975.
 9 Clark, M. M. *Young Fluent Readers*, 1976.
10 Davey, A. *Ballet Shoes or Building Sites.* Birmingham Library
    School Co-operative, 1979.
11 Rosen, B. 'Remarks.' *Children's Literature* 3, 1974, pp. 196–7.
12 Binder, L. *Bookbird* 13 (3) 1975, p. 27.
13 Smyth, J. *Times Educational Supplement* 11 November 1977, p.
    13.
14 *Library Association Record* 62 (10) 1960, p. 80.
15 Personal correspondence, 11 November 1976.
16 Butler, J. *Assistant Librarian* 69 (4) 1976, pp. 66–7.
17 Personal correspondence, 31 August 1975.
18 Personal correspondence, 11 July 1975.
19 Hill, J. *Children are People*, p. 118.
20 Pacey, P. 'Public Libraries and Subject Specialists: a personal
    view.' *Library Association Record* 76 (10) 1974, p. 202.
21 Shropshire County Library. *Children and Libraries*, p. 2.
22 Carroll, R. 'The Role of the Public Librarian.' *Selection at Work*,
    compiled and edited by Frank Baguley. Library Association,
    South Western Branch, 1977, p. 16.
23 Baguley, F., *comp. and editor. Selection at Work*, Library
    Association, South Western Branch, 1977, p. 39.
24 Day, A. 'Too precious a commodity.' *New Library World* 77
    (916) 1976, pp. 184–5.

25 Day, A. 'Sacred Cows Slaughtered in Keighley.' *New Library World* 78 (927) 1977, pp. 196–71.
26 *Sunday Express* 26 October 1975, p. 6.
27 *Aldershot News and Mail* 3 August 1976.
28 *Birmingham Evening Mail* 11 October 1977, p. 8.
29 *Birmingham Evening Mail* 21 October 1977, p. 11.
30 *Nottingham Evening Post* 29 September 1977, p. 6.
31 *The Guardian* 29 September 1977, p. 2.
32 *Library Association Record* 79 (11) 1977, p. 629
33 *Evening Argus* 4 May 1978, p. 11.
34 *Daily Telegraph* 25 April 1978, p. 10.
35 *Times Educational Supplement* 25th August 1978, p. 15.
36 Cullingford, C. *New Society* 9 August 1979, pp. 290–1.
37 *New Society* 6 September 1979, p. 524.
38 *Sunderland Echo* 23 April 1980, p. 9.
39 *Northern Echo* 23 April 1980, p. 5.
40 James, A. *Federation of Children's Book Groups Year Book* 6, p. 51.
41 Woods, M. *New Society* 19 September 1974, pp. 731–3.
42 Hollindale, P. *School Bookshop News* 3, 1975, p. 4.
43 Whitehead, F. *and others. Children's Reading Interests*, p. 48.
44 Kamm, A. *Choosing Books for Younger Children*, p. 9.
45 *Children's Book Review* 4 (1) 1974, p. 8.
46 *Times Literary Supplement* 4 April 1975, p. 364.
47 *Times Literary Supplement* 4 April 1975, p. 364.
48 *Children's Book Review* 5 (3 and 4) 1975, p. 93.
49 *The Guardian* 28 September 1978, p. 9.
50 *The Guardian* 6 December 1979, p. 11.
51 *New Society* 10 January 1980, p. 68.
52 *The Times* 5 March 1980.
53 Hollindale, P. *Choosing Books for Children*.
54 Alderson, B. *The Times* 16 October 1974, p. 7.
55 Cadogan, M. and Craig, P. *You're a Brick, Angela!*, p. 344.
56 Fisher, M. *Who's Who in Children's Books*, p. 109.
57 Ibid., p. 216.
58 Ibid., p. 259.
59 MacRae, J. 'A Different "Who's Who".' *Bookseller* 1 November 1975, pp. 2258–61.
60 *Times Literary Supplement* 29 September 1978, p. 1092.
61 Tucker, N. *Times Literary Supplement* 16 April 1970, p. 422.
62 *Times Literary Supplement* 1 October 1976, p. 1238.
63 *New Society* 20 August 1970, p. 337.
64 *Times Literary Supplement* 7 April 1978, p. 383.
65 McQuire, E. *Children's Libraries Newsletter* 11 (2) 1975, pp. 48–52.
66 Whitehead, F. *and others. Children and their Books*, 1977, pp. 228–35.

67 Hunt, P. *Signal* 15, 1974, pp. 123–4.
68 Hunt, P. *Children's Literature in Education* 30, 9 (3) 1978, pp. 143–50.
69 *Morning Star* 14 November 1975.
70 Ray, S. G. 'Attitudes in Children's Books.' *Bookbird* 14 (3) 1976, p. 55.
71 *New Statesman* 12 December 1980, p. 19.
72 *Observer Magazine* 26 February 1978, p. 44.
73 *The Guardian* 25 November 1975, p. 17.
74 *Yorkshire Post* 8 March 1980, p. 9.
75 *What the Children Like: a Selection of Children's Books, Toys and Games from the Renier Collection.* Victoria and Albert Museum, 1970.
76 *The Guardian* 6 September 1978, p. 9.
77 *Books for Your Children* 13 (4) 1978, p. 21.
78 Mace, E. *Growing Point* 19 (1) May 1980, pp. 2689–91.

II   ENID BLYTON AND THE CHILDREN

Chapter 7: Why Children like Enid Blyton's Books

1 Sykes, A. *Time and Tide* 43 (4) 1962, pp. 21–3.
2 Blyton, E. *The Author* 59 (1) 1958, p. 11.
3 Blyton, E. *New Statesman* 9 May 1959, p. 649.
4 Townsend, J. R. *Horn Book Magazine* 53 (3) 1977, pp. 346–55.
5 Leng, I. J. *Children in the Library*, p. 73.
6 Department of Education and Science. Central Advisory Council for Education (England) *Children and Their Primary Schools.* HMSO, 1967. (Plowden Report), para. 595.
7 Holbrook. D. *English for Maturity*, p. 53.
8 Leng, I. J. *Children in the Library*, p. 44, *and* Carsley, J. D. *British Journal of Educational Psychology* 27 (1) 1957, p. 19.
9 Ray, S. G. *Bookbird* 16 (3) 1978, pp. 2–5.
10 Leng, I. J. *Children in the Library*, p. 50.
11 Terman, L. M. *and* Lima, M. *Children's Reading*, p. 71.
12 Rankin, M. *Children's Interests in Library Books of Fiction*, p. 38.
13 Jenkinson, A. J. *What do Boys and Girls Read?*, pp. 175–6.
14 Carter, G. A. *Library Association Record* 49 (9) 1947, p. 218.
15 Dunlop, D. C. *Scottish Council for Research in Education Studies in Reading II*, pp. 81–105.
16 Leng, I. J. *Children in the Library*, p. 47.
17 Waite, C. A. *School Libraries in the 1970s*, p. 25.
18 Sourbut, B. *Lines* 2 (7) 1969, p. 4.
19 Leng, I. J. *Children in the Library*, pp. 82–3.
20 Harding, D. W. *English in Education* 1 (2) 1967, pp. 7–15.

21 Norvell, G. W. *The Reading Interests of Young People*, p. 66.
22 Leng, I. J. *Children in the Library*, p. 51.
23 Bentley, J. M. *Lines* 2 (7) 1969, p. 7.
24 Woods, M. *Lines* 2 (7) 1969, p. 14.
25 Tucker, N. *The School Librarian* 23 (2) 1975, p. 102.
26 Terman, L. M. *and* Lima, M. *Children's Reading*, p. 16.
27 Rankin, M. *Children's Interests in Library Books of Fiction*, p. 75.
28 Butts, D. *Use of English* 15 (2) 1963, pp. 87–90.
29 Whitehead, F. *and others. Children and Their Books*, pp. 77–8.
30 Woods, M. *Lines* 2 (7) 1969, p. 11.
31 Ellison, T. *and* Williams, G. *Reading* 5 (2) 1971, pp. 3–9.
32 Hanson, D. *New Society* 17 May 1973, pp. 361–3.
33 Woods, M. *Lines* 2 (7) 1969, p. 13.
34 *Use of English* 18 (1) 1966, p. 34.
35 Bateman, R. *The School Librarian* 15 (2) 1967, pp. 153–61.
36 Piaget, J. *The Moral Judgement of the Child.* 1932. Penguin, 1977, pp. 253–4.
37 Terman, L. M. *and* Lima, M. *Children's Reading*, p. 16.
38 Butts, D. *Use of English* 15 (2) 1963, p. 90.
39 Scott, W. J. *Reading, Film and Radio Tastes of High School Boys and Girls*, pp. 21–2.
40 Blyton, E. *New Statesman* 9 May 1959, p. 649.
41 Woods, M. *Lines* 2 (7) 1969, pp. 8–16.
42 Tucker, N. *Children's Literature in Education* 9, 1972, p. 55.
43 Harding, D. W. *English in Education* 1 (2) 1967, p. 10.
44 Terman, L. M. *and* Lima, M. *Children's Reading*, p. 16.
45 Spalding, E. *Books through Children's Eyes*, p. 19.
46 James, A. *Federation of Children's Book Groups Year Book* 6, 1974–5, p. 51.
47 Chambers, A. *School Bookshop News* 3, 1975, p. 19.
48 Warlow, A. *The Cool Web*, p. 91.
49 Rankin, M. *Children's Interests in Library Books of Fiction*, pp. 85–7.
50 Terman, L. M. *and* Lima, M. *Children's Reading*, p. 87.
51 Rankin, M. *Children's Interests in Library Books of Fiction*, p. 84.
52 Warlow, A. *The Cool Web*, p. 91.
53 Leng, I. J. *Children in the Library*, p. 61.
54 Dyer, C. *Lines* 2 (7) 1969, p. 16.
55 Leng, I. J. *Children in the Library*, p. 66.
56 Fenwick, G. *Educational Research* 17 (2) 1975, p. 148.
57 James, D. 'Promoting Voluntary Reading.' *The School Libarian* 26 (2) June 1978, pp. 118–22.
58 Scott, W. J. *Reading, Film and Radio Tastes of High School Boys and Girls*, p. 11.

59 Trease, G. *New Statesman* 9 May 1959, p. 650.
60 Rankin, M. *Children's Interests in Library Books of Fiction*, p. 60.
61 Warlow, A. *The Cool Web*, p. 92.
62 Blyton, E. *The Enchanted Wood*, p. 5.
63 Blyton, E. *Five on a Treasure Island*, p. 7.
64 Blyton, E. *First Term at Malory Towers*, p. 1.
65 Stranger, J. *The Author* 86 (2) 1975, p. 68.
66 Terman, L. M. *and* Lima, M. *Children's Reading*, p. 15.
67 Butts, D. *Use of English* 15 (2) 1963, p. 89.
68 Blyton, E. *New Statesman* 9 May 1959, p. 649.
69 Tindall, G. *New Statesman* 27 September 1974, p. 434.
70 *Use of English* 18 (1) 1966, p. 34.
71 Ibid., p. 38.
72 Leeson, R. *Books for Your Children* 10 (4) 1975, p. 16.
73 Woods, M. *Lines* 2 (7) 1969, p. 12.
74 *Spotlight* 1 (5) 1956, p. 6.
75 Roe, E. *Australian Library Journal* 13 (1) 1964, p. 8.

III THE WORK OF ENID BLYTON

Chapter 8: Critical Considerations

 1 Leeson, R. *Signal* 13, 1974, p. 9.
 2 Inglis, Fred. *An Essential Discipline: an Introduction to Literary Criticism*. Methuen 1968, p. 1.
 3 Hunt, P. *Signal* 15, 1974, pp. 121–2.
 4 Lewis, C. S. 'On three ways of writing for children.' *Only Connect*, p. 207.
 5 Whitehead, F. *and others*. *Children's Reading Interests*, p. 21.
 6 McKellar, P. 'Enid Blyton' *The Cool Web*, p. 224.
 7 Blyton, E. *Library Association Record* 51 (9) 1949, p. 285.
 8 Stoney, B. *Enid Blyton*, p. 208.
 9 McKellar, P. 'Enid Blyton.' *The Cool Web*, p. 223.
10 Blyton, E. *The Story of My Life*, p. 48.
11 Lewis, C. S. *An Experiment in Criticism*. CUP, 1961.

Chapter 9: Noddy and the Nursery Stories

 1 Welch, C. *Encounter* 10 (1) 1958, pp. 18–22.
 2 Blishen, E. *Where* 32, 1967, pp. 28–9.
 3 Blyton, E. *Noddy Meets Father Christmas*, p. 34.
 4 Ibid., p. 49.
 5 Ibid., p. 34.
 6 Welch, C. *Encounter* 10 (1) 1958, p. 19.
 7 Blyton, E. *Noddy Meets Father Christmas*, p. 30.
 8 Milne, A. A. *Winnie-the-Pooh*, p. 51.

9 Blyton, E. *Story Party at Green Hedges*, p. 29.
10 Ibid., p. 74.
11 Ibid., p. 72.
12 Green, R. L., *editor. The Hamish Hamilton Book of Other Worlds*, p. 100.
13 Blyton, E. *Story Party at Green Hedges*, p. 78.
14 Green, R. L., *editor. The Hamish Hamilton Book of Other Worlds*, p. 124.
15 Richards, I. A. *Practical Criticism*. Kegan Paul, 1929, p. 316.

Chapter 10: The Fantasy World
1 Norman, D. *Daily Mail* 29 November 1968.
2 Doyle, B. *Books and Bookmen* 14 (8) 1969, p. 24.
3 Tindall, G. *New Statesman* 27 September 1974, p. 434.
4 *The Guardian* 12 September 1974, p. 11.
5 Crago, M. *and* H. *Growing Point* 10 (7) 1972, p. 1868.
6 Blyton, E. *The Story of My Life*, p. 48.
7 Ibid., p. 50.
8 Geeen, R. L. *The Saga of Asgard*, p. 23.
9 Blyton, E. *The Enchanted Wood*, p. 161.
10 Nesbit, E. *The Phoenix and the Carpet*, p. 86.
11 Lewis, H. *The Ship that Flew*, p. 111.
12 Ibid., p. 112.
13 Blyton, E. *The Enchanted Wood*, p. 58.
14 Ibid., pp. 58–9.
15 Fisher, M. *Intent Upon Reading*, p. 147.
16 Blyton, E. *Adventures of the Wishing Chair*, p. 138.
17 Ibid., p. 208.
18 Streatfeild, N. 'About this book.' *Long Ago When I was Young*, by E. Nesbit, p. 15.
19 Blyton, E. *The Enchanted Wood*, pp. 84–5.
20 Nesbit, E. *Five Children and It*, p. 93.
21 Blyton, E. *Adventures of the Wishing Chair*, pp. 138–9.
22 Blyton, E. *The Enchanted Wood*, p. 6.
23 Nesbit, E. *Five Children and It*, p. 29.
24 Blyton, E. *The Enchanted Wood*, p. 177.
25 Nesbit, E. *Five Children and It*, p. 95.
26 Blyton, E. *Adventures of the Wishing Chair*, p. 170.
27 Ibid., p. 13.
28 Lewis, H. *The Ship that Flew*, p. 12.
29 Ibid., p. 18–19.
30 Nesbit, E. *The Phoenix and the Carpet*, p. 18.
31 Blyton, E. *Adventures of the Wishing Chair*, pp. 151–7.
32 Lewis, H. *The Ship that Flew*, pp. 148–9.
33 Nesbit, E. *The Phoenix and the Carpet*, pp. 34–56.
34 Nesbit, E. *Long Ago When I Was Young*, pp. 83–4.

35 Blyton, E. *The Enchanted Wood*, p. 175.

Chapter 11: Holiday Adventure Stories
 1 Blyton, E. *The Story of My Life*, p. 52.
 2 Blyton, E. *The Secret Island*, p. 121.
 3 Ibid., p. 110.
 4 Ibid., p. 37.
 5 Ibid., p. 39.
 6 Blyton, E. *The Adventurous Four*, p. 97.
 7 Ibid., p. 26.
 8 Ibid., p. 20.
 9 Ibid., p. 115.
10 Ibid., pp. 127–8.
11 Ibid., p. 67.
12 Ibid., p. 139.
13 Ibid., p. 140.
14 Ibid., p. 60.
15 Ibid., p. 28.
16 Streatfeild, N. *The Children of Primrose Lane*, p. 77.
17 Blyton, E. *Five on a Treasure Island*, p. 8.
18 Ibid., p. 9.
19 Tucker, N. *The School Librarian* 23 (2) 1975, pp. 101–9.
20 Blyton, E. *Five on a Treasure Island*, p. 106.
21 Ibid., p. 181.
22 Ibid., p. 97.
23 Blyton, E. *The Rockingdown Mystery*, p. 14.
24 Ibid., p. 37.
25 Trease, G. *Tales Out of School*, p. 107.
26 Blyton, E. *The Secret Mountain*, p. 136.
27 Haggard, H. Rider. *King Solomon's Mines*, p. 227.
28 Lewis, C. S. 'On Stories.' *The Cool Web*, edited by M. Meek and
      others. p. 78.

Chapter 12: Detective Fiction
 1 Blyton, E. *The Secret Seven*, p. 61.
 2 Ibid., p. 18.
 3 Blyton, E. *The Mystery of the Burnt Cottage*, p. 5.
 4 Ibid., p. 69.
 5 Fisher, M. *Intent Upon Reading*, p. 254.
 6 Lewis, C. Day. *The Otterbury Incident*, p. 94.
 7 Blyton, E. *The Mystery of the Burnt Cottage*, p. 69.
 8 Lewis, C. Day. *The Otterbury Incident*, p. 121.

Chapter 13: Circus Stories
 1 Spring, H. *Sampson's Circus*, p. 147.
 2 Streatfeild, N. *The Circus is Coming*, p. 263.

3 Blyton, E. *Mr Galliano's Circus*, p. 71.
4 Ibid., p. 79.
5 Blyton, E. *Come to the Circus*, p. 103.

Chapter 14: Family Stories
 1 Sykes, A. *Time and Tide* 43 (47) 1962, pp. 21–3.
 2 *Use of English* 18 (1) 1966, p. 38.
 3 Blyton, E. *The Children of Cherry Tree Farm*, p. 5.
 4 Ibid., p. 14.
 5 Morgan, A. *Ruth Crane*, p. 34.
 6 Blyton, E. *The Children of Cherry Tree Farm*, p. 104.
 7 Martin, C. *Books* 2, 1970, p. 27.
 8 Blyton, E. *The Family at Red-Roofs*, p. 46.
 9 Ibid., p. 48.
10 Blyton, E. *The Put-em-Rights*, p. 5.
11 Ibid., p. 71.
12 Ibid., p. 71.
13 Woods, M. *Lines* 2 (7) 1969, pp. 8–16.
14 Henriques, Basil. Foreword to first edition of *Six Bad Boys*,
       1951.
15 Blyton, E. *Six Bad Boys*, p. 6.
16 Ashley, B. *Terry on the Fence*, p. 16.
17 Blyton, E. *Six Bad Boys*, p. 158.

Chapter 15: Enid Blyton's World of School
 1 Stern, C. *Library Association Record* 38 (6) 1936, pp. 243–5.
 2 Trease, G. *Tales Out of School*, p. 107.
 3 Blyton, E. *First Term at Malory Towers*, p. 9.
 4 Stoney, B. *Enid Blyton*, p. 132.
 5 Ibid., p. 170.
 6 Blyton, E. *Last Term at Malory Towers*, p. 105.

Chapter 16: Critical Conclusions
 1 Moss, E. *Signal* 14, 1974, p. 68.
 2 Stranger, J. *The Author* 86 (2) 1975, pp. 67–9.
 3 Stranger, J. *Books for Your Children* 10 (3) 1975, p. 18.
 4 Peyton, K. *The Thorny Paradise*, p. 127.

Chapter 17: A Continuing Phenomenon . . .
 1 Richardson, J. *Birmingham Post* 2 October 1980, p. 4.
 2 *New Statesman* 1 February 1980, p. 178.
 3 Ibid., 19/26 December 1980, p. 53.
 4 *Library Association Record* 82 (2) December 1980, p. 569.
 5 *Times Literary Supplement* 28 March 1980, p. 358.
 6 *Folio* Winter 1980, p. 30.

7 *Television and the Family.* UK Association for the International Year of the Child and the University of London Department of Extra-Mural Studies, 1980, p. 45.
8 *The Guardian* 5 August 1980, p. 9.
9 Richmond, J. *The English Magazine* 5, 1980, pp. 25–8.

Bibliography of Sources Used

❦

The place of publication, if London, is not given. When more than one edition of a work has been consulted, details of all editions used are given. When a reprint has been used, the date of original publication is given. Where books and articles are known to have been written by the same person, the name of the author is given in one form only, although there may be variations in the original publication. Children's books are listed in a separate sequence.

Alderson, Brian. 'A long cool look at the controversial Miss Blyton.' *The Times* 18 September 1974.
'The Mallorys and the Medleys against the Famous Five,' *The Times* 16 October 1974, p. 7.
'Miss Blyton in the way of progress.' *The Times* 2 May 1973, p. 13.

Arbuthnot, May Hill. *Children and Books*. Chicago: Scott, Foresman, 1947. 4th edition, 1972. 5th edition (by Zena Sutherland), 1977.

Attenborough, John. *A Living Memory: Hodder and Stoughton Publishers 1868–1975*. Hodder & Stoughton, 1975.

Avery, Gillian. *Childhood's Pattern: a Study of the Heroes and Heroines of Children's Fiction 1770–1950*. Hodder & Stoughton, 1975.

Bateman, Robin. 'Children and humorous literature.' *The School Librarian* 15 (2) 1967, pp. 153–61.

Becker, May Lamberton. *Choosing Books for Children*. OUP, 1937.

Bentley, Judith M. 'Enid Blyton – what she meant to me.' *Lines* 2 (7) 1969, pp. 6–8.

Bethnal Green Public Libraries. *What are Children Reading Today?* Bethnal Green, 1946.

Bewick, Elizabeth. 'Children's fiction: the contemporary scene.' *School Library Review* 6 (1) 1952, pp. 6–11.

Billam, J. 'Jamie (Reading with deaf children).' *Books for Your Children* 4 (3) 1969, pp. 6–7.

Binder, Lucia. 'The sugar-sweet beginning.' *Bookbird* 13 (3) 1975, pp. 23–7.

Black, E. L. *and* Schofield, A. 'What do girls read?' *Times Educational Supplement* 13 June 1958, p. 986.

Blishen, Edward. 'Books in jeans and jerseys.' *The Guardian* 9 December 1970.
'Who's afraid of Enid Blyton?' *Where* 32, 1967, pp. 28–9.
Editor. The Thorny Paradise: Writers on Writing for Children. Kestrel Books, 1975.
Blyton, Enid. 'Letter to Stanley Dedman.' *Library Association Record* 51 (9) 1949, p. 285; reprinted in *Enid Blyton*, by Barbara Stoney, pp. 201–2.
The Story of My Life. Pitkins, 1952.
'Writing for children.' *New Statesman* 9 May 1959, p. 649.
'Writing for the young: the family story.' *The Author* 59 (1) 1958, p. 11.
'Blyton revisited.' *Lines* 2 (7) 1969.
Bourne, Richard. 'A comment on the cuts.' *Books for Keeps* 2, May 1980, pp. 4–5.
British Research Bureau and Market Information Services. *Child Readership Survey (8–15 Years).* Hulton Press, 1951.
Buchanan, E. 'Children's choice.' *New Library World* 72 (857) 1971, pp. 127–9.
Butler, Joan. 'All change?' *Assistant Librarian* 69 (4) 1976, pp. 66–7.
Butts, D. 'What do some boys and girls read and why?' *Use of English* 15 (2) 1963, pp. 87–90.
Cadogan, Mary *and* Craig, Patricia. *You're a Brick, Angela!'* Gollancz, 1976.
Capey, A. C. *and* Maskell, Duke, 'The ruder his words were, the more politely he spoke . . .' *The Haltwhistle Quarterly* 9, 1980, pp. 21–7.
Carsley, J. D. 'The interests of children (ages 10–11) in books.' *British Journal of Educational Psychology* 27 (1) 1957, pp. 13–23.
Carter, G. A. 'Some childish likes and dislikes.' *Library Association Record* 49 (9) 1947, pp. 217–21.
Chambers, Aidan. 'From Blyton to Doetovsky (sic).' *School Bookshop News* 3, 1975, pp. 18–9.
Introducing Books to Children. Heinemann Educational, 1973.
The Reluctant Reader. Oxford: Pergamon Press, 1969.
Clark, Margaret M. *Young Fluent Readers.* Heinemann Educational, 1976.
Colwell, Eileen. 'At the beginning.' *Signal* 13, 1974, pp. 30–7.
'Children's books today.' *Library Association Record* 54 (3) 1952, pp. 78–80.
'Twenty eventful years in children's books.' *Library Association Conference Proceedings* 1947, pp. 55–9.
Crago, Hugh *and* Crago, Maureen. 'A cupful of diamond juice.' *Growing Point* 10 (7) 1972, pp. 1866–9.

Crouch, Marcus. *The Nesbit Tradition: the Children's Novel 1945–1970.* Benn, 1972.
'Salute to children's literature and its creators: 21st birthday for Carnegie Medal.' *Top of the News* 1958, reprinted in *Readings about Children's Literature,* edited by E. R. Robinson, New York: McKay, 1966, pp. 183–8.
Treasure Seekers and Borrowers: Children's Books in Britain 1900–1960. Library Association, 1962. Reprinted with amendments, 1970.

Cullingford, Cedric. 'Why children like Enid Blyton.' *New Society* 9 August 1979, pp. 290–1.

Cutforth, J. A. 'The relation between mental development and children's reading.' *Library Association Conference Proceedings 1956,* pp. 71–4.

Darton, F. J. Harvey. *Children's Books in England.* Cambridge University Press, 1932; 2nd edition, 1958.

Davey, Angela. *Ballet Shoes or Building Sites.* Birmingham Library School Co-operative, 1979.

Day, Alan. 'Too precious a commodity.' *New Library World* 77 (916) 1976, pp. 184–5.

Dedman, Stanley C. 'Children's reading taste and some of the problems.' *Library Association Conference Proceedings 1949,* pp. 38–45.
'Reading tastes in children.' *The School Librarian* 4 (5) 1949, pp. 246–52.

Dixon, Bob. 'All things white and beautiful.' *Hard Cheese* 3, 1974, pp. 70–90. Reprinted in *Catching Them Young* vol. 1, pp. 94–127.
Catching Them Young. 2 vols. Pluto Press, 1977.
'The nice, the naughty and the nasty: the tiny world of Enid Blyton.' *Children's Literature in Education* 15, 1974, pp. 43–61. Reprinted in *Catching Them Young* vol.2, pp. 56–73.

Dohm, Janice. 'Enid Blyton and others: an American view.' *Journal of Education* 87 (1033) 1955, pp. 358–61. Reprinted in *Young Writers, Young Readers,* edited by B. Ford, pp. 99–106.

Doyle, Brian. 'Blyton and Biggles.' *Books and Bookmen* 14 (8) 1969, pp. 24–6.
The Who's Who of Children's Literature. Evelyn, 1968.

Dunlop, Doris C. 'Children's leisure reading interests.' *Scottish Council for Research in Education Studies in Reading II.* University of London Press, 1950, pp. 81–105.

Dyer, Christopher. 'Anatomy of a Blyton.' *Lines* 2 (7) 1969, pp. 16–18.

Egoff, Sheila *and others, editors. Only Connect: Readings on Children's Literature.* Toronto: OUP, 1969.

Ellis, Alec. *A History of Children's Reading and Literature.* Oxford: Pergamon Press, 1968.

Ellis, Alec. *How to Find Out About Children's Literature.* 3rd edition Oxford: Pergamon Press, 1973.

Ellis, Anne. *The Family Story in the 1960s.* Bingley, 1970.

'Reading in wartime.' *Books for Your Children* 3 (3) 1968, pp. 10–2.

Ellis, J. I. 'A reading survey by Warwickshire NATE.' *English in Education* 3 (1) 1969, pp. 31–6.

Ellison, T. *and* Williams, G. 'Social class and children's reading preferences.' *Reading* 5 (2) 1971, pp. 3–9.

Eyre, Frank. *20th Century Children's Books.* Longman for the British Council, 1952; revised and enlarged edition published as *British Children's Books in the Twentieth Century*, 1971.

Fazackerley, Joan. 'Sir John McKenzie Memorial Library, Upper Riccarton.' *New Zealand Libraries* 22 (8) 1959, pp. 179–85.

Fenwick, G. 'Junior school pupils' rejection of school library books.' *Educational Research* 17 (2) 1975, pp. 143–9.

Field, Colin. 'Enid Blyton, the teacher and children's reading interests.' *The School Librarian* 20 (3) 1972, pp. 204–6.

Fisher, Margery. *Intent Upon Reading: a Critical Appraisal of Modern Fiction for Children.* Leicester: Brockhampton Press, 1961; 2nd edition, 1964.

Who's Who in Children's Books: a Treasury of the Familiar Characters of Childhood. Weidenfeld & Nicolson, 1975.

Ford, Boris, *editor. Young Writers, Young Readers.* Hutchinson, 1960. Revised edition, 1963.

Fyleman, Rose. 'Poetry for children – then and now.' *Library Association Record* 36 (10) 1934, pp. 361–7.

Garner, Leslie. 'The heart of the matter.' *Sunday Times Magazine* 6 February 1976, p. 18.

Geary, B. *and* Haywood, M. E. *The Reading of Primary School Children in Brighton.* National Froebel Foundation, 1950.

Golding, William. 'Fable.' *The Hot Gates.* Faber, 1963. Reprinted in *The Cool Web*, edited by M. Meek *and others*, pp. 226–40.

Graham, Eleanor. 'The Bumpus years.' *Signal* 9, 1972, pp. 97–108.

'The Puffin years.' *Signal* 12, 1973, pp. 115–22.

Green, Roger Lancelyn. 'The golden age of children's books.' *English Association Essays and Studies* 1962. Reprinted in *Only Connect*, edited by S. Egoff *and others*, pp. 1–16.

Tellers of Tales. Edmund Ward, 1946; new enlarged edition, 1953; further revised edition, 1956; rewritten and revised edition, 1965; revised edition, 1969.

Greenfield, George. 'Phenomenon.' *Books* 2, 1970, pp. 24–5.

Hanson, Derek. 'What children like to read.' *New Society* 17 May 1973, pp. 361–3.

Harding, D. W. 'Considered experience: the invitation of the novel.' *English in Education* 1 (2) 1967, pp. 7–15.

Hazard, Paul. *Books, Children and Men*. Boston: Horn Book, 1944.
  4th edition, 1960.
Hildick, Wallace. *Children and Fiction*. Evans, 1970. Revised edition,
  1974.
Hill, Janet. *Children are People*. Hamilton, 1973.
Holbrook, David. *English for Maturity*. Cambridge University Press,
  1961.
Hollindale, Peter. *Choosing Books for Children*. Elek, 1974.
  'Does it matter what children read?' *School Bookshop News* 3,
  1975, pp. 3–5.
Hunt, Peter. 'The cliché count: a practical aid for the selection of
  books for children.' *Children's Literature in Education* 30, 1978,
  pp. 143–50.
  'Criticism and children's literature.' *Signal* 15, 1974, pp. 117–30.
'I remember, I remember.' *Times Literary Supplement* 6 December
  1974, p. 1370.
James, Anne. 'Success story: Enid Blyton.' *Federation of Children's
  Book Groups Year Book* 6, 1974–5, pp. 50–1.
Jeger, Lena. 'In large print.' *The Guardian* 24 May 1966, p. 18.
Jenkinson, A. J. *What Do Boys and Girls Read?* Methuen, 1940.
Jesson-Dibley, David, Atthill, Robin *and* Earl, Roland. 'What do they
  read?' *English* 13 (74) 1960, pp. 55–8.
Kamm, Antony. *Choosing Books for Younger Children*. Gloucester:
  Thornhill Press, 1977.
  'Malaysian interlude.' *Bookseller* 20 September 1975, pp. 152–4.
Karl, Jean. 'Paperbacks for children: an editor's viewpoint.' *Top of
  the News* 34 (1) 1977, pp. 63–6.
Kloet, C. *After Alice: a Hundred Years of Children's Reading in
  Britain*. Library Association, 1977.
Lane, M. *and* Furness-Lane, K. A. *Books Girls Read: a Survey of
  Reading Habits Carried Out in a Comprehensive School for Girls*.
  Society of Young Publishers, 1967.
Lawrence, E. 'Children's tastes in reading – a recent sample enquiry.'
  National Froebel Foundation Bulletin 147, 1964, pp. 2–11.
Leeson, Robert. 'Boom.' *Signal* 13, 1974, pp. 3–9.
  'Writing for today's children.' *Books for Your Children* 10 (4)
  1975, p. 16.
Leng, I. J. *Children in the Library: A Study of Children's Leisure-Read-
  ing Tastes and Habits*. Cardiff: University of Wales Press, 1968.
  'Children's reading.' *Library Association Conference Proceedings*
  1962, pp. 111–6.
Lewis, C. S. 'On three ways of writing for children.' *Library
  Association Conference Proceedings* 1952, pp. 22–8. Reprinted in
  Only Connect, edited by S. Egoff *and others*, pp. 207–20.
Lewis, Lorna. 'What Britain's children read.' *Wilson Library Bulletin*
  19 (8) 1945, pp. 552–3.

Library Association. *Books for Young People*. Group I. Under 11, 1952; revised edition, 1955.
Books for Young People. Group II. Eleven to Thirteen Plus, 1953; revised edition, 1954; 3rd edition, 1960.
Lines, Kathleen M. *Four to Fourteen: a Library of Books*. National Book League, 1940. 1st edition (sic), Cambridge University Press for the National Book League, 1950; 2nd edition, 1956.
Lock, Muriel. 'Problems of children's literature.' *Library World* 45 (520) 1943, pp. 153–5.
Lowry, Suzanne. 'Behind the green hedges.' *The Guardian* 12 September 1974, p. 11.
Mace, Elisabeth. 'Books and the young.' *Growing Point* 19 (1) 1980, pp. 2689–91.
McGill, Hilda. 'Juvenile and adolescent reading and readers.' *Library Association Record* 51 (8) 1949, pp. 236–40.
McKellar, Peter. 'Enid Blyton.' *Imagination and Thinking: an Analysis*. Cohen and West, 1957. Reprinted in *The Cool Web*, edited by M. Meek *and others*, pp. 222–5.
Correspondence between Peter McKellar and Enid Blyton is quoted in *Enid Blyton*, by Barbara Stoney, pp. 205–15.
McQuire, Elizabeth. ' "Home" versus "Dulce domum".' *Children's Libraries Newsletter* 11 (2) 1975, pp. 48–52.
MacRae, Julia. 'A different "Who's Who".' *Bookseller* 1 November 1975, pp. 2258–61.
Marsh, Gwen. 'Children's literature.' *Life and Letters* 47 (99) 1945, pp. 73–81.
Martin, Constance (née Stern, q.v.). 'South Sea bubble.' *Books* 2, 1970, pp. 26–7.
Meek, Margaret *and others, editors. The Cool Web: the Pattern of Children's Reading*. Bodley Head, 1977.
Meigs, Cornelia, *editor. A Critical History of Children's Literature: a Survey of Children's Books in English*. New York: The Macmillan Company, 1953. Revised edition, 1969.
Middlemiss, S. H. Books and libraries: a report of a survey in November 1964 of the use of books and libraries by pupils and students in some secondary technical schools and colleges of further education. Dissertation, School Librarianship Course, Birmingham Institute of Education, 1966. (Unpublished.)
Mitchell, L. J. 'Too precious.' *New Library World* 78 (920) 1977, p. 26.
Moss, Elaine. 'The adult-eration of children's books.' *Signal* 14, 1974, pp. 65–9.
Nesbit, E. *Long Ago When I Was Young*. Macdonald, 1966.
'Noddy a blight on libraries "down-under." ' *Library Association Record* 62 (10) 1960, p. 80.

Norman, Diana. 'Let's bring Noddy back from exile.' *Daily Mail* 14 September 1968.
'Noddy loses his oldest friend.' *Daily Mail* 29 November 1968.
Norvell, G. W. *The Reading Interests of Young People.* Boston: Heath, 1950.
Nottinghamshire County Library *and* Nottinghamshire County Youth Service. *The Reading Habits of Young People Aged 13–19.* Nottinghamshire Education Department, 1971.
P. F. P. 'What do they read?' *Librarian and Book World* 36 (5) 1947, pp. 99–100.
Payne, Margaret. 'Selection – or censorship? A children's librarian's approach to books.' *Books* 356, 1964, pp. 209–13.
Percival, A. 'Leisure reading by modern school children.' *National Froebel Foundation Bulletin* 143, 1963, pp. 1–10.
Petrie, Gillian E. The child's choice: to read or not to read. Thesis, City of Newcastle-upon-Tyne College of Education, 1972. (Unpublished.)
Peyton, K. M. 'On not writing a proper book.' *The Thorny Paradise*, edited by E. Blishen, pp. 123–7.
'Problems.' *Use of English* 17 (3) 1966, p. 199 and *Use of English* 18 (1) 1966, pp. 33–40. (Second issue contains contributions by Sister Margaret Mary, Nicholas Tucker, J. J. Pearce, D. W. Crompton, E. Hesk and John Werner.)
'Race, sex and class in children's books.' *New Statesman* 14 November to 19/26 December 1980 (6 consecutive issues) inclusive.
Rankin, M. *Children's Interests in Library Books of Fiction.* New York: Bureau of Publications, Teachers College, Columbia University, 1944.
Raphael, Frederick, *editor. Bookmarks.* Cape, 1975.
Ray, S. G. 'Attitudes in children's books.' *Bookbird* 14 (3) 1976, pp. 54–5.
Children's Fiction: a Handbook for Librarians. Leicester: Brockhampton Press, 1970; 2nd edition, 1972.
'Why do children read?' *Bookbird* 16 (3) 1978, pp. 2–5.
Richardson, Jean. 'The Blyton case.' *Birmingham Post* 2 October 1980, p. 4.
Richmond, J. 'What do 170 boys read?' *The English Magazine* 5, 1980, pp. 25–8.
Roddick, Jennifer. Children's reading. Birmingham Polytechnic, 1971. (Unpublished.)
Roe, Ernest. 'Why do children read?' *Australian Library Journal* 13 (1) 1964, pp. 3–14.
Rosen, Barbara. 'Remarks.' *Children's Literature* 3, 1974, pp. 196–7.
Scott, W. J. *Reading, Film and Radio Tastes of High School Boys and*

Girls Christchurch, New Zealand: Council for Educational Research, 1947.

Sheffield City Libraries. *A Survey of Children's Reading*. Sheffield, 1938.

Shropshire County Library. Children and libraries: report of Lilleshall staff course, 1975. (Unpublished.)

Smith, Lillian H. *The Unreluctant Years: a Critical Approach to Children's Literature*. Chicago: American Library Association, 1953.

Smith, W. H. and Sons Ltd. *Survey of Boys' and Girls' Reading Habits . . . Based on Questionnaires Completed by 8000 Boys and Girls*. Smith & Harrap, 1957.

Smyth, Joan. 'Enid Blyton tops reading list.' *Times Educational Supplement* 11 November 1977, p. 13.

Sourbut, Brian. 'Nothing to do with art.' *Lines* 2 (7) 1969, pp. 2–4.

Southwell, P. A. G. 'A junior school library.' *The School Librarian* 3 (12) 1947, pp. 351–6.

Spalding, E. L. *Books through Children's Eyes: the Story of a Children's Library*. Glasgow: House of Grant, 1960.

Sterck, Kenneth. 'Editorial note.' *Children's Literature in Education* 15, 1974, pp. 59–61.

Stern, Constance M. 'The reading interests of children.' *Library Association Record* 38 (6) 1936, pp. 243–5.

Stoney, Barbara. *Enid Blyton*. Hodder & Stoughton, 1974.

Stranger, Joyce. 'Why don't people read?' *The Author* 86 (2) 1975, pp. 67–9.

Sykes, Adam. 'The books that children love.' *Time and Tide* 43 (47) 1962, pp. 21–3.

Taylor, J. J. 'The voluntary book reading habits of secondary school pupils.' *Use of English* 25, 1973, pp. 5–12, 16.

Terman, L. M. *and* Lima, M. *Children's Reading: a Guide for Parents and Teachers*. New York: Appleton, 1925; 2nd edition, 1931.

Thompson, Anthony Hugh. *Censorship in Public Libraries*. Bowker, 1975.

Censorship in public libraries in the United Kingdom 1939–1971: a thesis submitted in the Faculty of Arts, the Queen's University of Belfast for the degree of Master of Arts, 1972. (Unpublished, but the basis of *Censorship in Public Libraries*.)

Thwaite, M. F. *From Primer to Pleasure in Reading*. Library Association, 1972.

Tindall, Gillian. 'Something nasty in the burrow.' *New Statesman* 27 September 1974, p. 434.

Townsend, John Rowe. 'Comment.' *Children's Book News* 4 (4) 1969, pp. 189–91.

'Peering into the fog: the future of children's books.' *Horn Book Magazine* 53 (3) 1977, pp. 346–55.

Written for Children. Garnet Miller, 1965; revised edition, Kestrel Books, 1974.

Trease, Geoffrey. 'Children's reading is changing.' *Books and Bookmen* 14 (8) 1969, pp. 23–5.

'The revolution in children's literature.' *The Thorny Paradise*, edited by E. Blishen, pp. 13–24.

Tales Out of School: a Survey of Children's Fiction. Heinemann Educational, 1949; 2nd edition, 1964.

'Writing for children.' *New Statesman* 9 May 1959, pp. 449–50.

Tucker, Nicholas. 'All things Blyton and beautiful.' *Times Literary Supplement* 16 April 1970, p. 422.

'The Blyton enigma.' *Children's Literature in Education* 19, 1975, pp. 191–7.

'Books your children read – a report.' *Where* 73, 1972, pp. 275–8, and *Where* 74, 1972, pp. 317–9.

(Contribution to) 'Problems.' *Use of English* 18 (1) 1966, pp. 33–40.

'A glutton for punishment.' *New Society* 12 March 1970, p. 446.

'How children respond to fiction.' *Children's Literature in Education* 9, 1972, pp. 48–56.

'Reading and personality.' *The School Librarian* 23 (2) 1975, pp. 101–9.

'What they read in 1975.' *Where* 115, 1976, pp. 94–5.

Editor. Suitable for Children? Controversies in Children's Literature. Sussex University Press, 1976.

Waite, Clifford. 'Books and other print resources: some principles and possibilities.' *School Libraries in the 1970s*, edited by Clifford Waite, pp. 16–27.

Editor. School Libraries in the 1970s. University of London, Institute of Education Library, 1972.

Warlow, Aidan. 'What the reader has to do.' *The Cool Web*, edited by Margaret Meek *and others*, pp. 91–6.

Welch, Colin. 'Dear little Noddy.' *Encounter* 10 (1) 1958, pp. 18–22. Reprinted in *New Zealand Libraries* 21 (9) 1958.

West Riding County Library. *Children's Questionnaire: Otley Branch Library*, 1962.

White, Dorothy Neal. *About Books for Children.* New Zealand Council for Educational Research in conjunction with the New Zealand Library Association, 1946; New York: OUP, 1949.

Whitehead, F. *and others. Children and their Books: Schools Council Research Project into Children's Reading Habits 10–15.* Macmillan, 1977.

Children's Reading Interests. Evans and Methuen Educational, 1975. (Schools Council Working Paper 52.)

Williams, Bernard. 'A junior school master meets Miss Blyton.' *Lines* 2 (7) 1969, pp. 5–6.

Williams, Gladys. *Children and Their Books*. Duckworth, 1970.

Wood, Anne. 'Editorial.' *Books for Your Children* 11 (4) 1976, p. 1.

Woods, Frederick. 'Letter.' *Journal of Education* 87 (1034) 1955, p. 404.

Woods, M. S. 'The uses of Blyton.' *New Society* 19 September 1974, pp. 731–3.

Woods, Michael. 'The Blyton line: a psychologist's view.' *Lines* 2 (7) 1969, pp. 8–16.

Wright, Peter. 'Five run away together – should we let them back?' *English in Education* 14 (1) 1980, pp. 16–22.

Yarlott, C. *and* Harpin, W. S. '1000 responses to English literature.' *Educational Research* 13 (1) 1970, pp. 3–11 *and* 13 (2) 1971, pp. 87–97.

Children's Books

The following list includes children's books mentioned in the text. Publication details of the original book edition are given: in the case of those books from which passages have been cited, details of the edition used are also given.

Comprehensive bibliographies of Enid Blyton's work are to be found in Barbara Stoney's *Enid Blyton*, pp. 221–44, in the compilation of which assistance was given by Joyce Chapman of Reading University Library, and in *Twentieth Century Children's Writers*, edited by Daniel Kirkpatrick (Macmillan, 1978), pp. 138–152.

Alcott, Louisa M. *Little Women: or Meg, Jo, Beth and Amy*. Boston: Roberts. 2 vols., 1868–9.

Ashley, Bernard. *Terry on the Fence*. OUP, 1975.

Ballantyne, R. M. *The Coral Island*. Nelson, 1857.

Bannerman, Helen. *The Story of Little Black Sambo*. Grant Richards, 1899.

Barrie, J. M. *Peter and Wendy*. Hodder & Stoughton, 1911; as *Peter Pan and Wendy*, 1921.

Blyton, Enid. *Adventures of the Wishing Chair*. Newnes, 1937; 8th edition, 1952.

The Adventurous Four. Newnes, 1941.

The Babar Story Book. Methuen, 1941; shortened version as *Tales of Babar*, 1942.

Before I go to Sleep. Latimer House, 1947; Leicester: Brockhampton Press, 1975.

Bom the Little Toy Drummer. Leicester: Brockhampton Press, 1956.

The Boy Next Door. Newnes, 1944.

The Brown Family: London to the Seaside and *Building a New House*. News Chronicle Publications, n.d.

The Castle of Adventure. Macmillan, 1946.

Child Whispers. Saville, 1922.

The Children of Cherry Tree Farm. Country Life, 1940; Armada, 1974.

The Children of Willow Farm. Country Life, 1942.

The Children's Life of Christ. Methuen, 1943.

The Circus of Adventure. Macmillan, 1952.
Come to the Circus. Newnes, 1948; Hamlyn Beaver, 1979.
The Enchanted Wood. Newnes, 1939; Dean, 1971.
The Family at Red-Roofs. Lutterworth, 1945; Armada, 1967.
The Famous Jimmy. Muller, 1936.
Fifth Formers of St Clare's. Methuen, 1945.
First Term at Malory Towers. Methuen, 1946; 1971.
Five Are Together Again. Hodder & Stoughton, 1963.
Five Fall into Adventure. Hodder & Stoughton, 1950.
Five Go Off to Camp. Hodder & Stoughton, 1948.
Five Go Off in a Caravan. Hodder & Stoughton, 1946.
Five Go to Demon Rocks. Hodder & Stoughton, 1951.
Five Have a Mystery to Solve. Hodder & Stoughton, 1962.
Five on a Treasure Island. Hodder & Stoughton, 1942; Leicester: Knight Books, 1967.
Five Run Away Together. Hodder & Stoughton, 1944.
The Green Story Book. Methuen, 1947.
Here Comes Noddy Again. Sampson Low, 1951.
The Island of Adventure. Macmillan, 1944.
The Land of Far-Beyond. Methuen, 1942; 1973.
Last Term at Malory Towers. Methuen, 1951.
Let's Garden. Latimer House, 1948.
Little Noddy Goes to Toyland. Sampson Low, 1949.
The Magic Faraway Tree. Newnes, 1943.
Mary Mouse and the Doll's House. Leicester: Brockhampton Press, 1942.
Mr Galliano's Circus. Newnes, 1938; Hamlyn, 1967.
More Adventures on Willow Farm. Country Life, 1942.
The Mountain of Adventure. Macmillan, 1949.
The Mystery of the Burnt Cottage. Methuen, 1942; Dragon Books, 1966.
The Mystery of the Strange Bundle. Methuen, 1952.
The Naughtiest Girl in the School. Newnes, 1940.
The Naughtiest Girl is a Monitor. Newnes, 1945.
Noddy Meets Father Christmas. Sampson Low, 1949.
Plays for Older Children. Newnes, 1940; *Plays for Younger Children.* Newnes, 1940; first published in one volume as *The Play's the Thing.* Nelson, 1927.
The Put-em-Rights. Lutterworth, 1946; Armada, 1974.
The Rockingdown Mystery. Collins, 1949; Armada, 1967.
Round the Clock Stories. National Magazine Company, 1945.
The Rubadub Mystery. Collins, 1952.
The Sea of Adventure. Macmillan, 1948.
The Secret Island. Oxford: Blackwell, 1938; Armada, 1964.
The Secret Mountain. Oxford: Blackwell, 1941; Armada, 1965.
The Secret of Killimooin. Oxford: Blackwell, 1943.

The Secret of Moon Castle. Oxford: Blackwell, 1953.
The Secret of Spiggy Holes. Oxford: Blackwell, 1940.
The Secret Seven. Leicester: Brockhampton Press, 1949; Leicester: Knight Books, 1967.
Shadow the Sheep-Dog. Newnes, 1942.
The Ship of Adventure. Macmillan, 1950.
Silver and Gold. Nelson, 1925.
Six Bad Boys. Lutterworth, 1951; Armada, 1968.
A Story Book of Jesus. Macmillan, 1956.
Story Party at Green Hedges. Hodder & Stoughton, 1949; Armada, 1976.
Twins at St Clare's. Methuen, 1941.
The Valley of Adventure. Macmillan, 1947.
Well Done, Noddy. Sampson Low, 1952.
The Wishing Bean and Other Plays. Oxford: Blackwell, 1939.
The Yellow Story Book. Methuen, 1950.
Brazil, Angela. *The New Girl at St Chad's*. Blackie, 1911.
Browne, Frances. *Granny's Wonderful Chair*. Griffith Farran, 1856.
Buckeridge, Anthony. *Jennings Goes to School*. Collins, 1950.
Burnett, Frances Hodgson. *The Secret Garden*. Heinemann, 1911.
   The Spring Cleaning. New York: Century, 1907; Stacey, 1972.
Cannan, Joanna. *A Pony for Jean*. The Bodley Head, 1936.
Carroll, Lewis. *Alice's Adventures in Wonderland*. Macmillan, 1865.
Coolidge, Susan. *What Katy Did*. Boston: Little, Brown, 1872.
Cresswell, Helen. *Jumbo Spencer*. Leicester: Brockhampton Press, 1963.
Crompton, Richmal. *Just William*. Newnes, 1922.
De la Mare, Walter. *Poems for Children*. Constable, 1930.
Garner, Alan. *The Owl Service*. Collins, 1967.
Garnett, Eve. *The Family from One-End Street*. Muller, 1937.
Graham, Eleanor. *The Children Who Lived in a Barn*. Routledge, 1938.
Grahame, Kenneth. *The Wind in the Willows*. Methuen, 1908.
Green, Roger Lancelyn. *The Saga of Asgard*. Penguin, 1960.
   Editor. The Hamish Hamilton Book of Other Worlds. Hamish Hamilton, 1976; *The Beaver Book of Other Worlds*. Hamlyn, 1978.
Haggard, H. Rider. *King Solomon's Mines*. Cassell, 1885; Penguin, 1958.
Haigh, Sheila. *Watch for the Ghost*. Methuen, 1975.
Kaestner, Erich. *Emil and the Detectives*. Cape, 1931.
Kingsley, Charles. *The Water-Babies*. Cambridge, 1863.
Lewis, C. Day. *The Otterbury Incident*. Bodley Head, 1948; 1966.
Lewis, C. S. *The Lion, the Witch and the Wardrobe*. Bles, 1950.
Lewis, Hilda. *The Ship that Flew*. OUP, 1939; 1965.

Lofting, Hugh. *The Story of Dr Dolittle*. Cape, 1920.

Macdonald, George. *The Princess and the Goblin*. Strahan, 1872.

Marryat, Captain. *Children of the New Forest*. Hurst, 1847.

Milne, A. A. *Winnie-the-Pooh*. Methuen, 1926; 1965.

Molesworth, Mrs 'Con and the Little People.' *Tell Me a Story*, 1875; *The Hamish Hamilton Book of Other Worlds*, edited by Roger Lancelyn Green.
   Christmas-Tree Land. Macmillan, 1884.

Montgomery, L. M. *Anne of Green Gables*. Boston: Page, 1908.

Morgan, Alison. *Ruth Crane*. Chatto & Windus, 1973.

Nesbit, E. *Five Children and It*. Fisher Unwin, 1902; Penguin, 1959.
   The Phoenix and the Carpet. Fisher Unwin, 1904; Penguin, 1959.
   The Wouldbegoods. Fisher Unwin, 1901.

Oman, Carola. *Robin Hood, the Prince of Outlaws*. Dent, 1937.

Opie, Iona *and* Peter. *The Oxford Book of Children's Verse*. OUP, 1973.

Ransome, Arthur. *Pigeon Post*. Cape, 1936.
   Swallows and Amazons. Cape, 1930.

Sewell, Anna. *Black Beauty*. Jarrolds, 1877.

Spring, Howard. *Sampson's Circus*. Faber, 1936.

Stevenson, Robert Louis. *Treasure Island*. Cassell, 1883.

Streatfeild, Noel. *Ballet Shoes*. Dent, 1936.
   The Children of Primrose Lane. Dent, 1941; Collins, 1966.
   The Circus is Coming. Dent, 1938; 1948.
   The House in Cornwall. Dent, 1940.

Tolkien, J. R. R. *The Hobbit*. Allen & Unwin, 1937.

Tozer, Katherine. *The Wanderings of Mumfie*. Murray, 1935.

Travers, P. L. *Mary Poppins*. Howe, 1934.

Treadgold, Mary. *We Couldn't Leave Dinah*. Cape, 1941.

Trease, Geoffrey. *Bows Against the Barons*. Lawrence, 1934.

Twain, Mark. *The Adventures of Tom Sawyer*. Chatto & Windus, 1876.

Wyss, Johann. *Swiss Family Robinson*. First English edition, 1814.

Index